The Humanization of Man

By Ashley Montagu

THE HUMANIZATION OF MAN

MAN IN PROCESS

HUMAN HEREDITY

THE CULTURED MAN

MAN: HIS FIRST MILLION YEARS

COMING INTO BEING AMONG THE AUSTRALIAN ABORIGINES

EDWARD TYSON, M.D., F.R.S. (1650–1708): AND THE RISE
OF HUMAN AND COMPARATIVE ANATOMY IN ENGLAND

MAN'S MOST DANGEROUS MYTH: THE FALLACY OF RACE

STATEMENT ON RACE

THE DIRECTION OF HUMAN DEVELOPMENT

THE NATURAL SUPERIORITY OF WOMEN

THE REPRODUCTIVE DEVELOPMENT OF THE FEMALE

ON BEING HUMAN

THE BIOSOCIAL NATURE OF MAN

DARWIN, COMPETITION AND COOPERATION

ON BEING INTELLIGENT

IMMORTALITY

EDUCATION AND HUMAN RELATIONS

ANTHROPOLOGY AND HUMAN NATURE

INTRODUCTION TO PHYSICAL ANTHROPOLOGY

HANDBOOK OF ANTHROPOMETRY

PRENATAL INFLUENCES

ANATOMY AND PHYSIOLOGY, 2 VOLS. (WITH E. STEEN)

Editor

STUDIES AND ESSAYS IN THE HISTORY
OF SCIENCE AND LEARNING

TOYNBEE AND HISTORY

THE MEANING OF LOVE

GENETIC MECHANISMS IN HUMAN DISEASE

INTERNATIONAL PICTORIAL TREASURY OF KNOWLEDGE

ATLAS OF HUMAN ANATOMY

CULTURE AND THE EVOLUTION OF MAN

ASHLEY MONTAGU

The Humanization of Man

THE WORLD PUBLISHING COMPANY

CLEVELAND AND NEW YORK

PUBLISHED BY The World Publishing Company
2231 WEST 110TH STREET, CLEVELAND 2, OHIO

PUBLISHED SIMULTANEOUSLY IN CANADA BY
NELSON, FOSTER & SCOTT LTD.

Library of Congress Catalog Card Number: 62-15707

FIRST EDITION

NOTE

Of the twenty-eight articles which have gone
into the making of this volume only sixteen have
previously been published. Grateful acknowledgment for permission to reprint is herewith
made to the editors of the journals in which
these articles first appeared. The sources are
given at the foot of the relevant pages.

Grateful acknowledgment is made to the fol-
lowing publishers for their kind permission to
reprint from the works indicated. Cambridge
University Press: *Man on His Nature* by Sir
Charles Sherrington. Harcourt, Brace & World,
Inc.: *The Cocktail Party* by T. S. Eliot, copy-
right, 1950, by T. S. Eliot. Holt, Rinehart and
Winston, Inc.: *Escape From Freedom* by Erich
Fromm, copyright 1941 by Erich Fromm.

TO
Edna
AND
Kenneth Macgowan

Contents

Introduction

IT HAS BEEN REMARKED by a certain pessimistic philosopher that man is, perhaps, Nature's sole mistake. The human brain, still another has avowed, is a knot designed to prevent the spinal cord from unraveling, a tumor characterized by a cancerous growth of pathogenic ideas which is taking man to certain extinction. A great many bomb-shelter-building individuals, in this apocalyptic age, would appear to agree. How little faith these have in man! How little they understand their own species! It is true that man is the only animal who blushes—or needs to. But his faults stem from the same sources as do his virtues. If he needs to blush he is capable of doing so, and if he is capable of error, as he is, he is capable of recognizing and rectifying his errors. Man endangers himself only when he refuses to face his errors or attempts to justify them. To err is human—but not so much, we have been told, as most human beings do. *Their* errors are something preternatural. But this is not so. Man is capable of more and greater errors than any other creature for the very same reason that he is capable of the discovery of the truth and of growing in wisdom. The reason lies in his supreme educability, the animal who is capable of learning more unsound as well as sound things than any other. The confusions from which man is at present suffering are compounded of sound and unsound ideas about himself, his nature, and the nature of the world in which he lives and has his being. Will man ever grow out of his confusions? Is there enough time left? There is an urgency about such questions which, perhaps as never before in man's history, call for the clearest kinds of answers.

9

I cannot claim in the present volume to have the answers to these questions, but in the essays here gathered together an attempt is made to light the way upon the road which I think may lead to the answers. During the last ten thousand years of man's increasingly complex urbanizing experience he has become more and more dehumanized. Some of the reasons for this, in the context of our own time and in our own land, are considered in this book. My hope is that these discussions may help the reader to see what has gone wrong, and what it is that requires to be done to put things right again. Americans have special problems, and for this reason the focus is on American culture and some of its values, images, and identities. Americans present a special case of the human quandary, and they have pressing problems to solve. Some of these problems are discussed in the following pages, and suggested solutions offered for the reader's consideration.

As one, who through reading, has learned and been influenced and caused to change, I hope that I am not unduly optimistic in the expectation that some readers of these pages will do likewise. Perhaps the idea before all others I would like the reader to re-consider is the notion that men are fallen angels who, in Adam's fall, sinned all. The idea of innate depravity seems to me to have been fiendishly damaging to man's growth in self-understanding. It is not difficult to understand why the idea of the innate nasti-ness of man should have had so wide an appeal. It is the simplest explanation of man's conduct. When the source of a trait can be attributed to innate factors, no further explanation or inquiry is necessary. When that attribution has centuries of secular, religious, and "scientific" authority to support it, and one's personal judg-ment is added to that host of imposing authorities, it is hardly likely to occur to anyone that the age-old doctrine of innate depravity is not only open to question but is demonstrably un-sound. The doctrine of innate depravity is a myth, one of the most cherished of the myths of Western man. Man, as in so much else, excels as a myth-making animal. The myths he creates are designed to satisfy his needs, and the need that is satisfied by the myth of innate depravity is the need for absolution from sin, for if sin is innately determined, then one can shift the burden of responsibility for it from oneself to one's innate heritage. Evil in the world is thus explained, and becomes easier to bear—and with a good conscience, much easier to do nothing about.

My own interpretation of the evidence, strictly within the domain of science, leads me to the conclusion that man is born good, and is organized in such a manner from birth as to need to continue to grow and develop in his potentialities for goodness. I define goodness as behavior calculated to confer survival benefits upon others in a creatively enlarging manner. I am aware of the fact that my ideas are eccentric, that they are highly unorthodox, and that in a former age I would have been burned at the stake for expressing them. Far from inspiring such incendiary reactions in anyone today, I find that the idea of the innate goodness of man, even though it is uncongenial to the temper of the times, meets with a fair amount of interest whenever it is expressed, though I should be the last to expect it to erode away, in a short time, the solidly entrenched traditional system of contrary views. Whether this erosion will ever occur will depend upon the number of individuals who are convinced that the traditional conception of the nature of human nature is unsound. I believe that it is demonstrably unsound, and in this book I have attempted to set out some of the reasons why I consider it to be so.

It is highly important, indeed urgently so, that we consider the possibility that our traditional ideas concerning the innate nature of man may be wrong and damaging, for I am convinced that underlying much of man's malfunctioning in the Western world is this unsound conception of human nature.

Some other highly popular and erroneous ideas and practices that contribute to the disordering of man, particularly in America —the ideas of freedom, the individual, culture and mental illness, love, the birth of babies, parents and children, values, marriage, the American character, the American woman, the beatniks, our foreign relations, the race problem, the atom bomb, games and character, and privacy—are all considered, I hope, sufficiently provocatively to stimulate the reader to do what requires to be done.

My first published article on the problem of race appeared in 1926. In the years that have elapsed since then I have grown more than ever convinced that racism is the most tragic of all the follies committed by man. It is one of the most awful of man's iniquities, and that it can anywhere in the world be still practiced or justified seems to me the most astonishing of all anachronisms. The truth is that worries, fears, and insecurities will, under certain conditions, almost invariably add up to some form of racism. It is because this is so that I have devoted some space in this book to the discussion of anxiety, personal fears, and other psychodynamic processes and their relation to racism.

It is what Americans do about race that will, I believe, ultimately determine the fate of the United States among the peoples of the world. The idea of equality is once more being challenged, and there are those who are sedulously attempting to confuse its meaning. We are told that egalitarians believe that all men and all races are biologically equal or that they are mentally equal. This is *not* what equality means. The idea needs to be restated. The equality of man does not imply identity but difference, the unique difference which by virtue of the fact that he is human entitles every man to the fullest realization of his differences irrespective of his membership of any group, whether ethnic or otherwise. The concept of equality does not even imply equality of opportunity, but rather opportunity according to the needs of the individual—not *denial* of opportunity, but provision of the fullest opportunity, and equality before the law. It is the quality in equality that matters, and quality knows no ethnic boundaries. The responsible citizen will be alive to the obligations which every form of inequality entail upon him. The good citizen is one who has a sense of personal responsibility for decency and justice. We must learn to cherish our differences as well as our likenesses. But if we would preserve our unique differences and encourage their development throughout the community of man, we must first acknowledge our basic similarities. The brotherhood of man is no longer a pious wish—it is a necessity for civilized survival.

ASHLEY MONTAGU

Princeton, New Jersey

PART I

Man Dehumanized and
Humanity Reclaimed

1. Our Changing Conception
of Human Nature

WHAT A FASCINATING BOOK could be written on the history of
theories of human nature! These theories have been as numerous
as the proverbial leaves of Vallombrosa, but curiously enough,
it was not until the beginning of the twentieth century that human nature really became a serious subject of scientific study.
Until that time human nature was mainly the province of theologians and philosophers.

The scientific study of human nature has, however, proceeded
along very different lines and has revealed a multiplicity of facts
which neither the theologians nor the philosophers even sur-
mised. There *are* some new things under the sun, particularly
about human nature, as the reader will, I believe, agree as he
reads this chapter. In the present chapter an account will be
given of some of the most significant research which has been
done, especially in recent years and even in recent months, which
throws a new light upon the nature of man in all his remarkable variety. I hope that the facts set out in these pages, and
their discussion, will serve as a challenge to social thinkers and
leaders of public opinion.

What Is Human Nature?

Our purpose is to attempt an answer to the question, What is

From *Impact* (UNESCO), vol. 3, 1952, pp. 219-232.

human nature? Definitions, however, are only properly meaningful at the end rather than at the beginning of an inquiry; the answer to our question, then, could be postponed till later, and, indeed, we shall have to postpone the full answer, for human nature can mean several different but mutually reconcilable things at one and the same time. Until we have explored the meaning of these different meanings and reconciled them under a unitary rubric, it will not be possible to make a brief readily understandable statement as to the nature of human nature. However, it is possible to say several meaningful things about human nature at once, and these should be said.

First, then, it should be said that no organism of the species so prematurely named *Homo sapiens* is born with human nature. This is the first, perhaps, of the rather startling findings about human beings and human nature: human beings are not born with human nature—they develop it. What human beings are born with is a complex of potentialities for being human, but being human is something one learns, it is not a status *with* which one is born—it is a status *to* which one is born; but to earn the status of being human one must learn it, otherwise one can never play the role of a human being.

This is a very important statement, for while for millennia human beings have been under the impression that human nature is something with which one is born, modern research has proved that this is unsound; indeed, it is worse than unsound, it is confused, and as Francis Bacon remarked, truth grows more readily out of error than it does out of confusion. The belief in the innate nature of human nature has been responsible for much personal, social, and political misunderstanding, and for an untold amount of human suffering; hence the very great importance, social and political, of a proper understanding of the facts about the nature of human nature.

The dictionary defines "human" as having the nature, qualities, or characteristics of man. What then are the specific qualities or characteristics and what is the peculiar nature of man which distinguishes him from all other creatures?

On the basis of his obvious physical characters man is described as a mammal of the order Primates, genus *Homo,* and species *sapiens;* so much for his physical classification, but what of his psychological classification?

A very strong case could be made out for the position that while every creature exhibiting the classificatory traits of mankind is *ipso facto Homo sapiens,* no such creature is really *human* until it exhibits the conduct of a human being. If it is true that one has to learn the kind of conduct which we know to be uniquely human, then any organism which fails to learn that conduct cannot be human. In a sense this is a sound argument, and it is important to raise it if only to examine it and put it in its proper place; such an examination will serve to throw much needed light upon what human nature should be understood to mean.

The organism *Homo sapiens* is normally born with the full equipment of potentialities for being human which are as much a species character of the genus *Homo* as are any of the uniquely hominid physical characters. In this sense the unique equipment of potentialities for being qualitatively human entitles every creature born with them—and we must take the physical characters of *Homo sapiens* as evidence of this—to be called *human.* One could make a distinction here, but I am not sure that it would serve any useful purpose: one could refer to man's physical characters as *hominid,* and to his mental characters as *human;* this would lead us to the quite indefensible position that while it is possible to be born a hominid, one is not necessarily therefore born human. This argument, however, would hold only in those exceptional instances in which a baby was born with all the physical characters of man, but for some abnormal reason lacking either human potentialities or the capacity to develop them.

The fact is that man is human by virtue of both his physical and mental characters. In the course of his evolution the two appear to have gone hand in hand. One should no more deny the status of being human to a newborn baby because it cannot talk, any more than one should deny it the status of being a member of the species *Homo sapiens* because it cannot walk in the erect position, as an adult does. The wonderful thing about a baby (as Faraday long ago pointed out) is its promise, not its performance, a promise to perform under certain auspices. A juvenile ape can do a great deal more than a juvenile human,[1] but the promise of the child far exceeds that of the brightest ape.

What are these potentialities with which every normal baby of the species *Homo sapiens* is born, potentialities which distinguish him from every other living creature? The answer is: a remarkably plastic capacity for learning to use complex symbols and symbol relationships.[2] A symbol is here taken to mean a meaning or value conferred by those who use it upon any thing. A sign, on the other hand, belongs to the physical world—it is a physical thing which indicates some other thing or event. A symbol belongs to the human world of meaning. It is generally agreed that newborn babies are incapable of symbol usage; it is an ability which they have to learn—if they are not taught it they do not learn it.

At this point we are ready for some clarification as to the meaning of human nature. Human nature means the uniquely human set of *potentialities* for being human with which the organism *Homo sapiens* is born. *Potentialities* must be stressed, for it is not being said here that the organism is born with a certain set of traits or characteristics; it is this latter assumption which is usually made, and it is here that the error creeps in when most people think of human nature, for what is generally erroneously assumed is that human beings are born with certain definite traits and characteristics which need only time if they are to develop, whereas the researchers of the last thirty years have increasingly convincingly shown that the biologically based traits and characteristics of the organism will to a very large extent be determined by the kind of cultural stimulation to which those potentialities are subjected.

What most persons have taken to be human nature is actually

<hr>

[1] W. N. and L. A. Kellogg, *The Ape and the Child* (New York, Whittlesey House, 1933); R. M. and A. W. Yerkes, *The Great Apes* (New Haven, Yale University Press, 1934); B. J. Benchley, *My Friends the Apes* (London, Faber and Faber, 1944); Cathy Hayes, *The Ape in Our House* (New York, Harper, 1951).

[2] See Ernest Cassirer, *An Essay on Man* (New Haven, Yale University Press, 1944); L. A. White, *The Science of Culture* (New York, Farrar Straus, 1949) pp. 22-39.

acquired behavior of the person; this may and usually does become a second nature, and this, too, could be called human nature, since it is a function of man's nature in interaction with his environment, but it must not be confused with man's inborn nature—and this is exactly where the confusion is usually made. The status to which *Homo sapiens* is born is humanity, but to be dynamically human, in other words to be able to play the role of a human being on the basis of the capacity which that status implies, is something that one learns. Now, since one always learns in a particular human environment, one's potentialities will develop according to the pattern of conditionings to which they are exposed. Hence, human nature may express itself or rather be made to express itself in many different forms. But the differences in these forms are not, so the evidence available to us at the present time indicates, determined by innate factors but by environmental ones; and this is what we meant when we said that the generally prevalent impression that human nature was something with which one was born was unsound.

Man is not born with the ability to speak any language, but he is born with a capacity or potentiality for speech. This potentiality will never develop in the absence of the proper stimuli; these stimuli will usually assume a form determined by a particular environment; so that what the organism learns to speak will be of purely social origin, just as the way in which he learns to eat will be socially determined.

We must ask the question: Is it human nature to speak a particular language? Is it human nature to eat with a knife and fork or with one's bare fingers? These questions should lead us to the answer we are seeking. Language, knives and forks, and fingers are all instruments for manipulating one's environment, but whereas fingers are natural, language and knives and forks are artificial; they are made by man, but they are not part of his nature, whereas fingers are. One would therefore say that it is natural to eat with one's fingers but unnatural to eat with knives and forks. Knives and forks are really artificially produced specialized hands and fingers. Obviously it is no part of the primary or innate nature of man to create artifacts. Science knows of no natural drive in man to make knives and forks or to speak Italian; whether one makes knives and forks and speaks Italian will depend entirely upon the cultural environment in which one develops. Australian aborigines neither use knives nor forks, nor do they speak Italian, not because they are unable to do so, but because they happen to be born into a cultural environment from which such instruments are absent and where their own language alone is spoken.

In short, how a person will behave, what he will do, think or say, what language he will say it in, and the artifacts he will prize will not be determined as much by his innate nature as by his acquired experience. And this gives us the answer we have been seeking: human nature consists of the unique potentialities for complex symbol usage with which the organism is born, potentialities which undergo development within the matrix of a stimulating cultural environment, the emergent results being a human being custom-made and tailored to the prevailing cultural pattern in which he has been conditioned. The process of learning the traditional cultural patterns is called *socialization.*

The socialization process is essentially cultural in character, and it is highly desirable to distinguish this from the natural endowment of potentialities with which the organism is born and which undergo development only under the operation of the socialization process. We may then call the natural endowment of human potentialities *primary human nature,* and the socialized development of those potentialities may be called *secondary human nature.* This is to recognize the fact that human beings are born with a certain equipment of potentialities for being human, and that this equipment is usually both developed and organized during the socialization process according to a certain cultural pattern. Human nature, therefore, consists of both primary and secondary elements, the innate *and* the acquired. In the past most errors have been committed by identifying the latter with the former.

All men are members of the species *Homo sapiens,* the same genus and the same species, and the primary human nature of all men is fundamentally similar. It is their secondary human nature which is frequently different. The differences in secondary nature are not due to any innate differences in character—at least there is no evidence that would suggest it. Instead, all the evidence indicates that the differences are due to variations in the history of cultural experience.[3] In short, human nature assumes secondary forms according to the pattern of the socialization process in which it has undergone development, and this pattern is determined by the cultural history of the group.[4]

Human Nature Begins To Be Influenced at Fertilization

In the tradition of Western civilization it is the custom to reckon age as beginning from birth; other civilizations, notably the Chinese, reckon age as beginning from fertilization or conception. Accumulating recent researches indicate that this is scientifically a very much more sound manner of reckoning age than our own. The tendency has been to think of the child being born as a sort of *tabula rasa*, without a previous history, and beginning life, as it were, for the first time at birth.

This viewpoint may be described not only as a vulgar error, but even more appropriately as a learned error. The teaching up to the present time in our scientific institutions has been that the fetus *in utero* is so carefully protected, so thoroughly insulated from virtually all stimulations originating in the mother or the outside world, that it develops autochthonously according to its own inner resources and the nutriment which it receives through the placenta. Since—so it was and is still being widely

[3] Franz Boas, *The Mind of Primitive Man* (New York, Macmillan, 1938); Ashley Montagu, *Man's Most Dangerous Myth: The Fallacy of Race*, 3rd ed. (New York, Harper, 1952).
[4] See Ralph Linton, *The Cultural Background of Personality* (New York, Appleton-Century, 1945); Branislaw Malinowski, *A Scientific Theory of Culture* (Chapel Hill, University of North Carolina Press, 1944); D. G. Haring, ed., *Personal Character and Cultural Milieu*, 3rd ed. (Syracuse, New York, Syracuse University Press, 1956); S. S. Sargent, *Culture and Personality* (New York, Wenner-Gren Foundation, 1949); C. Kluckhohn, H. A. Murray, D. Schneider, *Personality in Nature, Society, and Culture*, 2nd ed. (New York, Knopf, 1953); W. Coutu, *Emergent Human Nature* (New York, Knopf, 1949); John J. Honigmann, *Culture and Personality* (New York, Harper, 1954); Ashley Montagu, *On Being Human* (New York, Abelard-Schuman, 1950); Francis L. K. Hsu, ed., *Aspects of Culture and Personality* (New York, Abelard-Schuman, 1954).

taught—there is no nervous connection between mother and fetus, the mother's nervous states could not possibly influence the development of the fetus in any way; and since the placenta is a perfect semipermeable membrane which filtered out all but the very smallest molecules, not permitting even the mother's blood to pass as such to the fetus, it was evident how well insulated the fetus is.

With such a viewpoint concerning maternal-fetal relations it is no wonder that the prenatal period was considered irrelevant for the study of human nature. And yet, nearly a century and a half ago a great poet and thinker, Samuel Taylor Coleridge (1772-1834), wrote: "Yes—the history of a man for the nine months preceding his birth, would probably, be far more interesting and contain events of greater moment, than all the threescore and ten years that follow it."[5] It has taken science one hundred and fifty years to come somewhere near supporting Coleridge's "golden guess."

It is now a demonstrable fact that there is a very intimate relationship between the nervous system of mother and fetus; this connection is established through what is increasingly coming to be known as the neurohumoral system. The neurohumoral system is composed of the interrelated nervous and endocrine systems acting through the fluid medium of the blood (and its oxygen and carbon-dioxide content).[6]

We have good reason to think that an emotionally disturbed pregnant woman may communicate her emotional disturbance, at least in chemical form, to her fetus. The Fels Institute workers at Antioch College, Yellow Springs, Ohio, have found that emotional disturbances in the pregnant mother produce a marked increase in the activity of the fetus. They have also found that fatigue in the mother will produce hyperactivity in the fetus. Under severe emotional stress, especially during the later months of their pregnancies, these mothers will generally have babies who are hyperactive, irritable, squirming, feeding problems. Such an infant, says Sontag, "is to all intents and purposes a neurotic

---

[5] S. T. Coleridge, *Miscellanies, Aesthetic and Literary,* collected and arranged by T. Ashe (London, Bohn's Standard Library, 1885), p. 301.
[6] Ashley Montagu, *Prenatal Influences* (Springfield, Ill., Thomas, 1962).

infant when he is born—the result of unsatisfactory fetal environment. In this instance he has not had to wait until childhood for a bad home situation or other cause to make him neurotic. It has been done for him before he has even seen the light of day." [7, 8]

It is not being suggested that the mother's emotional states as such are transmitted to the fetus—this is almost certainly not the case. What does apparently occur is that the mother's emotional disturbance manifests itself in impulses which pass from cortex to thalamus and hypothalamus and proceed along the infundibulum to the pituitary gland. The latter then secretes various hormones directly into the blood stream which activate the glands in the rest of the body. And since most, if not all, of these hormones are of small enough molecular size, they will pass directly through the placenta into the fetus, and there act upon it.

It is now well established that the fetus is capable of responding to tactile stimuli, to vibrations, sounds, differences in pitch and tone, taste, and various gases. We thus have ample proof that the fetal organism is not completely insulated from the outside world. It is a great deal more sensitive to it than we had ever supposed.

Greenacre suggests that the evidence indicates the possible existence of preanxiety reactions in fetal life without necessarily any psychic content.[9] She suggests that traumatic stimuli such as sudden sounds, vibrations, and umbilical cord entanglements, and the like, including the "trip through the birth canal," may produce a predisposition to anxiety which, combined or not with

[7] L. W. Sontag, "Differences in Modifiability of Fetal Behavior and Physiology," *Psychosomatic Medicine*, vol. 6, 1944, pp. 151-154; L. W. Sontag and T. W. Richards, "Studies in Fetal Behavior," *Monographs of the Society for Research in Child Development*, vol. 3, 1938, pp. x-72; L. W. Sontag, "War and the Fetal Maternal Relationship," *Marriage and Family Living*, vol. 6, 1944, pp. 1-5.
[8] In addition, there is evidence that the mother's emotional disturbances are reflected through disturbances in nutrition in the skeletal system of the fetus. L. W. Sontag and L. M. Harris, "Evidence of Disturbed Prenatal and Neonatal Growth in Bones of Infants Aged One Month," *American Journal of Diseases of Childhood*, vol. 56, 1948, pp. 1248-1255.
[9] Phyllis Greenacre, *Trauma, Growth and Personality* (New York, Norton, 1952).

constitutional traumatizing birth experiences, might be an important determinant in producing the severity of any neurosis.

Even more important than these is Spelt's remarkable discovery that the human fetus, *in utero*, during the last two months of gestation, can be conditioned to respond to the sign—a vibrotactile conditioned stimulus—of a loud noise, the unconditioned stimulus.[10] Spelt's is the first successful experimental attempt to condition the human fetus *in utero*. Evidently, the fetus at seven months gestation age already has a sufficiently highly developed nervous system to be able to perform the operations necessary for learning.

Without dwelling any further upon these facts, it should be reasonably clear that by the time a fetus is born, it is highly probable that the genetic structure of its potentialities for being human have already been more or less greatly influenced by the environment in which they have undergone development; hence the primary human nature with which the organism *Homo sapiens* is born is not simply the genotypic potentialities that were laid down at fertilization, but more or less much modified expression of these potentialities.

Such findings, it will be readily granted, are of the first importance for the improvement of human welfare. The care of the child should, of course, begin with conception, if not before, and the best way of caring for the developing human being is caring for the mother during and after her pregnancy.

Heredity and Environment

Before proceeding with the discussion as to what the organism *Homo sapiens* is actually born with, a few words must be said concerning the spurious dissociation which has in the past been produced between what is in actual operation only arbitrarily separable, namely, heredity and environment. By "heredity" one usually refers to the innate inheritance of the organism, and "in-

[10] D. K. Spelt, "The Conditioning of the Human Fetus *in Utero*," *Journal of Experimental Psychology*, vol. 38, 1948, pp. 338-346.

nate" is usually defined as the unadulterated biological inheritance of the organism as determined by the genes, or hereditary particles in the chromosomes. The latter is usually referred to by geneticists as the *genotype*. The visible expression of the genotype is termed the *phenotype*. Now, the fact is that as the genotype always undergoes development within the complex medium of its environment, the environment to a greater or lesser extent always influences the development of the phenotype. Hence what the organism inherits, what its heredity in fact is, are both the genotype and the environmental factors which have formed it before birth. To disentangle what is due to genotype and what to environment, more especially where behavioral traits are concerned, is a task beset with unsolved difficulties. But it is clear that behavioral traits are due to a combination of genotypic and environmental facts with, by and large, environmental factors playing a dominant role. All other things being equal— which they seldom are—insofar as behavioral traits in man are concerned man's social heredity plays a more considerable role than does his physical heredity in establishing man's behavioral traits.

Since, then, the heredity of a person consists of the interactive effects of the innate potentialities for development within the particular environment, it follows that where we control environment we to some extent control heredity. This is an extremely important conclusion, for it tells us that the most effective way for human beings to influence the expression of the genotype is through the manipulation of the environment. Heredity in the genotypic sense may determine what we *can* do but environment determines what we *do* do.[11]

[11] L. C. Dunn and Theodosius Dobzhansky, *Heredity, Race and Society* (New York, New American Library, 1956); J. B. S. Haldane, *Heredity and Politics* (New York, Norton, 1938); L. Hogben, *Genetic Principles in Medicine and Social Science* (New York, Knopf, 1931); H. S. Jennings, *The Biological Basis of Human Nature* (New York, Norton, 1930); H. Kalmus, *Genetics* (London, Pelican Books, 1948); H. J. Muller, C. C. Little, and L. H. Snyder, *Genetics, Medicine and Man* (Ithaca, N. Y., Cornell University Press, 1947); Amram Scheinfeld, *The New You and Heredity* (Philadelphia, Lippincott, 1950); Ashley Montagu, *Human Heredity* (Cleveland and New York, The World Publishing Company, 1959).

Constitution

In view of the recrudescence of a constitutional school of human nature which attempts to link man's behavior with his physical traits,[12] it is desirable here to say a few words concerning the conclusions reached by scientists with respect to the nature of constitution. Constitution may be defined as the sum total of the structural, functional, and psychological characters of the organism. It may be regarded as the integral of genetic potentialities influenced in varying degrees by internal and external environmental factors. Constitution is more properly regarded as a process rather than as an unchanging entity. Constitution is not a biological given, a structure predestined by its genotype to function in a predetermined manner. The manner in which all genotypes function is determined by their interaction with the environment in which they operate.

All the relevant researches indicate that every genotype is a unique physico-chemical system comprising particular kinds of potentialities having definite limits. These limits vary from individual to individual, so that were the genotype to be exposed to identical environmental conditions, its interactive expressions would nevertheless continue to vary from individual to individual. In point of fact, the environmental conditions are never the same for two individuals—a fact which renders it necessary for us to remember that heredity is not merely constituted by the genotype, but by the genotype as modified by the environment in which it has developed. The fact cannot be too often reiterated that what the organism inherits is a genotype and an environ-

[12] See the works of E. A. Hooton: *The Twilight of Man* (New York, Putnam, 1939) and *Crime and the Man* (Cambridge, Harvard University Press, 1939). See also the works of W. H. Sheldon, *The Varieties of Human Physique* (New York, Harper, 1940); *The Varieties of Human Temperament* (New York, Harper, 1942); *Varieties of Delinquent Youth* (New York, Harper, 1949). For a criticism of the work of Hooton, see R. K. Merton and Ashley Montagu, "Crime and the Anthropologist," *American Anthropologist*, vol. 57, 1951, pp. 10-13; S. L. Washburn, "Physical Anthropology," *American Anthropologist*, vol. 53, 1951, pp. 561-563.

ment. Heredity is the dynamic integral of both, the resultant of the dynamic interaction between the two.

Finally, it has become quite clear that genes, the hereditary particles carried in the chromosomes, do not determine either characteristics or traits; what they determine are the responses of the developing organism to the environment. The genes the individual inherits are not, therefore, equivalent to predestination, but are amenable to the influences of the environment, and hence, to some extent, to human control.

Where the constitutionalists go wrong is in their claim that "structure determines function." Function is, of course, an aspect of structure, but as any elementary student of physiology should know, *the functions of structures* depend upon their particular character according to the environment in which they operate.[13] The constitutionalists consistently fail to understand the importance of the environment, especially in human development, and when everything is said and done and all other criticisms have been made, it is this that is the most fatal of all the criticisms.

With What Kind of Behavioral Equipment Is Man Born?

It is generally agreed that man is born free of those biological predeterminants of behavior which characterize other animals. Man is born without instincts.[14] In other words, man is not born with those psychophysical predispositions which cause other animals to respond in a particular manner to a particular stimulus accompanied by a particular emotion. The form of the nonhuman animal's reactions are predetermined; man has to learn the forms which his responses assume. While other animals are

[13] J. Needham, *Biochemistry and Morphogenesis* (New York, Cambridge University Press, 1942); C. H. Waddington, *Organizers and Genes* (New York, Cambridge University Press, 1940); J. T. Bonner, *Morphogenesis: An Essay on Development* (Princeton, Princeton University Press, 1952); E. S. Russell, *The Interpretation of Development and Heredity* (Oxford, Clarendon Press, 1930).

[14] L. L. Bernard, *Instinct, A Study in Social Psychology* (New York, Holt, 1924).

mostly creatures of habitat, man is the creature of habit—habits which he acquires from his culture. These habits are organized by his culture around a number of urges, drives, or basic needs, as they have been variously called. These terms are the merest labels for physiological conditions, the exact nature of which is far from being known. The basic needs are known by their functions rather than by their structure.

There is fairly general agreement as to the number and definition of basic needs. A basic need may be defined as a requirement of the organism which must be fulfilled if the organism and the group are to survive. The essential basic needs are oxygen, satisfaction of hunger and thirst, activity, rest, sleep, bowel and bladder elimination, sex, fear, and avoidance of pain. Malinowski has defined the concept of basic needs as the "environmental and biological conditions which must be fulfilled for the survival of the individual and the group." It is important to note that the definition of a basic need includes the group as well as the individual. The inclusion of the group in the definition of a basic need constitutes one of the most significant departures from and improvements upon the old concept of "instinct." It constitutes an explicit recognition of the fact that man, if not all other animals, functions in relation to a group, and that at least for human beings, functioning (behaving) apart from a group simply does not occur. When human beings behave socially it means that they have been socialized within a human group. If they have not been socialized within a human group, then they do not behave like human beings.[15] Indeed, a person becomes related to himself to the extent that he becomes related to the group.[16]

Malinowski, who was the first anthropologist to attempt a

[15] There are no examples of completely isolated human children—in spite of many published accounts to the contrary—but there are several recorded cases of children who have been almost completely isolated from human contact for several years. (These cases are discussed in Ashley Montagu, *The Direction of Human Development*, New York, Harper, 1955.) Such children completely fail to develop as human beings, and not alone this, but in most cases are psychically blind, and deaf, unable to walk or run, and unable to make more than the most elementary sounds.

[16] Erich Fromm, *Escape From Freedom* (New York, Rinehart, 1941) and *Man for Himself* (New York, Rinehart, 1947).

comprehensive theory of needs, set out the permanent vital sequences, as he called them, which are incorporated in all cultures, in a list of which we shall refer to but one impulse, as follows:

(a) Impulse	(b) Act	(c) Satisfaction
Hunger	Ingestion of Food	Satiation

This kind of sequence is rather too elementary and, in fact, unsound, because Malinowski has failed to perceive that the act leading to satiation (here in the case of hunger) is an indissoluble part of the process of satisfaction, and because there is rather more involved in the actual sequences than Malinowski's order suggests. A list of basic vital sequences prepared by the present writer follows on the next page.

The warning mechanism is a minimum physiological change which provides the organism with cues which enable it to anticipate the high pressor effects of depletion or excess. Thus, we generally drink before we become conscious of intense thirst, or indulge in activity long before we feel any intense need for it, and we breathe long before we feel the phobic stir which precedes each breath so faintly that we do not normally notice it.[17] The warning mechanism or minimum physiological cue enables the organism to anticipate its needs before the latter become too disturbing. Forestalling behavior therefore becomes possible.[18] We are warned long before there is any tissue depletion or experience of excess. The intervals between the warning activity and biochemical depletion or excess vary, the margin of safety varying from a few seconds in respiration to hours in water balance. The greater the interval the longer are the psychological complications which can be developed. The extent to which psychological processes can influence the various warning mechanisms varies widely.

Since the warning mechanisms operate through a phobiclike anxiety, failure to obtain the necessary satisfaction of the need

[17] Lawrence S. Kubie, "Instincts and Homeostasis," *Psychosomatic Medicine*, vol. 10, 1948, pp. 15-30.
[18] Ross Stagner, "Homeostasis as a Unifying Concept in Personality Theory," *Psychological Review*, vol. 58, 1951, pp. 5-17.

TABLE I
The Basic Vital Sequences

Warning Mechanism	Physiological Tension =	Urge or Need →	Satisfactions which leads to the act of →	Homeostasis
Accumulation of CO_2	Oxygen hunger	= Intake air →	Breathing →	Oxygenation of tissues
Periodic gastric waves	Hunger	= Ingest food →	Ingesting food →	Satiation
Dryness of mucous membranes	Thirst	= Intake liquid →	Intaking liquid →	Quenching
?	Sex	= Conjugate →	Conjugation →	Detumescence
Reduced organization	Fatigue	= Rest →	Resting →	Restoration of muscular and nervous energy
Excess energy	Restlessness	= Be active →	Activity →	Reduction of energy to equilibrium
?	Somnolence	= Sleep →	Sleeping →	Awaking with restored energy
Tonic disturbance	Bladder pressure	= Micturate →	Micturation →	Tension removal
Peristalsis	Colon pressure	= Defecate →	Defecation →	Tension removal
Autonomic activity	Fright	= Escape →	Escaping from danger →	Relaxation
?	Pain	= Avoid →	Avoidance →	Return to normal state
	Internal Excitation	= Craving →	Neuromuscular act →	Equilibrium

which develops serves to increase anxiety; as Kubie remarks, every basic need functions between the pressure of "normal phobic and normal compulsive psychologic processes which are the anlage of all pathologic distortions."[19]

Under certain conditions, the warning mechanism and the basic need may become detached from one another, so that the warning mechanism in the form, for example, of a sense of dryness may continue to operate even though the tissues are thoroughly hydrated. Or, vice versa, there may be a considerable amount of dehydration without any sense of dryness or thirst. Such dissociations are usually pathological. Anorexia, or chronic lack of appetite, is a well-known example.

It will now be readily understood how differences in conditioning and learning may affect the character of the basic needs and to some extent, therefore, the person's patterns of adjustments to the environment. This may be seen to be a matter of interaction of excitations or physiological tensions in the organism and the varying degrees of frustration or conditioning imposed upon their expression by the environment. This process is further complicated by the warning-mechanism interval which in relation to the need is also subject to cultural conditioning.

One of the prevailing myths of our Western tradition is the belief that a baby is born inheriting something of the ancestry of its lowly forebears, not only with respect to its physical traits but also with respect to its psychological traits. The alleged "aggressiveness" of animal nature, it has been held, is in part inherited by the young Homo sapiens. Freudian and Jungian psychology assumes the innate aggressiveness of man, and civilization is regarded by both as a more or less unsuccessful attempt to keep this innate aggressiveness within bounds.[20]

Freud's postulation of a "death instinct" is now generally discredited, but his use of the synonymous term, "the destructive instinct," still plays a considerable role in psychoanalysis and

[19] Kubie, p. 23.
[20] See Freud's Beyond the Pleasure Principle (London, Hogarth Press, 1922); The Future of an Illusion (London, Hogarth Press, 1928); Civilization and its Discontents (London, Hogarth Press, 1929); An Outline of Psychoanalysis (New York, Norton, 1949). See almost any of Jung's works and those of his followers.

writing influenced by it. This alleged "destructiveness" is identified with man's alleged inherited aggressiveness, and as a result one of the dominant views of human nature today is that man is born inherently aggressive.

This view is not scientifically corroborated. In fact, *all* the available evidence gathered by competent investigators indicates that man is born without a trace of aggressiveness. Dr. Lauretta Bender, through whose hands have passed literally thousands of children, finds in her capacity as a child psychiatrist that, far from being inborn, hostility in the child "is a symptom complex resulting from deprivations which are caused by developmental discrepancies in the total personality structure such that the constructive patterned drives for action in the child find inadequate means of satisfaction and result in amplification and disorganization of the drives into hostile or destructive aggression."[21]

The developmental directiveness of the organism is toward maturation in terms of co-operation. Bender calls it "the inherent capacity or drive for normality." And she adds, "The emphasis on the inborn or instinctive features of hostility, aggression, death wishes, and the negative emotional experiences represents a one-sided approach which has led our students of child psychology astray."

Professor Abraham Maslow makes much the same points in an important article. Maslow writes, "Those human impulses which have seemed throughout our history to be deepest, to be most instinctive and unchangeable, to be most widely spread throughout mankind, i.e., the impulses to hate, to be jealous, to be hostile, to be greedy, to be egoistic and selfish, are now being discovered more and more clearly to be acquired and *not* instinctive. They are almost certainly neurotic and sick reactions to bad situations, more specifically to frustrations of our truly basic and instinct-like needs and impulses."[22]

Professor Gardner Murphy writes, "As we watch behavior in early childhood, we no longer assume that each individual will

[21] Lauretta Bender, "Genesis of Hostility in Children," *American Journal of Psychiatry*, vol. 105, 1948, pp. 241-245.
[22] Abraham Maslow, "Our Maligned Animal Nature," *Journal of Psychology*, vol. 28, 1949, pp. 273-278, p. 276.

inevitably push himself ahead and crave every toy or every attention he can get; instead, we begin to ask if there is something in our society that does not satisfy the child's needs and, therefore, makes it aggressive."[23]

It seems that aggressiveness in a child usually develops as a response to frustration, that is to say, the blocking of expected satisfaction. The infant expects to have its needs satisfied; if those needs are not satisfied it feels frustrated, and normally reacts with aggressive behavior. More and more, aggression is coming to be regarded as a technique or mode of compelling attention to and satisfaction of one's needs.[24] This interpretation calls for a major change in the customary manner of dealing with aggression. Aggressive behavior in all human beings most frequently represents a response to frustration.[25]

As a result of the work of a large number of investigators (whose work is described in two pertinent books, Ashley Montagu's *The Direction of Human Development* and John Bowlby's *Maternal Care and Mental Health*) it is now indisputably clear that the satisfaction of a child's needs by its mother or a mother substitute is essential to its healthy physical and mental development. Physical satisfaction of the organism's needs is not enough; it must proceed from and be attended by the warmth and the love of another who is deeply interested in the child's welfare.

It is becoming increasingly clear that an infant is born not only with the need to be loved, but also with the need to love; he is certainly not born with any need to be aggressive.

This view of human nature makes a picture radically different from the traditional one, the one that conceives of man as born with an aggressiveness which must be suppressed or eradicated by the socialization process; the view that renders rationalizations

[23] Gardner Murphy, "Man and His Destiny," in *The Nature of Man*, A. W. Loos and L. B. Crow, eds. (New York, The Church Peace Union, 1950), p. 62.
[24] I believe that the late Ian B. Suttie was the first to point this out in his important book *The Origins of Love and Hate* (New York, Penguin Books, 1960). This book is, incidentally, perhaps the most original and best critique of Freudian psychoanalysis extant.
[25] John Dollard and others, *Frustration and Aggression* (New Haven, Yale University Press, 1939).

about the "innate warlikeness" of man, and circulates facile fallacies about man as a "brute." Modern research has shown this view of human nature to be erroneous. Man is not born evil or aggressive—he is rendered so. This being the case, it is incumbent upon us to realize that we can best change human nature for the better not by working on man's biological inheritance but by working on his social inheritance; by changing those conditions which produce disharmony in the person and a corresponding disharmony in his society. As Professor Warder C. Allee has said, "Despite many known appearances to the contrary, human altruistic drives are as firmly based on an animal ancestry as is man himself. Our tendencies toward goodness, such as they are, are as innate as our tendencies toward intelligence; we could do well with more of both."

The evolutionary school of thought that cited the "struggle for existence" and "the survival of the fittest" egregiously emphasized the competitive aspect of nature and virtually ignored the realities of co-operation and mutual aid, which play so great a role in ecology and the balance of nature.[26] The Darwinian view of nature fostered a view of human nature which was as readily accepted and just as heinous as the theory of nature that derived from an industrial civilization that advocated "rugged individualism" and "laissez faire."

Human nature fortunately holds considerably more promise for man than he has thus far been able to realize on a significant scale. A first step toward a fuller realization of that promise is a fuller understanding of his own nature.

[26] Ashley Montagu, *On Being Human* (New York, Abelard-Schuman, 1950); *Darwin, Competition and Cooperation* (New York, Abelard-Schuman, 1952); *The Direction of Human Development* (New York, Harper, 1955); Michael Graham, *Human Needs* (London, Cresset Press, 1951); W. C. Allee, *Co-operation Among Animals* (New York, Abelard-Schuman, 1951); S. J. Holmes, *Life and Morals* (New York, Macmillan, 1948); P. A. Sorokin, ed., *Explorations in Altruistic Love and Behavior* (Boston, Beacon Press, 1950).

2. Human Nature and Religion

WHAT IS HUMAN NATURE? Everyone has attempted to say, but no one has, in fact, known. Speculation and conjecture have been the rule and continue to be so today, the exceptions being the behavioral scientists who have, in recent years, been devoting themselves increasingly to the subject. Much research has yet to be done before we shall have most of the answers—we can, perhaps, hope to know *all* the answers in time. At the present time we know some of the answers, and some of us believe that we can give a fairly sound résumé of the nature of human nature in such a manner that it can be utilized as a working theory by which to help human beings develop their potentialities for being the warm, loving, healthy persons it is in the power of all human beings to be, and of all societies to encourage. I almost said "create," but while it is true that societies do, in a certain sense, create their members, and it is most important to understand that this is so, the term at this stage of our discussion would rather prejudice the true view of human nature which I shall endeavor to present in the following discussion. For human beings are in a very genuine sense already created as such at birth, and this is perhaps more important to understand first, before we understand how the process of postnatal creation occurs.

To come to the point at once: Contrary to the complex tradition concerning the nature of human nature which we of the Western world have inherited from the Hebrew-Greek-Christian tradition and its patristic commentators; from the sociopolitical

From *Journal of Existential Psychiatry*, vol. 1, 1961, pp. 441-454.

thinkers beginning with Thomas Hobbes (1651) and terminating with the Social Darwinists; from the Darwinian moralists up to the psychoanalytic view of the nature of man as presented in the writings of Freud and his school—a human nature which is conceived, in Hobbes's famous phrase, as "nasty, brutish, and short," which St. Paul declared as conceived in original sin, or as the Victorians put it, characterized by innate depravity, and as Freud said, a nature driven by the most powerful "urge to destruction"; contrary to this rather powerful complex of traditions, I, at least, read the scientifically established evidence as showing that man is born with a highly organized system of drives, all of which are directed toward development in terms of goodness, of love.

At the outset I desire to make it quite clear that I am presenting here my own interpretation of the available scientific evidence. I do so not because I wish to corner the market on the view of human nature which I hold, but simply because most students in the behavioral sciences have not yet had an opportunity to examine critically the theory of human nature which I am presenting. I should like it to be clearly understood that I am speaking for no other scientist or school. It is a rule of science that no theory can be accepted as proven until a number of independent scientists have verified and corroborated the theory by subjecting it to the proper tests. The facts which any one scientific worker may cite in support of his theory may be completely sound, yet the interpretation he gives to them may be wholly unsound. Since all scientific discussion is in the open domain, some time will have to elapse before the facts and their interpretation will receive the attention of a sufficient number of scientific investigators so that they become generally acceptable or not. The evidence has been presented in my book *The Direction of Human Development*.

I shall here be concerned with presenting that evidence in such a way as to point up its significance for an understanding not only of human nature but of religion. For if it is true that when that evidence is correctly interpreted it leads to the belief that all human beings are born good—good in the sense that they are born without one iota of aggressiveness or hostility or bad-ness or Original Sin or innate depravity, but with highly organized drives to confer the benefits of love upon all, including themselves—then it seems to me that we may have something of significance to offer for the proper understanding of the good life, of man's relation to the universe within which he finds himself. And that, I believe, has been something of the function of religion to reveal to man.

I speak here as a scientist, not as a man of religion. I wish to say at once that I believe that the man of science has more to offer concerning the understanding of the good life than has the man of religion. I have no faith in supernatural beings, but I do have faith, the faith that develops out of the kind of verifiable knowledge and wisdom which the scientific method makes possible. As Tennyson put it,

> There lives more faith in honest doubt,
> Believe me, than in half your creeds.

I have faith in science. I have faith in the belief that science will more efficiently solve the problems of human life than will any other discipline or approach. I believe that in the good society a man should be free to believe whatever he believes, but I also believe that in such a society it is the moral obligation of every man to take the greatest pains to prove his beliefs sound in such a manner that the highest degree of probability attaches to them as being in fact what he believes them to be, that is, as measurable by the measure of some verifiable standard.

I hope the reader will apply this same standard to everything he reads within the pages of this book.

Human babies are born with the desire for love, beyond and above all other needs. This means not merely that they need to be loved but that they also need to love others. As I see the evidence, love received by the infant is not only the best stimulus to its development, but the best stimulus to the development of its own potentialities for loving others. I see all the evidence supporting this conclusion and no evidence whatsoever which in any way renders it doubtful.

The baby is born desiring to love and be loved, two aspects of a unitary drive which we can only arbitrarily distinguish—

and the distinction is an important one—the baby wants to love as well as to be loved, because it needs to develop in the capacity to love, a development which will mark its good health. In other words, I am suggesting that the baby is born *good*, and that its birthright is development in terms of *goodness,* in terms of the ability to love. Whatever contributes to development along these lines is good for human beings, whatever retards or arrests development along these lines is undesirable and damaging to human beings. The evidence indicates that when the needs of the organism are lovingly satisfied the organism will develop as healthily as possible, that the organism which is loved will become a loving human being, harmonic, creative, and one that lives in the service of others as others have lived in his service.

Since love has been mentioned as a critically meaningful term, it is highly desirable that it be defined. In the vernacular, love may be defined as the communication to others of the attitude that one is all for them. Spelled out this means to communicate to others that one is so profoundly involved in their welfare, so deeply interested in their development that one will do all in one's power to contribute toward the stimulation and the development of their potentialities, first and foremost for becoming warm loving human beings, and secondly for the optimization of their innate capacities for developing as efficient and creative persons. This is love and it is also education, and in my view the two cannot be separated, unless one desires arbitrarily to distinguish the latter as the more formal part of the former. I speak here in the context of the making of human beings according to what I believe is their principal need.

What I have actually been saying is that human beings are born with an already built-in system of values, organismal values which have been biologically determined, and which one may disregard only at the extreme peril of the integrity of the person and the preservation of the race. These organismal values are the basic desires, needs, and interests of the organism, evolved over aeons of time and brought to their highest development in the human species. It is because man has to learn how to satisfy these needs, because he is the most plastic, the most educable of all living creatures, that man is the remarkable creature he is.

At the present time he is the unknown god—the god who lives in all of us but who has by almost all of us been overlooked. We have looked for that god in the heavens, in the firmament, when he has in fact been among us all the time, in each of us, in precisely the same place where miracles occur. The god within us all is the potentiality for goodness with which we are all biologically endowed, the potentiality for love. The organismal values are all oriented in the direction of love, this is the direction in which they seek development. The organismal values determine the limits and the kind of responses which the organism requires for healthy optimal development; they not only bridge the gap between what *is* and what *ought* to be, but they tell us what ought to be done if the organism is to develop in health and realize its potentialities. The basic needs are the evaluators of the environmental stimuli which come to the organism, and by observing these evaluators in action we find that they possess a directiveness which seeks satisfaction principally in terms of love. The satisfactions of the ingestion of oxygen, food, liquid, rest, activity, bowel and bladder elimination, and the like, are all optimally achieved in terms of love. From every relevant field of investigation the evidence is conclusive on this point.

We have, then, in the basic needs the Rosetta stone which enables us to read not only what human beings are born *as* but also what they are born *for*. Human beings are born with an organization of potentialities to develop all their capacities to the optimum through the stimulations of love; this is what they are born *as* and *for*. When human beings develop within the discipline of love they develop into ordered, harmonic, creative human beings according to their innate capacities—which set the limits, the biological limits, of development. When human beings are brought up in the matrix of confusion and disorder as most of them are in in the Western world, they become confused and disordered. One can no more make order in an individual by disordering him than by making order in the same way in the world. The world of humanity or inhumanity is the expression of the functions of human beings, and disordered human beings will make a disordered world. Ordered human beings will make an ordered world. Order and disorder in human beings is created in the home, principally by the masculine dominated values which are foisted upon the females who, with the best intentions in the world, succeed in disordering their children because they are not permitted to love them as they should, but "love" them by the criteria for love in such connections established by the false values of our society.

All of us in the Western world, and many elsewhere, have to learn the truth that the mother stands at the core of humanity. It is the mother, the loving mother, who teaches her children the most important of all the arts and sciences, namely, the ability to love, the development of the ability to love, so to behave always as to confer survival benefits upon all with whom one comes into contact in a creatively enlarging manner. Females are born already highly endowed with this capacity, males are born with the potentialities for its development, and it is principally from their mothers within the first six years of their lives that they have to learn how to love. We need to restore the mother to her inheritance as the educator of humanity.

We need to revise our conceptions of education, to distinguish between what passes for education today and instruction and techniques which are often confused with it. We need to understand that there is no education without love, the love that stimulates the potentialities of the individual toward development, the love which draws out those potentialities rather than the instruction which buries them under the detritus of pumped-in information. Education, in the light of what we have learned of the nature of human nature and what happens to human beings when they disregard the requirements of that human nature, education must be conceived as the discipline of the human being in making the best of his potentialities for being a warm, loving human being, and all techniques and information, the three R's, must be considered to play a secondary role. Love must be developed as the motivating force, and all else simply as a means to realizing the ends of that motivating force. In other words, what must be developed is an attitude toward life not merely of reverence but of the active participation in it in such a way as to confer survival benefits, at least, upon all human beings in a creatively enlarging manner.

What relevance has all this for religion? I think, in the first place, that it provides both a basis and a theme for belief and for action which all men can for the first time combine in accepting. In the second place, the demonstration of the nature of the organismal values provides a provable system of facts upon which an ethical code can be erected, for the organismal values tell us what men should do if they are to lead the good life. In the third place, the facts so generally referred to in this chapter render any appeal to supernatural agencies for the guidance of life upon this earth not only unnecessary but stultifying. In evaluating basic needs we are provided with a natural agency to which we can appeal for enlightenment as to the basic rules by which human beings should be educated in the conduct of life.

Love is God, *not* God is love. The belief in God cannot much longer, it seems to me, have any value for human beings. It is merely a means of postponing the reckoning, a means of avoiding the real issues and getting down to the business of realizing man's evolutionary destiny, which is to live in peace and good will, in creative harmony with all his fellow men.

Doctrines of innate depravity have done considerable damage to the development of humanity. Man does not need to look for salvation by repentance of his inherited sins, for he has inherited none within his biological structure; but he has inherited many through the social structures into which he has been born, and among the most reprehensible of these sins is the doctrine of innate depravity itself in the various forms which it has taken. Human beings are born with an ineradicable drive toward goodness. It may be completely repressed, but it cannot be extinguished. If there is a divinity in man it is this innate drive toward goodness, and it is the only divinity at the shrine of which human beings should worship. Indeed, unless they do they are likely to continue in the worship of false gods. The good man's religion is goodness.

At this point it may occur to some of my readers that if evil, hostility, aggressiveness, and violence seem to be a part of human nature, how then can one assert that they are not a part of human nature, as I do? The answer is very simple—as all answers tend to be once one has learned the facts. Evil is not inherent in human nature, it is learned. It is not human nature that is at fault, but human nurture. Aggressiveness is taught, as are all forms of violence which human beings exhibit. Warfare is no more a part of inherited human nature than is the carfare one is expected to pay. Both are learned activities.

But what of the naughtiness of children, is that learned, too? Do babies grow red and blue in the face, clench their little fists, and cry to high heaven because they have been taught to do so? The answer, surprising as it may seem to some, is yes. Even more surprising to some will be the statement that it is not natural for babies to cry at all unless they are disturbed, and that much of a baby's crying is taught him by those who do not know how to attend to his needs. The baby, infant, or child whose needs have been adequately satisfied will not normally cry. When a baby needs something and begins to make those signs and movements which he expects those who are supposed to be attending to his needs will recognize, but which we fail to recognize because we have lost the ability to understand the baby's language, and the pressure of his needs rises until it becomes unbearable, he becomes increasingly more distressed, frustrated, and responds by crying for attention. It is at this stage of affairs that we then run to him and attend to his need. We don't go to him when he first expresses the need, and this the baby learns, but we go to him when he can no longer bear the distress of nonsatisfaction of his need and he cries. This, too, the baby learns. In short, he learns that he cannot communicate with us more efficiently than by crying. He learns that we will come to him when he cries. And so when he wants us he cries.

Crying is a form of aggressive behavior, it is the elementary means of compelling attention. And, indeed, this is what most if not all hostility and aggression amounts to. Aggression is the expression of frustrated expectation of love. It is the expression of a pressing need for love. The way to meet aggression is not with further aggression, in the time-honored manner, but with love, with what aggression calls for, the response to the need for love. The fact is that we teach human beings to be aggressive by the simple device of denying them love in the multivarious ways in which we habitually, and often unconsciously, do so. Aggressiveness is not inborn but acquired. Indeed, whenever we observe aggressive behavior in any human being we should at once recognize that frustration of the need for love is at work in that person, that he is in need of love. And I would suggest that this is not only usually the case on the personal level, but on the community level, the national and international levels, and that what we need to apply more frequently than we have in the past on all these levels is the rule of love.

Aggressiveness, hostility, hatred, are nothing but forms of love frustrated, and so is evil. When the need for love in a human being, at any age, is being frustrated a wrong is being done. We can say this because, among other things, wrong conduct is the consequence of such behavior. Furthermore, we would expect it on theoretical grounds to be so—and we find it to be so.

It may be said that all I have succeeded in doing here is to provide something of a scientific validation for the Sermon on the Mount, and for similar sermons preached by others. If this is so, then it is certainly accidental, for I have certainly not arrived at my conclusions by any other route than by that of the scientist. If it is further claimed that I justify the findings of religion, I must put in something of a demurrer. The symbols of religion and the practice of reality I find do not coincide. In any event, I can see nothing in my conclusions which in any way can be said to support any existing traditional religion. On the contrary, my own conclusions lead me to believe that most of the traditional religions are actually antihuman, in that they contribute to the confusion of humanity rather than toward its enlightenment. From this characterization I would certainly exclude the reform and liberal representatives of many contemporary religions. But it seems to me that these latter representatives are, by the standard of what is traditionally considered a religion, much more in the camp of the secularists than they are in that of their own hardcore traditional churches.

My conclusions do not support a belief in God or in holy ghosts, nor in ritual or sacraments. My conclusions support only

the belief in the goodness of human beings, and in the probability
that if we love our children as we ought—and the "ought" refers
to a scientifically demonstrable "ought"—then we will for the
first time in our history begin to love our fellow human beings
as we ought. This way we will learn to live as if to live and
love were one—which I believe is the only true religion.

Science can make this belief a reality, and no existing religion
can, for the simple reason that science can teach men by what
means such a religion can be achieved, whereas religion does
not have the means. The churches have failed and their adherents
have failed the churches because neither of them had anything
better than confused means with which to attain their doubtful
goals. Science can clarify the means and verify it, and insure the
achievement of predictable goals, to the extent that anything
human is ever predictable. Peace on earth, good will to all men
is an achievable goal, and so is the love of one's neighbor as
oneself. But whereas for several millennia these goals have remained tragically unachieved in spite of much earnest striving,
they would be achievable within a few generations were the
findings of science applied concerning the nature of human
nature and of human society as we know them at the present
time.

The problem, however, is: How are we ever going to be able
to apply the findings of modern science to the solution of the
human problem? The answer can be immediate: Like charity,
one begins at home, with oneself, for one cannot mean very much
more to others than one means to oneself. One can, at the very
least, attempt to modify one's own conduct in the desired direction. At every level and by means of every possible approach
one can work to bring about those institutional changes in our
society, which will bring us nearer the desired goal. We can have
the process of maternity made better understood in the schools
in order that by the time females become mothers they shall be
fully prepared to do the right thing by their children. Our medical schools could be humanized, and the mechanization taken
out of them, even though the starch may remain in the white
coats of the doctors. But we don't need starch in doctors; what
we need is humanity. Our schools must be reorganized into insti-

tutions for the teaching of the theory and practice of human relations, and our colleges must carry on the good work of teaching and research in these areas.

It is, I consider, the moral obligation of every self-respecting person to make himself acquainted with the best that has been done, written, and thought on the subject of human relations—in the domain of science—and to apply this knowledge in every possible way. If a sufficient number of us will but do this I shall have no fear for the future of humanity or of religion.

3. Changes in Civilization That Affect Personal Fears and Anxieties

IT WAS PLATO WHO SAID that civilization is the victory of persuasion over force. By the measure of that statement, it will be generally agreed, we are either not at all civilized or only partially so. Plato was a philosopher. A psychiatrist or an anthropologist studying contemporary man might modify Plato's statement in the following way: civilization is the victory of reason over fear. He might add that true civilization involves being kind, and that the process of civilization is learning to be kind. If we reflect for a moment on the rephrasing of Plato's statement we will perceive that its meaning is essentially the same as that of the original statement. By "persuasion" Plato, of course, meant yielding to reason. And he was aware more than two thousand years ago that those who use force do so because they are afraid. We live in an age of violence because our civilizations, the societies in which contemporary civilized man lives, are full of people who are afraid and anxious. They are not afraid and anxious because the times are violent and threatening: the times are violent and threatening because they are afraid and anxious.

What are the changes in civilization, within the historic period, which have produced these personal fears and anxieties?

Before we proceed with the attempt to answer that question it should be made clear that fear and anxiety are nothing new upon the human scene, and that a certain amount of fear and anxiety has been characteristic of men everywhere. In fact without these responses, which are basic expressions of the organism, no human being could long survive. A certain amount of fear and anxiety are very necessary components of the human personality. The person who is not healthily fearful and anxious is likely to suffer a mishap of a lethal nature. It is good to be healthily afraid and anxious. But unhealthy fear and anxiety can be crippling and even fatal. And, indeed, it would appear that most persons in the civilized countries of the world are unhealthily fearful and anxious. As long as this condition continues, the problems of living confronting civilized man cannot be solved. It is therefore the most important of the tasks of modern man to find ways and means of not only reducing this fear and anxiety but of eliminating its particular kinds.

One of the acute problems which faces all people today is that of communication. When there is fear among people they mistrust one another and consequently do not speak to one another. In fact, fears not only cause man to distrust others, they also make man distrust himself. Fear is perhaps the greatest disturber of integrity. And when one distrusts oneself, disorganized behavior and hysteria are a frequent concomitant.

Nations behave like individuals because they are made up of individuals, and nations can be neurotic in much the same way that the individuals composing them are. Indeed, in 1925 there appeared a most interesting book by Mrs. Caroline E. Playne, entitled *The Neuroses of the Nations*. This is a most stimulating work, but it is only now, after more than a quarter of a century, that, thanks to the labors of psychologists, psychiatrists, psychoanalysts, sociologists, and particularly social anthropologists, the personality structure of whole peoples with particular reference to their relations to other peoples is being studied. For the first time we are learning, in a scientific manner, something about the conditions which enter into the formation of different personality types.

It is interesting to note that persons who were intimately

acquainted with the apparent conditions which led to World
War I were often clearly aware of its real causes. For example,
in a book published in 1921, Count Julius Andrassy writes:

> The real cause of the World-War was not conscious political
> determination, but the instinct of distrust and self-preservation.
> This statement is rendered plausible by the fact that the War
> was not declared because political determination and political
> aims failed to arrive at a compromise, and because all negotia-
> tions were utterly and finally futile; the War was brought about
> because, in the course of the negotiations, the feeling of distrust
> and the instinct of self-preservation led to military measures
> which were diametrically opposed to the instincts of self-preserva-
> tion and distrust of all the other States.[1]

Was it not President Roosevelt who, upon a famous occasion,
remarked that we have nothing to fear but fear itself?

Fear-ridden persons are neurotic, and a neurosis is a functional
attempt to adjust to a given set of conditions. A neurotic may
break down and become disorganized, detached from reality,
and under such conditions he may become very difficult to deal
with. Under such conditions nations frequently resort to violence,
to war; it has been suggested by Mrs. Playne that war develops
as a result of the nervous breakdown of nations. This is a very
suggestive thesis, but whether it is a fact or not, there is one
idea which must be dismissed at the outset, and that is the
notion that man is born with a will to power, an overriding desire to assert himself at the expense of others, that he is born
hostile and aggressive, and that it is the function of civilization
to discipline the brat so that he learns to control his allegedly
inborn aggressiveness and conforms to the requirements of his
society. The fears and anxieties that men exhibit are natural
and inborn, so run these claims, and they will always be with
us. The sensible thing is to recognize them and realize that
there will always be conflict between men, just as there will be
between nations. Wise men, so the argument runs, recognize
these indubitable realities, plan and prepare for all adversaries
and if necessary, for the peril of war.

---

[1] Julius Andrassy, *Diplomacy and the War* (London, Bale, 1921), p. 13.

These particular ideas constitute one of the principal sources and causes of contemporary man's fears and anxieties. Take, for example, the idea that human beings are born hostile and aggressive, and have to be disciplined into being good. This notion is very widespread in the Western world, and it is entirely false. Like most false ideas it has done an enormous amount of damage in the world, and caused the destruction of countless human beings. An acknowledgment and general acceptance of this stark fact through the efforts of educators and conscientious individuals would help diminish the personal fears and anxieties of future generations.

A society that believes children are born uncontrolled, evil, hostile, and egocentric will tend to discipline them according to the following representative dictates: "Spare the rod, spoil the child." "Let him learn early that he can't have what he wants." "The parents' word is the law." "Punish him if he misbehaves." "Make your love conditional upon his good behavior." "Don't pick him up when he cries or is in a tantrum, you'll spoil him." "Feed him by the clock, and keep him to a militarylike schedule so he will learn to grow up a good, dependable human being." The list of applicable phrases could be greatly extended, but these examples should suffice as fairly representative.

A consequence of this notion of Original Sin, as it were, is the creation of a regimen of systematically frustrated needs for the child. A frustration is defined as the thwarting of an expected satisfaction, and the result of such frustration is usually the production of hostility and aggressiveness. The fact is that the hostility which we find in children is not a congenital affliction but usually the hostility we ourselves have produced in them. It is an old device of humankind, first to produce a condition, and then to call it natural. A case in point is the inferiority which we impute to so-called minority groups, whose putative inferiority is subsequently regarded as "natural" or inherent. It is time we recognize that we have projected onto and produced in the innocent, defenseless, and utterly dependent child a hostility of which he is by nature guiltless. By treating him as if he were an aggressive, hostile brat we have made him so. By frustrating the child we have created fears and insecurities within him and have even made him doubt the reality of the love which has been offered him on such unattractive and conditional terms. Being so involved with ourselves that we almost involuntarily generalize our egocentric motives to the child because he is so completely dependent upon us and so demanding of our attention, we suppose the child to be the supreme egocentric. We are wrong.

The newborn infant is not an egocentric. In fact he has no ego. He acquires an ego from other egos, initially chiefly from the mother. What are usually confused with and taken for the infant's egocentricity are his dependency needs, which demand satisfaction by others and which cannot be satisfied by the infant himself. But in treating the infant as an egocentric we make an egocentric of him. An infant becomes egocentric when he is taught that most of his satisfactions are going to come from or be procured by himself. He is born with drives which make him behave as if he expected to receive satisfactions from others, and that is, of course, as it should be. Dr. Lauretta Bender, writing out of the fullness of her great experience as a psychiatrist, says: "The child acts as though there were an inherent awareness of his needs and there is thus the expectation of having them met. A failure in this regard is a deprivation and leads to frustration and a reactive aggressive response."[2]

The infant, in fact, is born with all its drives oriented in the positive direction of co-operation. It wants to co-operate and be co-operated with, for how is the former possible without the latter? Dr. Charlotte Bühler, one of our leading authorities on the psychology of children, testifies that co-operative behavior among children is more basic than competitive response. In the group of children under her observation, she noted that competitive responses did not make their appearance until about the third year.[3]

I must confess that there is precious little in the literature on the co-operativeness of babies. But as Dr. Lauretta Bender has

[2] Lauretta Bender, "Genesis of Hostility in Children," *American Journal of Psychiatry*, vol. 105, 1948, pp. 241-245.
[3] Charlotte Bühler, "Spontaneous Reactions of Children in the First Two Years," Proceedings and Papers of the 9th International Congress of Psychology, 1929, pp. 99-100.

said in the article from which I have already quoted, "The emphasis on the inborn or instinctive features of hostility, aggression, death wishes, and the negative emotional experiences represents a onesided approach which has led our students of child psychology astray." It is a sadly significant truth to have to acknowledge that one of the last branches of psychology to develop has been the study of the infant.

It should be fairly obvious that if the infant is born with drives which are mainly if not entirely co-operatively directed—that is to say, the drives are of such a nature that they demand satisfaction in order to establish a healthy equilibrium—then if his original drives are rewarded as he develops, the child exhibits increasingly more co-operative responses to those who sustain him. The child wants to be loved. To the extent that we inadequately love him we endanger his healthy development. A customary practice of the "best" and most highly paid pediatricians of a period now happily past—the subjection of infants to a clock schedule—is an illuminating example of Pope's aphorism, "A little knowledge is a dangerous thing."

Infants, children, and adults need no schedule. They need the discipline of love—the firmness that springs from love, not the ostensible love that springs from firmness.

We must realize that the changes which civilization has brought in our thinking and our way of life have often been determined by schools of thought which most scientists have accepted and which, therefore, the man in the street is inclined to follow. The notion that children are born aggressive was strongly reinforced by the formulation and misapplication of Darwinian ideas to man and his societies. Evolutionary jargon such as "The struggle for existence," "The survival of the fittest," "Nature red in tooth and claw," "The race is to the swift," "The weakest go to the wall," and similar shibboleths caused many people to believe that life in the jungle was a continuous war between animals. By association man, being an animal in origin and in fact, was thought to live in a world in which the relations with other men were ineluctably competitive. There was a struggle for existence not only between babies and men, but according to some late nineteenth-century biologists such as Wilhelm

Roux, even between cells! In any event, the doctrine of the struggle for existence found a ready translation from the biological into the social world in the form of Social Darwinism. Just as the fittest adapted themselves to their environment in the animal kingdom and survived, so those who best adapted themselves to the conditions of the nineteenth-century civilization became the fittest among men. So went the doctrine according to the gospel of Herbert Spencer and his followers.

One of the major changes in man's conception of human nature is the growing realization that he is not born aggressive, hostile, or evil, and that one is not therefore compelled to treat infants and children as if they were "wild animals"—which is another gross misconception—that have to be tamed and domesticated. The human infant is not a wild animal but a small, utterly dependent and defenseless creature seeking only to be loved, to be co-operated with. When a new understanding of the nature of human nature has become an established part of our culture, then we may hope to see a substantial reduction in personal fears and anxieties. For the myth of the intractable monster we must substitute the reality of the morsel of radiating defenseless life that wants to be loved and wants to love others. Our failure to recognize these truths has led us to what has at times seemed to be calculated enormities. Look, for instance, at the treatment of children in the supposedly enlightened centers of civilization.

At the present time more than 95 per cent of the babies in our cities are born in hospitals. In these institutions the baby is separated from the mother and put in a little crib in a nursery with a host of other babies. Each crib has a metal tag giving the child's name and number, as if he were a prisoner who had committed the crime of being born. The separation of the child from the mother is unnatural, unbiological, and psychologically detrimental to both. The baby particularly needs the warm comforting and extremely important physiological stimulation of the mother. The baby needs the mother because he is utterly dependent. He needs her cutaneous, or tactile, stimulation in order to develop his gastrointestinal and respiratory systems. The mother needs the contact of the baby for the sake of her own health and to promote her rapid recovery. Yet because we have largely thought of the convenience of the doctor, many mothers have readily agreed to the hospital because the stay there has provided a providential rest which was not otherwise attainable. Now that mothers are being encouraged to leave the hospital after a stay of a few days, things will perhaps begin looking up for babies. Certainly they are doing so with the development of "rooming-in" and natural childbirth. Also, there seems to be the increasing co-operation of a large body of workers in many different fields relating to child care.

Still there is a widespread lack of sympathy and understanding which does violence to the infant from the moment of his birth. We falsely assume that we are doing the right thing but often we do not. If we were guided by love and sympathy we would be more inclined to do the right thing even in the absence of empirical knowledge. Having had fear and anxiety produced in ourselves we go on producing them in those we ineffectually try to love. And this is because we live by a view of life which has been conditioned in us from early infancy, which is out of line with reality. That way of life is competitive. And it is to this competitiveness that I trace the origin of most of the fears and anxieties to which contemporary man is subject.

Just as one does violence to the naturally co-operative baby by frustrating him, so does one do violence to the nature of man when one puts him into the frustrative matrix of a competitive society. Man's inbuilt system of values and basic drives are directed toward co-operation, whereas the competitive societies in which we are socialized teach men to be aggressive, hostile, insecure, fearful, and anxious. We live in a competitive society, and it is that society which makes us afraid and anxious. What is a competitive society? A competitive society is one in which men strive against each other to achieve the goals upon which that society has set the highest premiums. And in a competitive society those goals are likely to be material ones—money, property, false prestige, and petty power. In such a society one competes because one is insecure, and because one seeks release from the tension of insecurity. It is supposed that release can be obtained by achieving "success." But "success" in these terms does not bring release from the tension of insecurity any more than does failure, as evidenced by the higher frequency of peptic ulcer and similar ailments among the "successful" than among the "failures."

Lawrence Frank has some germane comments in his illuminating essay, "The Cost of Competition." He writes of the impossibility of personal fulfillment through competition.

> One of the significant aspects of competition is this inability to attain any security in terms of the competitive activity in which it is sought. The reasons for this are more or less clear since competition denies any status that can be considered terminal; hence the competitors while always setting goals for themselves, are forced to a continual rejection of those goals when attained, in favor of a remote goal. This rejection is necessitated by the onward striving of others who threaten each goal as reached, but more imperatively by the individual's own personality that has set that goal only as a symbol. It is indeed remarkable how naively we have looked upon the ambition to be wealthy, politically powerful, or otherwise highly placed, as if the wealth or position were really significant to the individual.[4]

In a competitive society everyone will feel some insecurity, fear, and hostility because he is always threatened, supposedly or actually, by chance circumstances, by another person, or by his own disequilibrium and unpredictability. There is no one to depend upon, and so frequently those whom one thought one could lean upon turn out not to be rods but reeds. A competitive society consists of a striving crowd of individuals, *not* a co-operative community of persons, interrelated and interdependent in which all are engaged in a common enterprise. In such a competitive society every man is an island, essentially alone and afraid and anxious because he feels alone. Under such conditions he feels successful when he has been successfully aggressive. His aggressiveness may assume a variety of disguises, and it may even take the form of an apparent love or goodness.

There was a period in the Western world during which man felt more secure than he does today, because the society in which he lived was more firmly knit together by interest in and

[4] Lawrence Frank, *Society as the Patient* (New Brunswick, Rutgers University Press, 1948), p. 33.

respect for mutual endeavor and each other's welfare. I refer to the era of feudalism. I am not urging a return to the Middle Ages but I am trying to make a point which has been brilliantly made by Erich Fromm in his book *Escape From Freedom*.[5] Fromm has shown that the feudal economic system was based upon the principle of co-operation, and that it created measures to defend itself against incursions of the competitive spirit. Under this system men worked together, not against one another. With the rise of capitalism the co-operative organization gave way more and more to that of individualistic enterprise. Each individual had to go ahead and try his luck on his own. It was sink or swim. Others, who were not allied with him in a common enterprise, became competitors, and often, as Fromm says, he was faced with the alternatives of destroying them or being destroyed. Man has been expelled from the dependable world of co-operation and thrust into an uncertain, undependable world of competition. Today man is free—free to compete. He is free—free to be alone, threatened, isolated, estranged. He is free to feel insecure, power-less, doubtful, and anxious in a non-co-operative hostile world.

Is it any wonder that under such conditions men will look for any rod upon which to lean? Anything that will guarantee them security and freedom from anxiety is likely to make a successful appeal to them. Hitler exploited this knowledge to the limit.

It is impossible to talk of love and competition in the same breath. No amount of semantic jugglery can reconcile competition with co-operation and with love. If you are socialized in a competitive society you will become insecure, fearful and anxious, and unloving. If you are socialized in a co-operative society, in which men feel together and work together and are *for* each other, then you will be secure, unafraid and unanxious, co-opera-tive and loving. What makes men sick with fear and anxiety is the feeling of aloneness, anonymity, insignificance, alienation. As Bonaro Overstreet has said: "The one loss that a [person] cannot tolerate and remain in emotional health is the loss of good will between himself and his fellow humans. The fear and pain that distort his personality are those that come from actual or

[5] See Chapter 5 below.

anticipated rejection."[6] Man is most precariously dependent upon his fellow human beings for support, and what matters most to him is the quality of his human relationships. A point which cannot be too often made is that "Our extreme vulnerability where those relationships are concerned is a prime proof that we are 'members one of another.' "[7] In a society in which men are not for one another they are either indifferent to or against one another or both. Under these conditions men fall victim to acute anxiety and fear. Having made their tentative approaches to their fellow men and having been so often rejected, they fall ill with hostility. This is the normal response to continued frustration.

The basis of a thriving social life is the sensitivity of human beings to the behavior of their fellow men. If one individual responds to another with indifference or hostility, that other person becomes indifferent and hostile himself. And that is the present lamentable predicament of man in the highly competitive societies of the Western world.

The changes in civilization which have affected and continue to affect personal fears and anxieties revolve around the ethos of competition. The beginning of man's disintegration might be dated from the rise of commercialism. In itself it is nothing new in the world. It existed in ancient Egypt, Rome was diseased and finally died of it, and there have been other civilizations which have been fatally infected by the same plague. What is new in the world is the degree to which commercialism has developed and the extent to which the competitive ethos has infected the spirit of man. What progress men have made, spiritually, as human beings has been achieved in spite of competition *not* because of it. Commercialism has dehumanized and brutalized man; it has made a commodity of him to be manipulated and disposed of at ruthless whim. Commercialism has produced a form of society in which human beings are *used* and compelled to work at jobs whose only value resides in enabling them to continue to live—to live in an inhuman world. Consequently, in this commercial society there are millions of

[6] *Understanding Fear* (New York, Harper, 1951), p. 137.
[7] *Ibid.*, p. 138.

human beings who work at jobs which they detest and despise but who are shackled to them because they don't want to starve. This is madness and it drives millions of human beings mad. Sanity has been defined as adjustment to reality. But what kind of reality is this to which so many millions of human beings are called upon to adjust? What kind of a human being can one be after one has submitted oneself to the barbaric demands of such a society?

The accumulation of infant, childhood, adolescent, and adult frustrations produces a sizable quantity of hostility. Pushed around in childhood, human beings grow into adults who push others around. Human beings in such a competitive society are caught not in a trap, but in a large room from which there is no real escape. Flight is impracticable for there are walls to contain it, and like an animal which is pushed to the wall, human beings will fight when they cannot take to flight. And ours is a fighting society. The clawed hand may be concealed by a kid glove, and the grinning grotesques behind the hucksters' billboards may make you feel that they are giving you something you want when they are in reality depriving you of something you need. Isn't this the society in which a "sucker" is said to be born every minute? Is not this the society in which when one meets someone one asks oneself, What does this person mean to me? What can I get out of him? This is the society, is it not, in which one concentrates on meeting the "right" people instead of oneself *being* the right person.

One of the great sources of fear and anxiety in our culture is to be found in the fact that our society is a conflict-producing one. We bring up children in the teachings of Christianity or some other religion and teach them, at Sunday school at least, to love their neighbors as themselves. Yet at the same time we teach them to compete. In other words we bifurcate the psychological development of the person from his early years on and present him with a set of mutually irreconcilable principles and ways of life. We not only split the person's ego but we confuse it. One cannot worship God and Mammon at the same time, and those who try become sick hypocrites. The conflicting and mutually irreconcilable institutions which exist in our society put a great strain upon the adaptive capacities of most persons in the form of a running chronic conflict. There can be a breakdown of what Hans Selye has called the alarm-reaction system of the body. This is the system which is called into action under conditions of stress. Selye has shown that when this system is called upon too often it breaks down with resulting inability of the organism effectively to meet the conditions of stress. Hence a breakdown follows in one or more systems, or the total body system, of the organism. The person becomes apathetic, listless, loses his zest for living, and presents all the appearances of being, and in fact is, in a state of shock. Hence the great frequency of psychosomatic disorders in our day. In our present society there can be no temporizing between conflictful values. It is an either-or situation. To be a success in terms of both Christian ethics and those of the business world usually means knowing what is right and doing what is wrong—knowing what you should be, knowing what you would be, knowing what you could be, and refusing to face what you are.

We pay lip service to spiritual values but place our faith in material possessions. The prices of things are confused with the value of goods. On the one hand we tell people that they belong together but on the other we wean them from this idea from their earliest years. We separate the individual from his biological and social continuities with other human beings, and we try to make an individual of him increasingly, rather than increasingly a person who is thoroughly integrated with the community of his fellows. We teach our children that "I" is more important than "We," and in so doing we disorient and dislocate them; we make them feel alone when they should feel together.

To sum up: We are suffering from the disenfranchisement of humanity, from the absence of love and co-operation. We have been abject witnesses to the enthronement of a way of life whose monstrous issue is the disease of competition, a disease which is largely the effect of commercialism or industrialism. The commercial ethos vitiates human relationships, converts them into business affiliations. There is the business of "love" which is made copiously available by Hollywood and similar purveyors of this commodity. Love for innumerable people in our society has come to mean sex. Love without sex is to most of them inconceivable. Hence, one gets married on the basis of a conception of love which is something of a business arrangement. In return for the sex supplied by the female the male supplies a home. When sex begins to pall, a business meeting with a lawyer and the decision of a court will provide a divorce. This occurs in more than one out of every three marriages contracted in the United States, and in one out of four cases in the British Isles. Does one have children because one loves children? No. One has children because it's a kind of keeping up with the Joneses, the thing to do, like the engraved wedding announcements with the tissue paper carefully tucked in, in order, no doubt, to prevent the embossed ink from rubbing and thus giving the whole venture an ephemeral aspect. Children are the "proper" thing to have when one is married. And, of course, when one has them one likes them, for babies are the most endearing of all things. And so one likes and even "loves" them, but the brats have to be disciplined, and this is the point at which the pattern begins to repeat itself. The business of rearing children is conducted on business lines. If, say the parents, you do this for me I'll do that for you. It's a kind of trading. If you go on doing things that we don't like, say the parents, then we won't like you. So if you want to do business with us, you had better come across with the right behavior. We expect you to deliver the goods if you're to receive payment. Even worse, thy communicate to their children that they have made an investment in them and they expect a profit, that is, they expect their children to be better than they are themselves.

Of course this is an exaggeration, but is there not some truth in it? There is, in fact, something of this in all cultures, but the culture of the United States is perhaps that in which the business of trading in human relationships has gone furthest in modeling itself on technological relationships.

Technology and industry are admirable and desirable things in their proper place. Wherever their place may be, it is certainly not in the area of human relationships. On the other hand, technology and industry are in vital need of more human relations. Technology and industry must be humanized, and we must eliminate the technologizing and industrializing of human relations. Human society must not be based on economics. Economics must be based on human society. In other words, it is not on economics that human societies must be based but on human relations. When we have fully realized the significance of this fact and put our knowledge into action we shall be in a position to control better all those changes in civilization which affect personal fears and anxieties.

4. Freedom and the Individual

THE INDIVIDUAL IS A MYTH. There are no individuals. There are many persons, however, who try to be individuals, who endeavor to live their lives separate and apart from their fellow human beings. Frequently they live their individual lives without thought or consideration of the effects of their individualism upon their fellow men. Such persons are psychically disfigured, disintegrated, and disoperative, and they are the producers of disintegration and disoperation among their fellow men not only in the societies in which they immediately live, but also among their fellow men in far distant places, among human beings whom they have never seen and often of whom they have never heard. The effects of "rugged individualism," American or any other variety, are likely to be widespread and particularly devastating to those peoples of the world who have been unprepared for its effects. The impact of smallpox and measles upon those who have no immunity is as nothing as compared to the disastrous effects of the Western doctrine and practices of "individualism" upon these peoples.

The victim of the diseases of "individualism," who has inherited the pathogenic idea from his ancestors, is in a far better position to resist its effects than are those people of this earth who have never been afflicted by the pathogenic ideas or perhaps had long ago in their history completely eliminated them. Because we of the Western world have developed a certain immunity to the disorder of individualism, we are at once both endangered by that immunity and in a position to do something constructive about it. Unless we do so we stand a good chance of eliminating our-

61

selves altogether. The idea of individualism is a pathological one, and, as I have said, we have developed an immunity to it: hence the idea itself will not kill us. What will kill is are the consequences of that idea, the acts to which that idea leads.

An individualist is one who attempts to live essentially for himself. Why does he attempt to do so? Not because he is inherently driven to do so, but because he has been conditioned in a social environment in which the values which he is taught to respect are those of "individualism." Man for himself, for if he is not for himself—he is taught to believe—who will be? No, he learns to argue that life is a struggle and those who have what it takes survive, and those who haven't—don't. This is the principle by which most men in the Western world live today. It is the Golden-Plated Rule, "Do unto others what will enable you to advance yourself without consideration of the effects of your conduct upon anyone or anything else."

So to live is to destroy the freedom of others as well as of oneself. It is not to be wondered at that the individualist fails to understand the meaning of freedom. He becomes, instead, increasingly more authoritarian, one who wishes to destroy freedom because freedom increases his anxiety, an anxiety which arises in part from a half-conscious awareness of what he ought to do, but which he will not or cannot do. Since he is not free to enjoy freedom himself, the individualist conscientiously sees to it that freedom for others is constricted as far as possible. The individualist is rigidified. He dare not deviate from the rigid course which has largely been set for him and which he must maintain for himself. The individualist is a person whose individualist values have become congealed at an early stage in his development in a matrix which is essentially contrary to his individualist values. For every human being is born a co-operative creature and remains ineradicably so throughout life. Nevertheless, insofar as conduct is concerned it is possible to bypass the co-operative drives and repress them in favor of individualistic or competitive ones. Individualism is a sickness because it is a disorder of a system, the human organism, which is originally organized and oriented in the direction of relatedness—the very opposite and contradictory of individualism.

The organism is conceived in a system of relatedness, in the relationship to the mother during prenatal development, and in relatedness to the mother and increasingly to others during the postnatal period. It is because a person derives his self and develops it through his interrelationships with other selves that there is not nor can there ever be such a thing as an individual— separate and apart from other selves. Every self is derived from and is constituted by other selves, and it is for this reason that every human being necessarily forms a network of social interrelationships from which he cannot possibly extricate himself without doing considerable damage both to himself and to his society in the process.

It is one of the greatest of errors to assume—for it is nothing more than an erroneous assumption—that the older a person grows the more of an "individual" he grows to be. On the contrary, the older a person grows the more complex does the network of his social relationships become, and the more deeply involved does he become with society. In other words, he becomes less and less of an individual and more and more of a person.

This is most definitely not to say that the older the person grows the more and more anonymous or undifferentiated he becomes. On the contrary, the more the person becomes involved in his fellows and in his society, the more of a person he becomes, the more he is differentiated, for there is nothing like the interstimulation of association with one's fellow human beings for developing to the maximum one's potentialities for being human, and for being what one uniquely is. A person is a unique organization of interpersonal or social relationships—unique, because every person begins with a unique primary nature or system of potentialities which through the unduplicated history of experiences which their possessor undergoes become organized into a unique personality. The identity of the person consists of the meaningfulness of his interrelationships.

The human state is in the social state, and the antihuman state is that of the individualist, the rigidified creature who must cleave to his undeviating course because of his fear that if he does deviate from that course he will be lost. This is the creature

who is himself virtually completely unfree, who has no inner
resources of freedom, but who is conditioned by imperatives
from which he dare not depart. This is the authoritarian personality, the personality who likes to command and to be commanded. Children who have been brought up in authoritarian
families, no matter in which land they may be, are likely to develop as authoritarian personalities. Adorno and his co-workers
in their studies on Californian college boys and girls, and Schaffner, Levy, and others[1] have found this to be so in German subjects. Other studies on democratic and authoritarian families in
the United States yield the same conclusions, namely, that the
kind of conditioning which the child receives within his family
largely determines his personality structure with respect to freedom and authoritarianism. The democratic family situation leads
to a freely organized personality, the authoritarian family to an
authoritarian personality.[2] Levy, most interestingly, found that
even in the same German family, as the attitudes become less
authoritarian with the birth of successive children, so did the
personalities of the children, so that the first-born male, for example, was usually found to have become a violent Nazi, the
second-born son a member of the Nazi party, but not as violent
a Nazi as the first-born, whereas the third-born son either became a token member of the party but was in fact opposed to it
or avoided joining altogether.

In short, the results of such investigations as have thus far
been made indicate that both tyrants and free men are made,
where so much else is, largely in the home. I say "largely" in the
home because there is good reason to believe that while the
home is the major factor in producing such personality differences, the playmates of the child and also the school play a not
inconsiderable role in the conditioning of his attitudes.

If we would have men and women in this world who will

[1] T. W. Adorno and others, *The Authoritarian Personality* (New York,
Harper, 1950); B. Schaffner, *Father Land* (New York, Columbia University
Press, 1948); D. M. Levy, "Anti-Nazis: Criteria of Differentiation," in A. H.
Stanton and S. E. Perry, eds., *Personality and Political Crisis* (Glencoe,
Free Press, 1951), pp. 151-227; D. Rodnick, *Postwar Germans* (New Haven,
Yale University Press, 1954).
[2] See pp. 91-94 below.

be capable of understanding the meaning of freedom, who will be capable of living their lives in freedom, then the home is the principal institution upon which we must focus our attention. And as practically all investigators in this area have agreed, if parents will but adequately love their children, the best of all foundations will have thus been well and truly laid for the development of human beings who will be free of all rigidities and therefore free and open to understand all the experiences which life will bring them.

5. Escape From Freedom

ERICH FROMM's *Escape From Freedom* is one of the most important books published in our time. Important, not so much because of any novelty in the views which the author expresses, but because he has written a book in which, for the first time, the conditions which lead to the strange individualistic–anti-individualistic conduct of modern man are set out and penetratingly discussed. The subject is, of course, a large and complex one, and its study has involved many years of labor on the part of Dr. Fromm. It is not at all unlikely that the present volume will have a wider and deeper influence upon modern thought than the projected larger work, for *Escape From Freedom* will always be read as the essence of the author's considered conclusions. Scholars, who will want to verify the evidence, will alone need to go to the larger work.

The whole of Dr. Fromm's thesis is stated in these words:

> We see that the process of growing human freedom has the same dialectic character that we have noticed in the process of individual growth. On the one hand it is a process of growing strength and integration, mastery of nature, growing power of human reason, and growing solidarity with other human beings. But on the other hand this growing individuation means growing isolation, insecurity, and thereby growing doubt concerning one's own rôle in the universe, the meaning of one's life, and with all that a growing feeling of one's own powerlessness and insignificance as an individual.

> If the process of the development of mankind had been har-

From *Psychiatry*, vol. 5, 1942, pp. 122-129.

monious, if it had followed a certain plan, then both sides of the development—the growing strength and the growing individuation would have been exactly balanced. As it is, the history of mankind is one of conflict and strife. Each step in the direction of growing individuation threatened people with new insecurities. Primary bonds once severed cannot be mended; once paradise is lost, man cannot return to it. There is only one possible, productive solution for the relationship of individualized man with the world: his active solidarity with all men and spontaneous activity, love and work, which unite him again with the world, not by primary ties but as a free and independent individual.

However, if the economic, social and political conditions on which the whole process of human individuation depends, do not offer a basis for the realization of individuality in the sense just mentioned, while at the same time people have lost those ties which gave them security, this lag makes freedom an unbearable burden. It then becomes identical with doubt, with a kind of life which lacks meaning and direction. Powerful tendencies arise to escape from this kind of freedom into submission or some kind of relationship to man and the world which promises relief from uncertainty, even if it deprives the individual of his freedom.

European and American history since the end of the Middle Ages is the history of the full emergence of the individual. It is a process which started in Italy, in the Renaissance, and which only now seems to have come to a climax. It took over four hundred years to break down the medieval world and to free people from the most apparent restraints. But while in many respects the individual has grown, has developed mentally and emotionally, and participates in cultural achievements in a degree unheard of before, the lag between "freedom from" and "freedom to" has grown too. The result of this disproportion between freedom *from* any ties and the lack of possibilities for the positive realization of freedom and individuality has led, in Europe, to a panicky flight from freedom into new ties or at least into complete indifference.[1]

The analysis and demonstration of this thesis is most successfully carried out.

[1] Erich Fromm, *Escape From Freedom* (New York, Farrar and Rinehart, 1941), pp. 35-37.

In his analysis of medieval society Fromm shows that the feudal economic system was based upon the principle of co-operation as consciously opposed to the principle of competition. Under this system men worked together, not against one another. With the rise of capitalism the principle of co-operation gave way more and more to that of individualistic enterprise. "Each individual must go ahead and try his luck. He had to swim or sink. Others were not allied with him in a common enterprise, they became competitors, and often he was confronted with the choice of destroying them or being destroyed."[2]

Instead of the limited bounded world of co-operation each person is now thrust into an unlimited, unbounded world of competition. He is free—free to compete, free not to co-operate. He is free, free to be threatened, isolated, estranged—free to feel insecure, powerless, doubtful, anxious, and alone in a non-co-operative hostile world.

Is it any wonder that he looks for props to lean upon and leaders who will restore to him that feeling of solidarity which comes with the identification with others?—Which comes with the merging of oneself in others, so that one ceases to be an isolated person serving as a target for the blows of life? This merging of the personality in the group seems to me a perfect example of withdrawal from reality into the realm of fantasy. For with the group or the mob one can do without a feeling of responsibility what one would only dream of doing as a person.

When the group with which one identifies oneself provides such a host of fantasies as the Nazi party, the conflicts of millions of confused, unhappy isolated men will immediately be reduced by joining such a fantastic group.

On a lesser and more human scale this has happened before in Germany. This occurred in the eighteenth century when, years after Luther had deprived the Germans of Roman Catholicism, which had so effectively nourished their mysticism and ministered to their sense of beauty while commanding their belief, Winckelmann went to Rome and discovered the classical spirit

[2] *Ibid.*, p. 61.

in Greek sculpture.[3] Luther destroyed the mythological element in Christianity, and from the date of that event to the present day the Germans have been seeking for some new mythology wherewith to replace it. By clearing the way for a more purely rational interpretation of the world, Luther failed to foresee that by withdrawing the experience of the mystical, the metaphysical, the poetic, and the dramatic, he was building for a time when the people would be glad to embrace a mythology whose barbarity would have appalled him. One may never deprive mankind of its feeling of unity with the world and with nature and with man without providing another set of such metaphysical beliefs—unless one is ready to brook disaster. As Renan wrote:

> The serious thing is that we fail to perceive a means of providing humanity in the future with a catechism that will be acceptable henceforth, except on the condition of returning to a state of credulity. Hence, it is possible that the ruin of idealistic beliefs may be fated to follow hard upon the ruin of supernatural beliefs and that the real abasement of the morality of humanity will date from the day it has seen the reality of things. Chimeras have succeeded in obtaining from the good gorilla an astonishing moral effort; do away with the chimeras and part of the factitious energy they aroused will disappear.[4]

Dr. Fromm has overlooked this episode in the history of Germany, even though it principally affected the more cultured classes. But the discovery of the Greek classical spirit was for them as significant, and in many ways as similarly valued, a discovery as was Nazism for all the classes of modern Germans.

Luther is treated at some length by Dr. Fromm, who points out that although Luther gave the Germans independence in religious matters, he none the less involuntarily contributed to their basic insecurity by depriving them of their traditional props. This is a view which is clearly supported by Miss Butler in the volume already referred to. And who is not familiar with those

---

[3] For an admirable discussion of this subject see E. M. Butler, *The Tyranny of Greece over Germany* (New York, Macmillan, 1935).
[4] Ernest Renan, *The Future of Science, Ideas of 1848* (London, Chapman and Hall, 1891), p. xviii.

modern men and women who very simply express what is for them the prop function of religion in the words, "Why, if I didn't have God to fall back upon, where *would* I be?"

Protestantism did a great deal to destroy the confidence of man in God's ever-ready, proplike, unconditional love.

Thus, from the secular and the spiritual sides man, from the Reformation on, has been more and more isolated, thrown back upon himself. Man was deprived of the security he had enjoyed, of the unquestionable feeling of belonging, and he was torn loose from the world which had satisfied his quest for security both economically and spiritually. He felt alone and anxious.

Now what seems to me of rather more than ordinary interest, in more than one way, is the fact that in Western civilization children are still brought up to believe that they live in a co-operative world, in which they have but to co-operate to secure the proper rewards. The family is, of course, the child's conception of a co-operative unit, where he has but to be in evidence in order to have practically his every need taken care of. Is there not a strange disequilibrium here? And is not this factor a significant one in contributing to the social neurosis of the person in later years?

I am myself completely in favor of the education of children in co-operative principles, and I am entirely in favor of a society which is run upon such principles. But where, as in Western societies, such principles function only upon an ideal plane, and in actual practice are replaced by the principles of competition to the death, it is nothing short of a deliberate deception and a calculated desire psychically to shock, to create an alleged working conception of life to which life as it is lived by men does not correspond.

Many hope, and some believe, that the co-operative spirit of love which pervades, and is, the pattern of family relationships, will some day be extended to interfamily and all interpersonal relationships. Yes, let parents teach their children this, but also teach them the brutal facts about the world in which they live. Prepare them, but do not continue to deceive them.

As the editors have written in *Psychiatry:*

Youth is the victim everywhere. Even in America, his lot grows increasingly difficult. It has never been so easy to see that this is a world for the ageing, that people are born to carry on the ideals of their elders, not to go forward in freedom towards the horizon of undreamed of things to come.

In America, the average youth from 9 to 13 embodies the ideals of a glorious society. Thereafter, socio-sexual necessities compel him to relapse to the prevailing pattern of juvenile competitive society the earmark of which is the active struggle for power. The creative biosocial strivings are strong in the preadolescent personality. The symbol activity is oriented towards the achievement of collaborative, sympathetic group life, with interest in understanding the rich field of individual variation.[5]

While society continues to be run on the principles of big business, of competition and exploitation, where men are treated as less valuable than machines, good for a certain needed time, and then when no longer required to be thrown upon the dust-heap, to starve, to degenerate, to die, to—who cares what?—is it not time that psychiatrists assume their full social obligation, and inform society of the disasters which will inevitably overtake a community run upon such principles?

During my first winter in New York, in 1927, and in many winters subsequently, I saw a man, sleeping, as I thought, on the sidewalk. It seemed to me a strange place to choose for a sleep. But what interested me more than the man were the passers-by. They didn't even cast a glance in the direction of the recumbent form. They seemed quite dissociated from his, and from everyone else's, existence. That afternoon, passing by the same place, the man was still where I had first seen him in the morning. He was blue-green in the face, and I saw at once that he was dead. No one apparently had taken the trouble to inform the police, and nobody cared. The only difference, it seemed to me, between this man and those who had passed him by was that he was dead while they were reaping the benefits of oxygenated blood. Of course, there were more differences, but for all practical purposes that seemed to me the principal difference,

[5] "Responsibility"—an Editorial, *Psychiatry*, vol. 2, 1939, p. 600.

and in my weaker moments it seems to me the only difference even now. For the dead man was a completely and thoroughly isolated unit, and so, more or less, seemed those units who, in isolation, were passing him isolatedly by.

"I cannot become involved," seems to be the human principle today. "I must look after myself, and let others look after themselves, for if I won't look after myself who will?" Who will, indeed? Is there anything else under such circumstances that a man can do? Yes, he can follow the first leader, and join the first party, that promises to look after him and his—that promises to give him security, substantiality, meaningfulness, love. What is a so-called freedom worth which leads to insecurity, anxiety, and insignificance, compared to this other freedom to live? Very little, indeed. And so one joins the party.

Is it as simple as that? Dr. Fromm does not see that it is really any more complicated than that. Nor do I. Of course, there is vastly more to be said upon the subject; Dr. Fromm has said a good deal of it, and said it very well.

Dr. Fromm shows that modern society affects man simultaneously in two distinct, yet inseparably linked, ways: he becomes more independent, self-reliant, and critical, and he becomes more isolated, alone, and afraid. And the tragedy of modern man is that his very independence, self-reliance, and critical abilities all combine to render him more and more isolated, alone, and afraid. Most people do not, of course, fully realize the situation, but they do realize with all the power for life that is within them that somehow, sometime, they must escape from the burden of a freedom so complete that they are left completely alone. This negative freedom they must exchange for a positive freedom.

Those who will read Dr. Fromm's book will not doubt what requires to be done. What they will doubt is whether the proper action will be taken in time to prevent disaster.

Until the educational systems have been reorganized from top to bottom, there is, in my judgment, little hope of ever achieving a well-equilibrated personality, for even a significantly small proportion of mankind.[6]

---

[6] For a beautiful and cogent exposition of these principles consult the essay on "American Democracy" by George Norlin in his admirable volume of

In order to bring about a reform in the educational systems it will first be necessary to secure the proper political representation in the houses of legislation. In order to achieve that it will be necessary to educate the voter to be able to evaluate evidence for himself. And there is the vicious circle! But I do not believe that it is completely vicious. Unless, however, men of humanitarian vision and culture assume more responsible social attitudes and conduct than the majority of them have done in the past, that circle will remain, unbroken and vicious.

Men are the victims of the world they create. They must become masters. It is for mastery of mind over matter, of the spiritual over the material, that they must be taught to strive. This can only be achieved through education. Violent revolution will not achieve this. Revolution always breeds reaction. If anyone doubts this let him but study the history of Europe and America since the French Revolution. Let him study the history of the world since the Russian Revolution of 1917. True reforms come only by evolutionary, not by revolutionary, means.

Apropos of all this, Dr. Fromm has many profound and illuminating things to say.

> The irrational and planless character of society must be replaced by a planned economy that represents the planned and concerted effort of society as such. Society must master the social problem as rationally as it has mastered nature. One condition for this is the elimination of the secret rule of those who, though few in number, wield great economic power without any responsibility to those whose fate depends upon their decision. . . .
>
> Only if man masters society and subordinates the economic machine to the purposes of human happiness and only if he actively participates in the social process, can he overcome what now drives him into despair—his aloneness and his feeling of powerlessness. Man does not suffer so much from poverty today as he suffers from the fact that he has become a cog in a large machine, an automaton, that his life has become empty and lost its meaning. The victory over all kinds of authoritarian systems will be possible only if democracy does not retreat but takes the

essays and addresses, *Things in the Saddle* (Cambridge, Harvard University Press, 1940).

offensive and proceeds to realize what has been its aim in the minds of those who fought for freedom throughout the last centuries. It will triumph over the forces of nihilism only if it can imbue people with a faith that is the strongest the human mind is capable of, the faith in life and in truth, and in freedom as the active and spontaneous realization of the individual self.[7]

I completed reading *Escape From Freedom* in a week. During the following month I read several other books, and what struck me with understandable force in each of these volumes was the clear and unmistakable recognition of the essential aloneness of Western man. It seems very evident that educated men and women are becoming more and more aware of the principal disorder from which they together with their fellows are suffering.

Here, for example, is a passage from Eleanor Dark's delightful historical novel *The Timeless Land*, a work which is, incidentally, the most sympathetic and penetrating account of the workings of the mind of the Australian aboriginal which has ever been written.

Cunnembeilee is an aboriginal girl who has become the "wife" of the escaped convict Andrew.

> Nothing in her association with the white man had disturbed Cunnembeilee so much as his mysterious detachment. He was the first human being she had ever known who was isolated—a solitary individual, existing, incomprehensibly, without background or relations. Even his single name, An-droo, told her nothing, whereas among her own people a man's names were his testimonial, his letter of introduction, and his genealogical tree, all in one. Her vocabulary was rich in names for the different kinds and degrees of kinship, and implicit in every name were functions and responsibilities and taboos, so that from birth one was secure, embedded in the pattern of tribal organization, one's place ready-made, one's guardians appointed, one's duties clearly defined.
>
> She was profoundly uneasy in her fear that her child might be deprived of this rich and reassuring background. Father's relations he had none; and mother's relations were, so far, denied to him. No longer, she was determined, should they be denied. Her brothers should see him. He should be given, even if only

[7] Fromm, pp. 272, 276.

for a little while, now and then, his rightful place as a member of his mother's tribe.[8]

In her preface Mrs. Dark writes of the Australian aborigines:

> The race is nearly gone, and with it will go something which the "civilized" world has scorned too easily. . . . we, nine-tenths of whose "progress" has been a mere elaboration and improvement of the technique, as opposed to the art, of living, might have learned much from a people who, whatever they may have lacked in technique, had developed that art to a very high degree. "Life, liberty, and the pursuit of happiness"—to us a wistful phrase, describing a far-away goal—sums up what was, a taken-for-granted condition of their existence.[9]

In the Gifford Lectures for 1937-1938, *Man on His Nature*, the great neurophysiologist, Sir Charles Sherrington, writes:

> He [man] feels afresh that in himself for the first time a product of the process of evolution perceives that process and reads its own making. It is as though the door of Nature had been pushed ajar and man were peeping through, there to get a glimpse at his own story and some fresh understanding of himself. His reading of the world and of himself in it had before been a different one. In several ways his fuller knowledge has spelt disillusion, disenchantment. In him evolving mind has got so far as to become critical of life. He feels the curse as well as the blessing attached to "zest-to-live." He is impressed by a cruelty inherent in the economy of life. He is disillusioned the more to find he is a part in that same dispensation. The Regime is, if he ask his "heart," one for which he cannot seek his heart's approval. There was the old parable of the Fruit of the Tree and the Expulsion from the Garden. With knowledge of good and evil, paradise was lost. To look on with understanding at what is passing in life's world and to be a party to it is complicity in war against his "values." Lessons from the old sub-human existence enjoined on him at least what to avoid. But ancient trends die hard. He himself is often still just one more agent of

---

[8] Eleanor Dark, *The Timeless Land* (New York, Macmillan, 1941), p. 438.
[9] *Ibid.*, footnote pp. viii-ix. In this connection consult Ashley Montagu, *Coming Into Being Among the Australian Aborigines* (New York, Dutton, 1938), pp. 343-350, and "The Socio-Biology of Man," *The Scientific Monthly*, vol. 50, 1940, pp. 483-490.

suffering to others. He must escape further from those ways of life. He must try to shed from his gene complex some sub-human ingrained elements. The mill he has been through ground out its products in the main by retaining above all the interests of "self." He was a successful product of that process. Looking at it, as the founder of these lectures would in these lectures have him, by that same mode of thought which he employs for science, but infusing into the view so won, as again the founder of these lectures would have him do, his moral aspirations, there arises for him a dilemma and a contradiction. The contradiction is that he is slowly drawing from life the inference that altruism, charity, is a duty incumbent upon thinking life. That an aim of conscious conduct must be the unselfish life. But that is to disapprove the very means which brought him hither, and maintains him. Of all his newly-found values perhaps altruism will be the most hard to grow. The "self" has been so long devoted to itself as end. A good man's egotism, it is said, is altruism. Perhaps that indicates a stepping-stone on the way.

Marked out it would seem, to be leader of life upon the planet, more, willy-nilly set so, he yet has none to seek guidance from. None of whom to ask a question. What wonder his religions seek to supply a Higher Being to meet his need in this? The sole counsel he can take, and he must seek it to the uttermost, is with the facts. He will need all his qualities. His kind must co-operate together to the last man.

Man's spirit thus yearns for company, comradeship, angels— even demons. His mediaeval thought had judged him a thing apart, but never allotted to him a loneliness such as this he now is conscious of. Nothing at all outside himself with which he can commune on what is next his heart. Was it not Kant who wrote, "I declare I am much moved toward the presence of immaterial beings in this world, to put my soul with them."

Perhaps a like sentiment bred the weariness which Goethe found insufferable in the materialism of his time, "its Cimmerian grey." Facing this, in comparison with himself limitless, "surround," which is fraught with good and evil but is, it would seem, unaware of either, man now knows enough of it to know that itself and he are none the less parts of one and the same. There was a time when he nursed the notion that he stood a thing apart, even somewhat after the manner of an Olympian or of one of the host of heaven. He was wont to think of man and

Nature as two contrasted empires. He thought of himself as an exception to the order of the rest; not a wheel geared in with the other wheels. "Most of those who have written on the ways of men have done so as though those ways were no part of Nature. As though forsooth they were not controlled by the general laws of the universe. As though they were something outside Nature."[10]

And there is a great deal more on the values of fellowship and co-operation, which the reader must go to the original volume for himself.

A perhaps not altogether unconscious recognition of what has here been illustrated is suggested by Eric Linklater who, in his autobiography, writes of the pleasure he found in submission and discipline, as a recruit during World War I,

> . . . drill on the football field, and the discovery that in a disciplined response to orders there is a curious pleasure—submission is a feminine thing, a Christian thing, an aspect of perversion and a military necessity, and being all these is perhaps a normal thing—but also there was the little pleasure of exhibitionism, because often our friends were watching us. So proudly we slapped our rifles and blew to their full extent our exiguous willing chests.[11]

And now let me quote a few lines from a rare little book by that relentless critic of his fellow Englishman, Sir Richard Burton. This work, a long poem, entitled *Stone Talk*, was pseudonymously published in 1865. It has recently been reprinted at San Francisco.

Whew!

> A most eccentric race are you
> Islanders; as the Germans dream
> You all so many islands seem
> Cut off from the rest of human kind.[12]

[10] Charles Sherrington, *Man on His Nature* (New York, Macmillan, 1941), pp. 382-384. This book is in the present writer's opinion one of the greatest works of our century.
[11] Eric Linklater, *The Man on My Back* (New York, Macmillan, 1941), p. 20.
[12] Frank Baker [Sir Richard Francis Burton], *Stone Talk*, Reprint Series No. 24, Occasional Papers, San Francisco, California State Library, 1940.

Going back some years I find a clear recognition of the malady of Western man in an article by C. E. M. Joad, in which the following significant passage occurs.

In England the men of this generation have lost their religion. It has evaporated and, withdrawing, has left a vacuum. Without some cause in which to lose themselves, some creed in which to find themselves, or some loved object of value for which to sacrifice themselves, men live lives without point and purpose. Recognizing nothing which can raise them out of the selfish, little pit of vanity and desire which is the self, they are led to turn their thoughts inwards to find in themselves at once the sole object of interest and the sole criterion of value. As a result they live tired and tiring lives, play solely for their own hands, and endeavour to find in self-satisfaction and the gratification of sense a sufficient aim and purpose for living. The symptoms of the *malaise* in terms of disillusion, cynicism, undue introspectiveness, hysteria and neurosis are familiar.[13]

One of the best introductions to this spiritual malaise of the twentieth century is Routh's *Towards the Twentieth Century*.[14] But I must cease quoting, for this tract is already longer than it should have been. Let me, then, refer in a footnote to some of the books from which I should have liked to quote.[15]

---

[13] Cyril E. M. Joad, "What Eastern Religion Has to Offer to Western Civilization," *The Aryan Path*, vol. 1, 1930, pp. 16-19.
[14] Harold Victor Routh, *Towards the Twentieth Century* (New York, Macmillan, 1937).
[15] Hugh l'Anson Fausset, *The Proving of Psyche* (London, Jonathan Cape, 1929); C. Delisle Burns, *The Horizon of Experience* (New York, Norton, 1934); Karl Jaspers, *Man in the Modern Age* (London, George Routledge, 1933); Henry Chester Tracy, *Towards the Open* (London, Chatto and Windus, 1927); Johan Huizinga, translated from the Dutch by Jakob Hermann Huizinga, *In the Shadow of Tomorrow* (New York, Norton, 1936); George Gorden Coulton, *Inquisition and Liberty* (New York, Macmillan, 1938); Karl Mannheim, *Man and Society in an Age of Reconstruction* (New York, Harcourt, Brace, 1940); Thomas Henry Howells, *Hunger for Wholiness* (Denver, The World Press, 1940); Ruth Nanda Anshen, ed., *Freedom, Its Meaning* (New York, Harcourt, Brace, 1940); Oscar Cargill, *Intellectual America* (New York, Macmillan, 1941).

6. Culture and Mental Illness

IT IS NOT, I think, too often pointed out that contemporary psychiatric theory and the development of modern cultural anthropology evolved at about the same time. That the cross-fertilizing effects of the two fields have been considerable and mutually beneficial has been gratifyingly clear for more than a generation. That the reciprocal interstimulation will continue in depth on an ever-widening horizon is already evident. The mental health of both disciplines will, in the future, depend to a considerable extent on this continuing agreeable relationship. Something of what has thus far been achieved as a result of the ethno-psychiatric interdisciplinary approach to the study of mental health and illness will, I hope, be made evident in what follows.

We are to discuss culture and mental illness. Let this be taken to mean that I shall not only be discussing the influence of culture on mental illness, but also the influence of mental illness upon culture. The latter is an approach which, it seems to me, has received altogether too little attention.

Perhaps we might commence with some working definitions of our terms. By *culture* we understand the man-made part of the environment: man's symbols, ideas, values, traditions, institutions, pots and pans, and technology. As the late Sir John Myres put it, culture is what remains of man's past working on his present to shape his future.

By *mental illness* we may perhaps understand a more or less gross, more or less persistent, failure of social adaptation. It

From *The American Journal of Psychiatry*, vol. 118, 1961, pp. 15-23.

should be made clear at the outset that the term *mental illness* as used here refers to functional mental disorder, and not to organically originating mental illness. It is understood that genetic factors and, probably, prenatal factors are each classes of variables which, under certain cultural conditions, are capable of making a significant contribution to the incidence of mental illness. By *mental health* we shall mean the ability to love and to work, or if you like, the balance between anxiety and its resolution.

It should be understood that with the development of human culture man has entered a new zone of adaptation, in which, through the socialization process, he learns what is expected of him and what he may expect from others. He internalizes the norms and acquires a working knowledge of his culture as a whole. While no one in any culture ever develops a mastery of every aspect of the culture, in different cultures and in different segments of the same culture there exist significant differences in both the quantity and the complexity or quality of the cultural variables, a good many of which the average member of such a culture is able to command. In general, nonliterate cultures (the so-called "primitive" cultures) are both quantitatively and qualitatively less demanding of their members than literate cultures, at least this would appear to be so. The individual is simply not assaulted by so many and so various stimuli or expected to know and do as much as the average member of literate cultures.

It is an open question whether we do not have in this difference a significant factor in producing the differences in the frequency and distribution of the various forms of mental illness. Is it possible that the sheer weight, recurrence, and complexity of the innumerable variables which the person has to master in a complex society constitute if not the sufficient conditions, then at least some of the necessary conditions in contributing to the incidence of mental illness of various kinds in societies culturally so weighted? The strain of life under highly complicated and stressful conditions of existence can play havoc with the human organism, and it seems to me reasonable to suppose that the less stressful a culture is upon the individual the less likely is there to be mental illness in such a culture. The evidence of cultural anthropology supports this relationship.

In every culture there probably exist differences among individuals of a genetic and constitutional nature in the ability to adjust to the stresses and strains of the load of cultural competencies they are required to carry. But when that has been said one has said very little, for the role played by the genes is extremely difficult to measure, and constitution is itself the dynamic expression of the interaction between genetic and environmental factors. It is a massive task, which no one has yet undertaken for any population, to tease out and determine to what extent genes and to what extent environmental influences are responsible for the individual's response to the cultural load which is placed upon him.

The environmenetal factors begin to be operative upon the organism from the moment of conception, and even before. By "before" I refer to the influence exercised by environmental factors upon ova and sperm before conception. We know that environmental factors operative during the prenatal period are capable of producing what Pasamanick has called a *continuum of reproductive casualty,* which ranges all the way from death to transitory minimal cerebral defects; I believe that in connection with mental illness we shall have to consider the possibility that different cultures provide the conceptus with different prenatal environments sufficiently varied to affect the individual's subsequent behavioral development. The influence of prenatal factors upon behavioral development is a fascinating subject which has only just begun to come under investigation. The cultural aspect of the subject remains virtually completely untouched. Neither the anthropologist nor the social biologist, nor, it should be added, has the psychiatrist, devoted any significant attention to this area of human experience. And yet the experiences of the human organism during the first 267 days of its life *in utero* may turn out to have a highly important bearing upon the epidemiology of mental illness. The culturally determined differences in the pregnancy experience of women in different cultures may well result in differences in predisposition to mental illness of the individual in different cultures.

There is evidence that in our own culture babies born to mothers who have had disturbed pregnancies, at birth already exhibit behavioral disturbances. I refer to the work of Sontag in this country and of Stott in England. Intrauterine convulsions of the fetus have been described in mothers who were emotionally disturbed, and there is evidence that the fetus can be sufficiently emotionally disturbed *in utero* to develop a peptic ulcer and be born with it. May it not be that the differences in cultural experience during pregnancy in different cultures constitute a significant factor in the etiology of mental illness?

A period very differently handled in various cultures and which, it may be suggested, is possibly critically productive of differences in the predisposition to mental illness is the first year of postnatal life. There is a good deal of evidence which indicates that the first postnatal year, and especially the first six months, is a very much more sensitive and vulnerable period than has hitherto been supposed, and that cultures which fail to recognize this are likely to exert a damaging effect upon the development of the individual. The evidence is both interesting and convincing, and a good deal of it has been summarized in Bowlby's World Health Organization report *Maternal Care and Mental Health* and in Montagu's *The Direction of Human Development*. Recently I have come to view man's gestation period as not being completed till about eight to ten months after he is born, that is, about the time when he begins to crawl. *Uterogestation* is terminated, in my view, principally because the size of the fetal head reaches the maximum size consonant with its ability to pass through the birth canal. The fetus must be born when it is born if it is to survive, but its gestation must continue outside the womb, a process which I have called *exterogestation,* similar to that of the marsupial. If this interpretation of the facts is correct, then it should be clear that the human infant during its first year is in a very much more precarious position in relation to the world into which it is born than we had previously supposed. Mother and child continue to form a symbiotic unit at birth. Birth is wrongly interpreted as an interruption of that unity, a unity which should continue for many months after birth, and which both mother and infant are reciprocally designed to continue. Contact with the mother's body, the baby's visual experience of that body, the support she gives, the breast-feeding that should continue for at least nine months, all these are indispensably necessary conditions for the well-being and healthy development of the infant. Any culture which discourages its mothers to behave in this manner is likely to contribute in a major way to the predisposition to mental illness in its members. The extreme dependency of the infant must be met with all the responses it calls for. Unless these are provided the results may be subsequently catastrophic. Whether such satisfactions are afforded the infant is a matter which in every society is culturally determined. Hence, here is a basic relation between culture and the incidence of mental illness.

At this point it is perhaps necessary to say that no culture is completely homogeneous, in the sense of providing or being the same for each of its members. There are differences of status, roles, class, caste, and the like. There appear to be interesting differences in the frequencies, and in some cases even in the kinds, of mental illness, associated with such social differences. This has been clearly demonstrated in Hollingshead and Redlich's ten-year study of the New Haven community, *Social Class and Mental Illness*. Among the five social classes distinguished by these investigators, the results showed "the lower the class, the greater the proportion of patients in the population." Class differences in type of mental illness followed the rule "the higher the class the more neurosis and the less psychosis, or inversely, the lower the class the more psychosis and the less neurosis." But, as Hollingshead and Redlich point out, these differences may be an artifact of the different ways psychiatrists are utilized by the classes. Also genetic and constitutional factors may play a role. However this may be, Hollingshead and Redlich have made out a good case for the view that "who becomes a psychiatric case, particularly if neurotic behavior is involved, depends in large part upon where one is in the class structure." Similar findings have been reported by Kaplan, Reed, and Richardson on the prosperous Wellesley, Massachusetts, population, and the "below average" Whittier Street area of Boston.

Class and caste, and even religious differences within any culture, often become as significantly different from each other as are the differences between different cultures. This is not a new observation. Anyone of any experience of life has repeatedly made it, and it was quite clearly stated in 1845 by that remarkable anthropologist Benjamin Disraeli when, in his programmatic novel *Sibyl*, he says, "I was told that the Privileged and the People formed Two Nations," (Bk. IV, Chap. 8), the "Two Nations," of course, being the upper and lower classes of nineteenth-century England.

In America, Jurgen Ruesch finds that the preponderance of psychosomatic conditions in the lower middle class, "the culture of conformance and excessive repressive tendencies," may be explained as due to the lack of expressive facilities, hence the solution of psychological conflicts through physical symptom formation. In the lower classes, hostility frequently tends to express itself through accidents, fractures, and traumatic disease. The upper classes, "with overbearing superego traditions" manifest a relatively large frequency of neuroses and psychoses, especially of the manic-depressive type.

Lemkau, Tietze, and Cooper in their study of the relation between mental illness and socioeconomic status in America found that schizophrenia tends to be the mental illness most common among social isolates, such as unskilled workers, farmers, or lone urban residents, and manic-depressive illness being most prevalent among professional, religious, socially prominent, and other groups of persons who have strong idealistic, interpersonal, and community involvements.

Every culture requires the acceptance of a certain number of fundamental values. This requirement in many cultures, if not in all, is itself generative of stress in some individuals who, from constitutional, temperamental, or other reasons are unable to adjust to such values. In some cultures, such as our own, the attempt is made to socialize the individual in irreconcilable and mutually conflicting values. For example, the accidents of history have made Americans the heirs of the Hebraic-Christian tradition ethically, and of successful competition within the framework of American social evolution. A great many individuals break down from the effects of unsuccessfully struggling to reconcile the Sermon on the Mount or its equivalent with the principle of competition. Others find no difficulty in harmonizing the two. As a consequence of carrying the burden of such conflicting values why do some individuals break down, while others do not, exhibiting, at most, only minor symptoms? Until a great deal more research has been done, it will not be possible to return a satisfactory answer to this question.

Where the culture provides institutionally sanctioned outlets for the reduction or resolution of the stresses it creates, or where the individual can find these for himself without too much strain, mental illness is likely to be avoided by those who can utilize these outlets. Those who cannot are likely to become behaviorally ill under the strain.

In a small atoll society of 250 people such as that of the Ifaluk in the Central Carolines of Micronesia, where the climate is pleasant, land and sea produce an abundance of food, and the work required of anyone is neither long nor strenuous, it is not difficult for anyone to live up to the paramount values of the culture: kindliness, co-operation, and nonaggression. Spiro tells us that no one could remember a single instance of murder, rape, robbery, or fighting (with one exception). Hostility finds an outlet through individual and cultural fantasy, that is, through dreams and legends. Religion provides another outlet for hostility through its good and bad ghosts (*alus*). But even on Ifaluk mental illness sometimes occurs, and there were three such cases in which, interestingly enough, a dominant characteristic was the subdued aggressiveness of each affected individual. Spiro attributes the repressed hostility and anxiety of the Ifaluk individual to the peculiarities of Ifaluk infantile experience—largely the morning bathing of the helpless infant in the cold water of the lagoon—water so cold that adults avoid it until the sun has warmed it and it becomes bearable. All else is overindulgence until four years of age, when children's emotional needs are both ignored and rejected.

Why do the vast majority of Ifaluk manage to avoid mental illness? The answer, according to Spiro, appears to be the sanctioned outlet that religion primarily affords. Aggression is displaced upon the malevolent ghost, the *alus*. Another important means of reducing hostility and anxiety and satisfying the Ifaluk's dependency needs is the institution of the chieftainship. As the paramount Ifaluk chief put it,

> The chiefs are like fathers here. Just as an empty canoe is tossed about by the waves and finally sinks, so, too, a society without chiefs is tossed about by conflict and strife and is destroyed. If a father asks his son not to behave badly, the latter may not obey him since he may not respect him highly. But all people obey the words of the chiefs, since they are feared and respected by all. The chiefs' duty is to see that the people behave well. The chiefs must constantly tell the people to be good, or else the society, like the canoe, would be destroyed.[1]

In the United States quite a number of people felt the same way about Franklin Delano Roosevelt. When he died in 1945 it was for millions as if a protecting father had died. The importance of making a strong identification with a parental figure in the development and maintenance of mental health is today, I believe, abundantly clear.

The Ifaluk fear to lose the love of their chiefs and do everything in their power to maintain it. And this is the main incentive to conformity to the ethos of co-operation and kindliness which the chiefs so prominently personify. The chief is a warm, loving, parental figure. The love and praise given by the chiefs provide the essential satisfaction and security of which the individual was deprived as a child.

Perhaps the Ifaluk has achieved an approximation to the Welfare State from which other societies could learn a thing or two. At any rate, the Ifaluk do afford an interesting case history which may help us to understand better by what cultural devices mental illness could be kept to a minimum in any society. The indications are that emotional stress, anxiety, and conflicting values must be as minimal as possible, but since such experiences are not wholly avoidable the culture should provide institutionally sanctioned means for the expression of aggression and the reduction of anxiety, as well as support for the dependency needs of the individual. It is interesting to note that in the Western world mental

[1] M. Spiro, "Cultural Heritage, Personal Tensions, and Mental Illness in a South Sea Culture," in M. K. Opler, ed., *Culture and Mental Health*, p. 165.

illness is least frequent among the subscribers to that religion which makes a real attempt to satisfy these requirements, namely, the Catholic. This suspicion was corroborated by the findings of Hollingshead and Redlich on the population of New Haven, although they found that among the lowest-class Catholics there were more frequently psychiatric patients than among either Jews or Protestants. Why this should have been so remains an interesting but unanswered question.

Fairly clear-cut evidence of the relation between culture and mental illness is to be found in a culture which flourishes in our very midst, namely, that of the Hutterites. The Hutterites have a reputation for peace of mind, and many who have written on them have been lastingly impressed by this quality. Eaton and Weill and their co-workers, on first contact with them were struck by the generally prevailing atmosphere of relaxation, contentment, co-operativeness, and absence of manifested anxiety. Upon investigation, in the summer of 1951, it was found that out of a Hutterite population of 8,542 people, 199, or 1 out of every 43 living Hutterites, were then mentally ill or had been previously.

The total number of schizophrenics was nine, manic-depressives thirty-nine, there were fifty-three with neuroses, sixteen with psychophysiological disorders, and six with personality disorders.

Withdrawal in so well knit a group as the Hutterites is difficult, and this Eaton and Weill suggest may explain the fewness of schizophrenics. On the other hand, depression appears to be an intensification of a culturally supported normative trend.

Among the Hutterites no cases have been known to occur of psychoses due to drugs, alcoholism, or syphilis. There were no psychopathic personalities. Murder, arson, violent physical assault, or sex crimes were quite unknown in this group. Only two persons showed moderately severe character disorders. Divorce, separation, or even family quarrels were rare. Violence, panic, and severe regression are uncommon, even among psychotics; suicide was extremely rare.

Eaton and Weill conclude that the facts justify the generalization that Hutterites tend to internalize their problems rather than project them into their relationships with other people. Under stress, they are much more likely to be antiself than antisocial.

The socialization process and communal indoctrination supports this normative behavior tendency. This emphasizes submission of the individual to community expectations, the principle of personal guilt and pacifism.

Such findings have led to the formulation of the hypothesis of specific cultural relevance with respect to the epidemiology of schizophrenia and manic-depression, to wit, as we have already seen, schizophrenia is the disorder of social isolates and manic-depression the disorder of the socially involved. At the same time the structure of Hutterite society does seem to show rather clearly the kind of cultural factors that are operative in relation to the production of individual and social disorganization or nondisorganization.

It is fairly evident today that all human beings at some time during their early development possess the potentialities for behaving in schizophrenic, manic, depressive, obsessive, or anxiety patterns. Whether an individual will respond to his behavioral environment, that is, his cultural environment, with one pattern of behavior or another will depend very much upon the pressures of that cultural environment, making all necessary allowances for genetic and constitutional factors. Some cultures produce more and more severe forms of these responses than others, and the cultural stresses that do so may vary in their nature in different cultures. In some cultures mental illness is institutionalized, by which is meant not that the individual is put into an institution as a sick man, but rather that he and his behavior are incorporated into the society as a normal part of it. The person whom we would regard as normal in our society would be regarded as sick in such a culture. The diabolical, hostile, paranoid Dobuans of northwestern Melanesia make a virtue of treachery and ill will, and would regard anyone who deviated from this pattern as utterly unfit to deal with the malignancies of this cutthroat world. Malignancy and hostility are therefore institutionalized as the ethos of Dobuan culture—it is a way of life.

Similarly, the Balinese, in a culture in which the food and material goods are adequate, war and crime at a minimum, the arts highly developed, the traumatizing experiences of childhood turn the Balinese into schizoid personalities. From about five or six months of age, and steadily becoming more definite as the child grows older, the mother continually tantalizes and teases the child. She stimulates him to show emotion, love or desire, jealousy or anger, and then turns away, as the child in rising passion raggingly and despairingly implores emotional response from her. The discouragement of interpersonal emotion is systematic. The child never attains a climax of emotional response, and the resulting withdrawal is seen in a lack of responsiveness which is established by the age of three or four. The relationship to people remains distant, wary of the expression of too much feeling. When he is frightened, the Balinese falls into a soft sleep from which it is difficult to wake him. When he has to wait he may curl up into a fetal position and fall asleep. Within his own highly elaborate system of time and space he moves relaxedly and with grace; in an unknown situation he is unable to act at all. On tests, the Balinese respond like schizophrenics, yet they are fully functioning members of their community.

Responding to a question raised by Lauretta Bender, "How many schizophrenics can a society absorb and survive?" Margaret Mead says:

One might say that Bali had been able to absorb a much higher number of those who would be schizophrenic in other societies, until their special potentialities, seen now as one variant of human nature, had helped develop a social order that was self-perpetuating. To this all children born in Bali were exposed, they, in turn, absorbing, in posture and gesture and capacity to move within a highly protected, symbolic system, something of the special gifts, the special vulnerabilities, the special sensitivities of the potentially schizophrenic, fitting in with the phrasing that "schizophrenia is not so much a disease as a way of life." In studying Balinese culture, the details of childhood experience may be seen as a way in which a culture perfectly adapted to the particular constitutional needs of schizoid individuals is communicated to all human children, involving far greater trauma for some than for others, subduing all to a state where they do not threaten the pattern, and developing an insatiable demand for symbolic rather than immediate satisfactions, turning the schizoid hunger for a meaningful pattern into an appetite for the practices of living arts.[2]

The important thing to note here is that in Bali the schizoid habitus has become institutionalized and that it has given Balinese culture its essential character in the arts, in interpersonal relations, and in religion. This has been discussed by others elsewhere; here it must suffice to say that the arts, interpersonal relations, and religion are all greatly influenced by the prevailing psychosis— using that word to mean no more than "a state of mind"—and each of these cultural activities and institutions affords the individual abundant opportunities for the maintenance of his own self-homeostasis.

Thus, we begin to perceive how mental illness may to a large extent condition the institutionalized forms of emotional expression such as religion, pageantry, painting, carving, puppet-making, music, the dance, drama, narrative, and the like. For in Bali it seems quite clear that these forms of emotional expression are designed to fit the requirements of the individual's emotional needs.

The effects of mental illness upon the structure and functioning of society is a matter which in our own time has assumed the dimensions of a world-important problem—no less than the problem of the survival of mankind itself. The question is, How behaviorally deranged can a society get before it endangers its own survival and that of others? Before that question can be answered we must dispose of the doubt as to whether it is possible for a society to be behaviorally deranged, and consider whether the phrase is only a figure of speech. I recall a brilliant book by an Englishwoman, Caroline E. Playne, *The Neuroses of the Nations*, published in 1925. It was thirty years before its time. I read it in 1925, and I also read the reviews. I was impressed by the book, but not by the reviews, which were largely scornful. How could a nation be neurotic? Neuroses applied to individuals, not to such complex entities as nations. This was the main criticism of what was otherwise conceded to be a well-

[2] Margaret Mead, "Some Relationships Between Social Anthropology and Psychiatry," in Franz Alexander, ed., *Dynamic Psychiatry*, pp. 439-440.

written and interesting book. Only eight years were to pass, or if you like twenty, for Mrs. Playne's analysis of the German and the French neurosis to receive full corroboration from the tragic denouement of events. But meanwhile Mrs. Playne's book and her examination of national neurosis has been forgotten. I should like briefly to quote her thesis in her own words. She writes:

> The study on which we embark of the national group-minds of the two great continental representatives of Western civilization, France and Germany, is an examination of the nature of the limitation which in their case "held up" the generation who lived at the beginning of the twentieth century. And the contention is that the special limitation of human nature which hindered the progress of this generation was the failure of men's nervous systems to adjust themselves to the ever-increasing strain of life under highly stressed and complicated conditions of existence. Out of this failure of adjustment arose nervous excitement, nervous depression, general irritation, resulting in anger and passion. Primitive passions burst forth, accompanied by emotions of instinctive type. The effect of this upthrust of ancient and obsolete furies into the newer order was so turbulent, that . . . they swept the masses out of the path of reasonable advancement and plunged them into a series of group-neuroses.[3]

Whatever one may think of Mrs. Playne's explanation of the dynamics involved, it took the spectacle of Nazi Germany to convince some observers, at least, that a whole nation could be mentally ill, for how otherwise would it be possible to account for the behavior of the Hitlers, Goerings, Goebbelses, Himmlers, Eichmanns, and countless others like them but by the history of the average German's behavior? Those who had known many Germans and who ever gave the matter any thought, like those German exiles Heine and Nietzsche, were aware of what the Germans subsequently proved themselves capable. One does not have to read the memoirs of Nazi generals or concentration camp commandants to know that the cultural conditioning of a majority of the Germans was such as to make rigid, fearful, emotionally shallow and humanely arid, obeisant and obsequious creatures, who were never happier than when commanded or commanding.

[3] Caroline E. Playne, *The Neuroses of the Nations*, pp. 18-19.

The parallel between German family structure and the structure of German political life is now something of a cliché of the psychiatry of peoples. Dr. Bertram Schaffner has discussed this subject in his aptly titled book *Father Land: A Study of Authoritarianism in the German Family*. The manner in which the adult German personality is formed within the German family in great part serves to explain that personality. The fear and respect, *Ehrfurcht*, inculcated for the father, the obsessional sense of duty, *Pflicht*, which seems to serve the German as a substitute for what is elsewhere known as a conscience, the absence of love, the subservience of women, the commanding position of the father, the word of the father as inflexible law, the unquestioning obedience expected of children and inferiors, the emphasis on work, the thoroughness and attention to detail, the fear of failure, the discipline and regulation, the enforced passivity of the child, the lack of freedom, and the like, would be enough in themselves to explain why the Germans are Germans.

No analysis can be attempted here of the historical conditions which caused German culture to develop in this way, but if there is one man who deserves a major share of the discredit that man is Martin Luther. It was not, however, one man, but many who were responsible for Germany's totalitarian development. Germany was and still is a nation of little Hindenburgs, Ludendorffs, and Hitlers. They are turned out as regularly and as invariably as a pattern made to a template. The patterning of the German personality has on two occasions already had the most devastating consequences for millions of human beings, and it may be predicted that it will again—just as it may be predicted that all American attempts to democratize the Germans will fail. The Americans helped the Japanese to achieve a democratic revolution that had already long been in the making. But can a nation of little Hitlers be taught democracy? I believe not. Democracy is something one learns in the home. It is not simply a political doctrine. Politics is life, and political attitudes are founded in the home. "Do you imagine" wrote Plato in *The Republic* "that constitutions grow at random 'from stone to stone,' and not from those characters of the men in cities which preponderate and draw the rest of the cities after them?" The characters of "the men in the cities" are determined by the agencies that shape them within the family. Democracy in Germany can come about, if at all, only by gradual evolution, and only after the German family has democratized itself. As things are today there is hardly a German who really understands the meaning of democracy.

The comparative psychiatry of cultures and of nations would be a fascinating topic to pursue further. It is a subject in the making. Each nation has its own psychosis, and some of them happen to be more dangerous than others. I hope I have said enough in this chapter to suggest that it is a subject worthy of our closest attention.

I have thus far spoken of the influence of cultural factors upon the incidence of mental illness. I should now like to say something about the influence of the mental illness that prevails in any culture upon the condition of that culture. It should be clear that in a culture in which there are as many sick individuals as there are in Dobu that such a society must either ultimately destroy itself or change its character. Dobu is a remarkable example of what happens to a culture when virtually everyone in it is mentally unbalanced. Mental illness becomes the norm of behavior, and in a short time there remains no one in such a society who is able to perceive that such behavior is, in fact, socially maladaptive and destructive. The parallel to some Western societies is rather deadly, and we in the Western world have to ask ourselves, before it is too late, whether it may not be that at the present time we stand at the very edge of doom because mental illness has become endemic among us and institutionalized as a way of life. We have to ask ourselves how mentally fit are those men in our culture who occupy high office and influence the lives of millions of others?

We have to consider whether motivations which move many men to acquire political power are not generated by something less than the desire to be of help to mankind, and we have, in addition, to consider whether the citizens who make it possible for such persons to realize their drive for power are not perhaps as sick as those they elect.

Mental illness, it would seem, has not been uninfluential in the appearance of certain forms of art, architecture, and literature, not to mention many of the things that are said and done through the usual form of these arts.

A culture such as that of the United States, which not only permits but encourages the employment, for example, of newspaper columnists who are clearly mentally ill, in which such men grow to riches, fame, and even respect, evidently caters to the deep-felt needs of mentally sick individuals. This is further evident in the nature of the entertainments favored by the masses, in which murder, violence, rape, and sexuality form the staple article of diet, and in the plays having morbid and perverted themes for their plots. It would appear that it is no longer the blind who are leading the blind into the ditch, but the mentally ill who are leading the mentally ill and contributing to the secularization of even greater numbers of mentally ill.

We stand much in need of a social psychiatry which will devote itself to the study of the causes and cure of the mental illnesses of cultures.

BIBLIOGRAPHY

Bateson, Gregory, and Mead, Margaret. *Balinese Character*. New York. Special Publications of the New York Academy of Sciences, vol. 2, 1942.
Belo, Jane. *Trance in Bali*. New York. Columbia University Press, 1960.
Benedict, Ruth. *Patterns of Culture*. Boston. Houghton Mifflin, 1934.
Bowlby, John. *Maternal Care and Mental Health*. World Health Organization Monographs. New York. Columbia University Press, 1951.
Eaton, Joseph, and Weill, Robert J. "Some Epidemiological Findings in the Hutterite Mental Health Study," in *Interrelations Between the Social Environment and Psychiatric Disorders*. New York. Milbank Memorial Fund, 1953.
Ebenstein, William. *The German Record: A Political Portrait*. New York. Farrar and Rinehart, 1945.
Ellenberger, H. "Cultural Aspects of Mental Illness." *American Journal of Psychotherapy*, vol. 14, 1960, pp. 158-173.
Erikson, Erik, H. *Young Man Luther*. New York. Norton, 1958.
Fortune, R. F. *The Sorcerers of Dobu*. New York. Dutton, 1932.

Gladwin, T., and Sarason, S. B. *Truk: Man in Paradise.* New York. Wenner-Gren Foundation for Anthropological Research, 1953.
Halliday, J. L. *Psychosocial Medicine.* New York. Norton, 1948.
Haring, D. G., ed. *Personal Character and Cultural Milieu,* 3rd ed. Syracuse, New York. Syracuse University Press, 1956.
Hollingshead, August B., and Redlich, Frederick C. *Social Class and Mental Illness.* New York. Wiley, 1958.
Honigmann, John J. *Culture and Personality.* New York. Harper, 1954.
Hsu, Francis L. K., ed. *Aspects of Culture and Personality.* New York. Abelard-Schuman, 1954.
Kaplan, B., Reed, R. B., and Richardson, W. "A Comparison of the Incidence of Hospitalized and Non-Hospitalized Cases of Psychoses in Two Communities." *American Sociological Review,* vol. 21, 1956, pp. 472-479.
Kardiner, Abram. *The Individual and His Society.* New York. Columbia University Press, 1939.
Leighton, Alexander H. *An Introduction to Social Psychiatry.* Springfield, Ill. Thomas, 1960.
Lemkau, P. V., Tietze, C., and Cooper, M. "Mental Hygiene Problems in an Urban District." *Mental Hygiene,* vol. 25, 1941, pp. 624-646.
—— "A Summary of Statistical Studies on the Prevalence and Incidence of Mental Disorder in Sample Populations." *Public Health Reports,* vol. 5, no. 53, pp. 1909-1927.
Lindemann, E. "The Wellesley Project for the Study of Certain Problems in Community Mental Health," in *Interrelations Between the Social Environment and Psychiatric Disorders.* New York. Milbank Memorial Fund, 1953.
Linton, Ralph. *The Cultural Background of Personality.* New York. Appleton, 1945.
—— *Culture and Mental Disorders.* Springfield, Ill. Thomas, 1956.
Mead, Margaret. *From the South Seas.* New York. Morrow, 1939.
—— "Some Relationships Between Social Anthropology and Psychiatry," in Franz Alexander, ed., *Dynamic Psychiatry.* Chicago. University of Chicago Press, 1952, pp. 401-448.
—— and Wolfenstein, M., eds. *Childhood in Contemporary Cultures.* Chicago. University of Chicago Press, 1955.
Montagu, Ashley. *The Direction of Human Development.* New York. Harper, 1955.
—— *Prenatal Influences.* Springfield, Ill. Thomas, 1962.
—— "Neonatal and Infant Immaturity in Man." *Journal of American Medical Association,* vol. 178, 1961, pp. 156-157.

Myres, John L. *Political Ideas of the Greeks*. New York. Abingdon Press, 1927.

Opler, Marvin K. *Culture, Psychiatry, and Human Values*. Springfield, Ill. Thomas, 1956.

────── ed. *Culture and Mental Health*. New York. Macmillan, 1959.

Pasamanick, Benjamin. "Epidemiologic Investigations of Some Prenatal Factors in the Production of Neuropsychiatric Disorder," in *Field Studies in Mental Disorder*. New York. Grune and Stratton, 1961.

────── "A Survey of Mental Disease in an Urban Population." *Archives of Psychiatry*, vol. 5, 1961, pp. 151-155.

Playne, Caroline E. *The Neuroses of the Nations*. London. Allen and Unwin, 1925.

Rapp, Don W. "Childrearing Attitudes of Mothers in Germany and the United States." *Child Development*, vol. 32, 1961, pp. 669-678.

Ruesch, Jurgen. "Social Techniques, Social Status and Social Change," in C. Kluckhohn, H. A. Murray, and D. Schneider, eds., *Personality in Nature, Society, and Culture*. New York. Knopf, 1950, pp. 123-136.

Sontag, L. W. "The Significance of Fetal Environmental Differences." *American Journal of Obstetrics and Gynecology*, vol. 42, 1941, pp. 996-1003.

────── "War and the Fetal Maternal Relationship." *Marriage and Family Living*, vol. 6, 1944, pp. 1-5.

────── "Differences in Modifiability of Fetal Behavior and Phsyiology." *Psychosomatic Medicine*, vol. 6, 1944, pp. 151-154.

Spiro, M. "Cultural Heritage, Personal Tensions, and Mental Illness in a South Sea Culture," in M. K. Opler, ed., *Culture and Mental Health*. New York. Macmillan, 1959, pp. 141-171.

Stott, D. H. "Evidence for Prenatal Impairment of Temperament in Mentally Retarded Children." *Vita Humana*, vol. 2, 1959, pp. 125-248.

────── "Physical and Mental Handicaps Following a Disturbed Pregnancy." *Lancet*, vol. 1, 1957, pp. 1006-1012.

────── "Some Psychosomatic Aspects of Casualty in Reproduction." *Journal of Psychosomatic Research*, vol. 3, 1958, pp. 42-55.

PART II

Education and the Family— The Didactic Dimensions of Love

7. A Scientist Looks at Love

THE STUDY OF LOVE is something from which scientists, until very recently, have shied away. With the increase, however, of interest in the origins of mental illness in this century, more and more attention has begun to be paid to the infancy and childhood of human beings. What has been revealed by these investigations is that love is, without any question, the most important experience in the life of a human being.

What is love? One of the most frequently used words in our vocabulary, the major theme of art in all its aspects, the principal industry of Hollywood and of countless magazines, the thing with which human beings are most concerned all their lives, the most important experience in the world, *love* is something about which most of us, at this late date, are still extremely vague. One has only to ask one's friends what they understand by "love" to discover how unclear the idea remains in the minds of many people. Even when a fair definition is achieved the meaning of love in its full significance is rarely understood.

In this chapter I should like to set out some of the findings about the nature and meaning of love as scientists have revealed them.

The dictionary tells us that love is a feeling of deep regard, fondness, and devotion. Robert Louis Stevenson said that love was a passionate kindness. One could go on quoting hundreds of statements about love, and they would all be true as far as they go, but none of them go far enough because while they provide the skeleton, they miss the vital essence of the meaning of love. This essential meaning one can discover only by studying the origins and development of love as they are manifested in small children, in the newborn baby and every stage of childhood, and finally in adolescents and in adults.

There is a widespread belief that a newborn baby is a rather selfish, disorganized, or unorganized, wild kind of creature which would grow into a violently intractable savage if it were not properly disciplined. Contrary to this widely held belief, modern scientists find that far from being such an unorganized barbarian the newborn baby is one of the most highly organized creatures on the face of the earth, and organized not for brattishness but for love.

The newborn baby is organized in an extraordinarily sensitive manner, most delicately attuned to receive all those stimulations which will creatively contribute to its development. Far from wanting to be disciplined in the usual meaning of that word, it wants to be loved. It behaves as if it expected to be loved, and when its expectation is thwarted—that is, frustrated—it behaves in a grievously disappointed manner.

There is now good evidence which leads us to believe that not only does a baby want to be loved, but also that it wants to love, that all its drives are oriented in the direction of receiving and giving love, and that if it doesn't receive love it is unable to give it—as a child or as an adult.

From the moment of birth the baby needs the reciprocal exchange of love with its mother. From the very outset the baby is capable of conferring great benefits upon the mother—*if* the maternal-infant relationship is not disturbed. It has now been thoroughly established that if the baby is left with the mother and put to nurse at her breast, three problems which have bedeviled obstetricians for many years, and what is more important, have been responsible for much tragedy and unhappiness, are in most cases solved at once. These are hemorrhaging from the womb after birth, the beginning return of the uterus to normal size, and the completion of the third stage of labor by the ejection of the placenta. These problems are solved in the majority of instances by putting the baby to nurse at the mother's breast. The hemorrhage is reduced and the uterus begins its return to almost normal size within a matter of minutes, and the placenta becomes detached and is ejected. There are almost certainly other benefits which the nursing baby confers upon the mother, not the least of which are probably psychological. The baby is in turn, of course, also benefited; among other things, such a baby is practically never a feeding problem.

Understanding just these things helps us to understand better, or begin to understand, the meaning of love, *if* the nursing maternal-infant relationship and its effects in any way involve the elements of love. It has, I believe, universally been acknowledged that the mother-infant relationship perhaps more than any other defines the very essence of love. If that is so, then on the basis of the findings I have already described we may tentatively define love as *the relationship between persons in which they confer mutual benefits upon each other.* This is a broad definition and might be said well to describe the relationship which exists between an insurance company and the insured. Bearing in mind the physiological benefits which accrue to mother and child, perhaps we could try again and state that *love is the relationship between persons which contributes to the welfare and development of each.*

The "welfare" given the mother in the cited example consisted of reduced hemorrhage, the initiation of the reduction to normal size of the maternal uterus, and the completion of the third stage of labor. In the baby there are established good feeding habits, and there is a healthy development of the gastrointestinal, genito-urinary, and respiratory tracts—indeed, of all the sustaining systems of the body. Scientists have learned most about love from the study of the mother-infant relationships. Let us proceed to the discussion of *how* and *what* they have learned about the nature and meaning of love.

Survival is of the first importance, without it nothing else matters, but survival alone is not enough—human beings need and should receive much more. If children are to grow in health and harmony, then they must experience more than the mere physical satisfaction of their needs. A baby is a beginning human being, and his birthright is development—development of his psychological and spiritual as well as his physical potentialities for being human. The mere satisfaction of his physical needs will not bring about such development—such satisfaction may secure survival, but in most cases it is doubtful whether it will even secure that.

We now know that babies which are physically well nurtured may nevertheless waste away and die unless they are also loved. We also know that the only thing that can rescue such babies when they are dying is love. We now know, beyond cavil or question, that love is an essential part of the nourishment of every baby, and that unless human beings in their early stages of development are loved they will not grow and develop as healthy organisms. It has taken the independent observations of a number of physicians and other investigators to ascertain the relationship between the infant's need for love and his capacity to survive.

It may come as a surprise to many readers to learn that because this relationship was not understood during the first two decades of this century, the majority of infants under one year of age who entered hospitals and similar institutions never emerged from them alive. This shocking infant death rate was discussed at a meeting of the American Pediatric Society in 1915. Dr. Henry Chapin reported on ten infant asylums located in the United States in which, with one exception, *every* infant under two years of age died! Dr. R. Hamil of Philadelphia, at the same meeting, remarked with tragic irony that he "had the honor to be connected with an institution in Philadelphia in which the mortality among all the infants under one year of age, when admitted to the institution and retained there for any length of time, was 100 per cent. That is, no infant admitted under one year of age lived to be two years old." Dr. T. S. Southworth of New York City, said, "I can give an instance from an institution which no longer exists in which on account of the very considerable mortality among the infants admitted, it was customary to enter the condition of every infant on the admission card as hopeless. That covered all subsequent happenings."[1]

Many other such reports could be quoted from other American authorities as well as from institutions abroad, but those given above should be enough. In the late twenties Dr. J. Brennemann of New York City recognized the ill effects caused by an absence

[1] H. D. Chapin, "A Plea for Accurate Statistics in Infants' Institutions," *Transactions of the American Pediatric Society*, vol. 27, 1915, pp. 180 ff.

of mothering and established a rule in his hospital that every baby should be picked up, carried about, amused, and "mothered" several times a day.[2] A most illuminating experience is related by Dr. Fritz Talbot, who visited the Children's Clinic in Düsseldorf, Germany, some fifty years ago. Dr. Talbot noticed a fat old woman wandering about the ward with a baby on her hip. Inquiring of the chief of the Clinic, he was told, "Oh, that's Old Anna. Whenever we have a baby for whom everything we could do has failed, we turn it over to Old Anna. She is always successful."[3]

Drs. Ruth and Harry Bakwin, of Bellevue Hospital Pediatric Division, have graphically described what happens in hospitals as a result of the lacklove experiences which children undergo there:

> The effect of residence in a hospital manifests itself by a fairly well-defined clinical picture. A striking feature is the failure to gain properly, despite the ingestion of diets which are entirely adequate for growth in the home. Infants in hospitals sleep less than others and they rarely smile or babble spontaneously. They are listless and apathetic and look unhappy. The appetite is indifferent and food is accepted without enthusiasm. The stools tend to be frequent and, in sharp contrast with infants cared for in the home, it is unusual for 24 hours to pass without an evacuation. Respiratory infections which last only a day or two in the home are prolonged and may persist for weeks or months. Return to the home results in defervescence (disappearance of fever) within a few days and a prompt and striking gain in weight.[4]

The emotional deprivation suffered by infants in hospitals may do vastly more damage than the physical condition which brought them there. The infant can suffer no greater loss than the privation of its mother's love. There is an old Talmudic proverb which has it that since God could not be everywhere he created mothers. There have been several important studies of

[2] J. Brennemann, "The Infant Ward," *American Journal of Diseases of Children*, vol. 43, 1932, p. 577.
[3] *Ibid.*
[4] Ruth M. and Harry Bakwin, *Psychologic Care during Infancy and Childhood* (New York, Appleton-Century, 1942), p. 295.

the effects of the absence of mother-love within the past decade.

Dr. Rene Spitz of New York City has reported on children confined in two different institutions. They were studied simultaneously during the first year of life. Both institutions were adequate in all physical respects, providing equivalent housing, asepsis, food, and hygiene. In both, infants were admitted shortly after birth. The institutions differed in but one factor—the amount of affection offered. In the first institution, called "Nursery," the infants were cared for by their own mothers. In the second institution, called "Foundlinghome," the children were raised from the third month by overworked nursing personnel, each nurse in charge of from eight to twelve children. The absence or presence of emotional interchange between mother and child formed the one independent condition in the comparison of the two groups.

The response to this condition showed up in many ways, but perhaps most comprehensively in what is called the Developmental Quotient. The Developmental Quotient represents a measure of the total development of six sectors of the personality: mastery of perception, bodily functions, social relations, memory and imitation, manipulative ability, and intelligence. At the end of the first year, though the "Foundlinghome" infants had a developmental quotient of 124 to start with, and the "Nursery" infants a developmental quotient of 101.5, the deprived "Foundlinghome" infants declined to a developmental quotient of 72, while the "Nursery" infants rose to 105. At the end of the second year the D.Q. had fallen in the "Foundlinghome" group to an astonishing low of 45!

As Dr. Spitz remarks:

> We have here an impressive example of how the absence of one psychosocial factor, that of emotional interchange with the mother, results in a complete reversal of a developmental trend.
> It should be realized that the factor which was present in the first case but eliminated in the second, is the pivot of all development in the first year. It is the mother-child relation. By choosing this factor as our independent variable we were able to observe its vital importance. While the children in "Nursery" developed into normal healthy toddlers, a two-year observation of "Foundlinghome" showed that the emotionally starved children never

learned to speak, to walk, to feed themselves. With one or two exceptions in a total of 91 children, those who survived were human wrecks who behaved either in the manner of agitated or apathetic idiots.[5]

A comparison of the mortality rates in the two institutions is striking and significant. During five years of observation involving 239 children who had been institutionalized for one year or more, "Nursery" did not lose a single child through death; whereas in "Foundlinghome" 37 per cent of the children died during a two years' observation period. Death, Dr. Spitz states, is but an extreme consequence of the general physiological and psychological decline which affects children completely starved of emotional interchange.

Drs. Ralph Fried and M. F. Mayer of Cleveland, in a study[6] of dependent and neglected children at the Cleveland Jewish Orphans Home, found the severest disturbances in growth and development to be in these emotionally impoverished derelict children. The child that has been inadequately loved, neglected, or abandoned by its parents, exhibits socio-emotional disturbances which are reflected in his growth and development. Drs. Fried and Mayer conclude that "socio-emotional adjustment plays not merely an important but actually a crucial role among all the factors that determine individual health and physical well-being . . . it has become clear that socio-emotional disturbances tend to affect physical growth adversely, and that growth failure so caused is much more frequent and more extensive than is generally recognized."

Dr. Griffith Binning, in a study[7] of 800 Canadian (Saskatoon) children, found "that events in the child's life that caused separation from one or both parents—death, divorce, enlistment of a parent—and a mental environment which gave the child a feel-

[5] Rene Spitz, "Anaclitic Depression," *The Psychoanalytic Study of the Child*, vol. 2 (New York, International Universities Press, 1947), pp. 313-342.
[6] Ralph Fried and M. F. Mayer, "Socio-Emotional Factors Accounting for Growth Failure of Children Living in an Institution," *Journal of Pediatrics*, vol. 33, 1948, pp. 444-456.
[7] Griffith Binning, "Peace Be on Thy House," *Health*, March/April, 1948, pp. 6-7, 28, 30.

ing that normal love and affection was lacking did far more damage to growth than did disease," indeed, that such an environment "was more serious than all other factors combined." Dr. Binning was able to show that where disease has affected growth "in most cases the reason is the emotional tension arising from the disease and its manner of treatment rather than the disease itself."

Drs. N. B. Talbot, E. H. Sobel, B. S. Burke, E. Lindemann, and S. S. Kaufman, of Massachusetts General Hospital, Boston, in a study[8] of fifty-one children who exhibited stunted growth, but in whom no physical abnormalities could be found to account for their dwarfism, found that "the majority were undernourished because of anorexia [chronic lack of appetite] due to either emotional disturbances or mental deficiency or a combination of both, in addition to such factors as parental poverty and ignorance. In the 51 so studied there was a high incidence of rejection by the mother, emotional disturbances and delinquency in mothers, marked poverty at home. Fourteen per cent had severe emotional reactions with chronic grief and anorexia attributable to broken homes brought about by death, divorce and desertion."

Drs. H. Lihn, Karl Menninger, and M. Mayman of the Menninger Clinic, Topeka, Kansas, have found that in the infant and childhood histories of adult chronic osteoarthritic patients, there was, without exception, the experience, in varying degrees, of being ignored, neglected, or rejected by their overburdened or inconsiderate parents. Often these patients were the victims of early desertion and of the arid emotional conditions of the orphanage.[9]

There exists much additional research along the same lines,[10] but that given above should be sufficient to indicate that emotional deprivation during childhood may result in severe retardations in growth and development of the total organism. The

[8] N. B. Talbot and others, "Dwarfism in Healthy Children: Its Possible Relation to Emotional Disturbances," *New England Journal of Medicine*, vol. 236, 1947, pp. 783-793.

[9] H. Lihn and others, "Personality Factors in Osteo-arthritis," in *Life Stress and Bodily Disease*, H. G. Wolff and others, eds., (Baltimore, Williams & Wilkins, 1950), pp. 744-749.

[10] For a review of that research see Ashley Montagu, *The Direction of Human Development* (New York, Harper, 1955).

effects upon the development of personality and behavior of a lacklove infancy appear to be even more severe.

Criminal, delinquent, neurotic, psychopathic, asocial, and similar forms of unfortunate behavior can, in the majority of cases, be traced to a childhood history of inadequate love and emotional instability. Findings on this score have been surveyed in a United Nations World Health Organization report entitled *Maternal Care and Mental Health*. Dr. John Bowlby, the English psychiatrist who prepared the survey, had published one of the earliest studies on the relationship between maternal love and juvenile delinquency.

In a study[11] of forty-four juvenile thieves Dr. Bowlby found that a large proportion exhibited an inability to establish affectionate relationships with other persons, and displayed what he termed "the affectionless character." Fourteen of the forty-four delinquents were of this type, and of these fourteen, twelve had suffered a prolonged separation from the mother at an early age. These affectionless characters were significantly more delinquent than the other thieves, "constituting more than half of the more serious and chronic offenders."

Drs. Fritz Redl and David Wineman of Detroit have much the same story to tell in their book *Children Who Hate* (Glencoe, Illinois, Free Press, 1951), as does Dr. Frank Cohen of New York in his book *Children in Trouble* (New York, Norton, 1952).

Show me a murderer, a hardened criminal, a juvenile delinquent, a psychopath, and a "cold fish," and in almost every case I will show you the tragedy that results from not being adequately loved during childhood. When the infant's expectation of emotional warmth and love is thwarted, he may turn in upon himself for any satisfactions he can secure. If his crying goes unnoticed he may begin to weep through his skin, and break out in many kinds of skin disturbances; or he may begin to weep and wheeze through his lungs in the form of asthma, or he may break out in ulcers of the stomach—yes, in infancy, not only in adulthood. In short, in order to attract the attention he so much desires and

[11] John Bowlby, "Forty-Four Juvenile Thieves: Their Characters and Home Life," *International Journal of Psychoanalysis*, vol. 25, 1944, pp. 19-53, 122, 154-178.

needs, he will resort to every conceivable means at his disposal. On the psychological level this will usually take the form of behavior calculated to elicit the required attention. We generally call such behavior "aggressive." But when it is fully understood we find that aggressive behavior is, in fact, nothing but love frustrated, a technique for compelling love. Hence, it should be very clear that the best possible way in which to approach aggressive behavior in children is not by further aggressive behavior toward them, but with love. And this is as true not only for children but for human beings at all other ages.

Why do criminals so often enjoy having their photographs in the papers? Is it not perhaps for the same reason that they have committed their crimes? Is it not because these were the only ways they knew how to gain the attention they had been denied, and at the same time to revenge themselves upon the society which had let them down, disillusioned, deserted, and dehumanized them?

Why do rejected children often steal from their mothers? Dr. Adrian Vander Veer offers an explanation:[12] "The stealing usually has very little to do with money . . . the stealing really means that the child is trying to get something, in a vague way, that he knows he hasn't got, which something is his mother's love. If this delinquent pattern becomes marked enough, it may form the foundation for later more generalized anti-social behavior, all sorts of crimes, for example, stealing from persons who are not in the family." Dr. Vander Veer is more emphatic. He says that maternal rejection may be seen as the "causative factor in almost every type and every individual case of neurosis or behavior problem in children."

The mother does not necessarily have to be the biological mother of the child; any human being whether female or male, as long as he is capable of giving the child love, may be the equivalent of the real mother. All investigators are agreed that the importance of the mother—biological or surrogate—lies in the fact that she is the first representative of humanity with whom the child comes into association and through whom it usually receives

[12] A. Vander Veer, *The Unwanted Child*, Publication of the Illinois League For Planned Parenthood, Chicago, April 10, 1949, pp. 3-12.

the satisfaction or expects to receive the satisfaction of its needs. The child constructs its picture of the world largely through the experience it has with its mother. According as the mother is loving or unloving, the child will feel that the world is loving or unloving.

Endowed at birth with all the necessary drives for developing as a loving harmonic human being, the child learns to love by being loved. When it is not loved it fails to learn to love, but responds instead with protesting behavior, with rage and aggression, then with despair, and finally with the abandonment of all faith and hope in human beings. These are not mere statements concocted out of a desk thinker's head, but the conclusions of the workers at The International Children's Centre in Paris under the leadership of Drs. John Bowlby and Jenny Roudinesco. Such children, the children who have not been adequately loved, grow up to be persons who find it extremely difficult to understand the meaning of love; they are awkward in their human relationships, "cold fish," they tend to be thoughtless and inconsiderate; they have little emotional depth; hence they are able to enter into all sorts of human relationships in a shallow way and drift from one marriage to another with the greatest of emotional ease. They are "affectionless characters" who suffer from a hunger for affection. Awkward and ineffectual in their attempts to secure it, they often suffer rejection and end up by becoming more embittered than ever, finding themselves in the paradoxical situation of hating people because they want to love them, but having attempted to love them have been repulsed, and so end up by hating them. One such affectionless character who was apprehended by the police for having killed an entire family of five strangers exclaimed, "The whole world hates my guts, and I hate the whole world's guts." This youth had never been loved by anyone; whenever he made the attempt he was misunderstood and rejected. He served several prison terms and was so full of hate that his next crime could easily have been predicted . . . and prevented. Our society, murderously logical, corrected the wrongs thus done by murdering the murderer.

Many such unloved children avoid coming into overt conflict with society by making the required external adjustments, but they still remain cold, desolate, and hungry for love. Such children as adults often seek ways of achieving power, as if by so doing they may be able to force others to love them. Unhappily for them and for many others whom they may involve in their schemes, they rarely succeed. Such persons wreak much havoc upon their fellow human beings when, as in the case of such unloved creatures as Adolf Hitler, Mussolini, and Stalin, they attain positions of great wordly power. It was quite evident that the tragedy these men brought to the world was principally due to the incapacity of these creatures to love or to understand the meaning of love. Had they understood the meaning of love, had they been taught how to love by having been loved themselves, they could not possibly have behaved as inhumanly as they did. To love your neighbor as yourself requires first that you be able to love yourself, and the only way one learns that art is by having been adequately loved during the first six years of one's life. As Freud pointed out, this is the period during which the foundations of the personality are either well and truly laid—or not. If one doesn't love oneself one cannot love others. To make loving order in the world we must first have had loving order made in ourselves.

We are now, perhaps, in a better position to understand the meaning and importance of love for human beings and for humanity. Nothing in the world can be more important or as significant. Let us, then, set out the characteristics as best we can, of love—the conditions which must be fulfilled if we are to agree that the state of love exists.

1. Love is not only a subjective feeling which one has, an emotion, but a series of acts by means of which one conveys to another the feeling that one is deeply involved, profoundly interested, in him and in his welfare. In this sense love is demonstrative, it is sacrificial, it is self-abnegative. It always puts the other first. It is not a cold or calculated altruism, but a feeling of deep involvement in the other.

2. Love is unconditional, it makes no bargains, it trades with no one for anything, but conveys the feeling, the in-the-bones belief to the other that you are all for him, that you are there to give him your support, to contribute to his development as best you can, because the other is what he is, *not* because he is

something you want or expect him to be, but because you value him for what he is as he is.

3. Love is supportive, it conveys to the other that you will never commit that supreme of all the treasons that one human being can commit against another, namely, to let him down when he most needs you. Love promises that you will always be present to support the other, no matter what the conditions you will never fail him; that you will neither condemn nor condone, but that you will always be there to offer your sympathy and your understanding, and that whatever the other needs as a human being he shall have, even though it may be a firm no. Love means that you will be there to help him say yes to life, and to have all his needs for love satisfied.

If a human being can convey this complex of feelings to another, then the state of love for that other can be said to exist.

The nature of love has perhaps never been more beautifully described than by the Elizabethan dramatist George Chapman (1559-1634) in his play *All Fools* (1605):

> I tell thee, Love is Nature's second Sun,
> Causing a spring of virtues where he shines;
> And as without the Sun, the World's great eye,
> All colours, beauties both of Art and Nature,
> Are given in vain to men; so without Love
> All beauties bred in women are in vain,
> All virtues born in men lie buried;
> For Love informs them as the Sun doth colours;
> And as the Sun, reflecting his warm beams
> Against the earth, begets all fruits and flowers;
> So Love, fair shining in the inward man,
> Brings forth in him the honorable fruits
> Of Valour, wit, virtue, and haughty thoughts,
> Brave resolution, and divine discourse.

From the evidence thus far available it seems clear that love is indispensably necessary for the healthy development of the individual. Love is the principal developer of one's capacity for being human, it is the chief stimulus to the development of social competence, and the only thing in the world that can produce that sense of belongingness and relatedness to the world of humanity which every healthy human being develops. And what is health? Health is the ability to love and the ability to work. And what is love? Love is the quality which confers survival benefits upon others, and upon oneself, in a creatively enlarging manner.

Love is creative—creative both for the receiver and the giver, and greatly enriching the lives of both. When we understand the meaning of love we understand that it is the only thing in the world of which one cannot give anyone too much. The counterfeit thing is not the real thing—overprotectiveness and "smothering" are often mistaken for love when they are in fact often disguises for hostility. Genuine love can never harm or inhibit, it can only benefit and create freedom and order. Love has a firmness and discipline of its own for which there can be no substitute. No child can ever be spoiled by love, and there are few if any human problems which cannot be most efficiently solved by its application.

Scientists are discovering at this very moment that to live as if to live and love were one is the only way of life for human beings, because, indeed, this is the way of life which the innate nature of man demands. We are discovering that the highest ideals of man spring from man's own nature, that what is right for man is what is right for his nature, and that the highest of these innately based ideals is the one that must enliven and inform all his other ideals, namely, *love*. This is not a new discovery in the world; what is new is that scientists should be rediscovering these truths by scientific means. Contemporary scientists working in this field are giving a scientific foundation or validation to the Sermon on the Mount and to the Golden Rule: To do unto others as you would have them do unto you, and to love your neighbor as yourself.

We have left the study of love to the last, but now that we can begin to understand its importance for humanity, we can see that here is the area in which the men of religion, the educators, the physicians, and the scientists can join hands in the common endeavor of putting man back upon the road of his evolutionary destiny from which he has wandered so far away—the road which leads to health and happiness for all humanity, peace and good will unto all on earth.

8. Should Babies Be Born at Home?

SHOULD BABIES BE BORN AT HOME? What a question! Where else should they be born, if not in the home? The hospital? But I had thought that a hospital was a place where one went for relief from sickness or injury. I would not have thought, had I not known it to be the fact, that the most important event in the life of a family, the birth of a child, was best celebrated away from the home, away from the family, in a hospital—in a hospital to which the sick and the injured go. Is pregnancy a sickness? Is the birth of a child a disease? Is the arrival of a new baby something in which the rest of the family should not share? Is it bad for the mother, or for anyone else, if birth takes place in the home?

Most persons in the vicinity of middle age who read this chapter were probably born at home. I was, and so were most of my friends. The vast majority of human beings alive at this moment were born at home, and the vast majority of births in the world taking place at this moment are occurring in the home. In the greater part of Europe most births still take place in the home. How, then, does it come about that in the United States the greater number of births take place in the hospital? In the larger cities of this country well over 90 per cent of the births take place in the hospital.

The history of this development will not long detain us. It is largely the doing of the medical profession. To our doctors we probably owe as much, if not more than, to any other profession for the all-round general improvement in the health of Americans, the virtual elimination of many diseases, the reduction in the

113

virulence of others, decreased maternal and infant mortality rates, and the increase in longevity. The average American male may expect to live to be sixty-nine years of age, the average American female may expect to live to be seventy-five years of age—almost exactly double the expectation of life one hundred years ago. All this is largely the doing of the medical profession. But somehow this progress has been achieved at the cost of an increasing specialization and mechanization of the practice of medicine. The much esteemed old family doctor, the general practitioner, over the course of the years got to know his family and his patients so intimately that he couldn't but help knowing them and treating them as human beings. Today the horse-and-buggy doctor has been replaced by a specialist who is an authority on either the right or the left nostril, but not on both, and to whom the patient is a set of symptoms to which a body happens to be attached. Many doctors seem to have forgotten that the care of the patient begins with caring for the patient. The general idea seems to be to treat as many patients as possible. This tendency results in an arrangement whereby if the doctor can persuade his patients to go to a particular hospital he can see them all there without the necessity of having to run all over the place, and as a consequence see fewer patients than he could by this arrangement. Furthermore, the hospital offers the doctor relief from many obligations which he would otherwise have to carry out himself; a good deal of the drudgery associated with the practice of medicine is taken over by the hospital. This is particularly the case where birth is concerned.

In the hospital the obstetrician doesn't even have to be present when the baby is born. If he can manage to be present, well and good, but if he happens to be elsewhere when the baby is about to be born, an intern or any nurse on the service will do just as well. If the baby is to be born at home it is imperative that someone who knows how to deal with the situation be at hand. In our own time we have somehow grown to believe that this person must be the obstetrician.

One can readily understand and sympathize with the physician's desire to have his patients in the hospital for the delivery of their babies—it is a great convenience for the doctor, but is it good for anyone else? Is it, eventually, good for the doctor himself? Is it good for the baby, for the mother, for society? The answer to all these questions, as I shall endeavor to show, is in the negative.

I have heard a great many women say they wouldn't dream of having the baby anywhere else but in the hospital because the period of their confinement in the hospital is about the only time they ever get a real rest. Of course, with the advent of ambulatory obstetrics when the mother is required to go home on the fourth or fifth day, this incentive to go to the hospital has largely been removed. But, then, there are all the other reasons.

First, there are the objections which come from many doctors who look upon the recommendation that mothers should go back to the home to have their babies as some form of madness. The most frequent objection that comes from the medical profession is in the form of the question, What do you do in case of emergency? In the hospital you have everything immediately available, at home practically nothing is available. The answer to that question is: emergencies are the exception rather than the rule. There is good reason to believe that the present rate of "emergency" would be reduced in the parturient mother and child were she to have the baby in the home. In any event, insofar as emergencies are concerned, these are best met in the home, where the mother is surrounded by the loving care of her family, her husband, perhaps other members of the family, and the children—the children who are so often looked upon as being "in the way." Love cannot do what penicillin can do, but what penicillin cannot do love alone often can. Be that as it may, what of all those physical emergencies which may arise during labor, during the birth, and after the birth of the child? How are they to be dealt with in the home?

The answer is simple enough. In all communities every doctor would report to a central agency the approximate date at which every woman known to him professionally is expected to have a baby. At the appropriate time a fully equipped mobile birth unit would be stationed outside the home where the baby was to be born, so that any emergency could be dealt with then and there, or if necessary the patient taken to the hospital—but the latter should be the last resort rather than the first. A small addition to the community taxes would be more than sufficient to cover the cost of such a service, and it would be very much less costly to the family than the cost of hospital care during the most uneventful stay there. Every town has a fire-fighting apparatus which can be called into action at a few minutes' notice. With an impending birth we have a notice of months, weeks, and days during which to prepare for any possible emergency—an emergency which will in by far the majority of cases not occur. Emergency mobile birth units will be far less expensive to maintain and service than fire trucks—and at least as useful. The equipment of the mobile birth unit will include a highly qualified midwife-nurse able to deal with all but the worst emergencies. In England "Flying Squads" fully equipped and ready to go anywhere on obstetrical service at a moments notice have been available for years.

And speaking of midwife-nurses. In the United States the midwife has become so rare a phenomenon as to be on the verge of extinction. We don't need midwives, say many obstetricians. On the other hand, I think we need to revive this ancient and noble profession. With that charming insouciance which we Americans so often exhibit, we are sometimes inclined to identify the United States with "civilization." But the fact is that there are many other lands worthy of that description in which the vast majority of human beings are brought into the world by midwives. During September 1954 the International Confederation of Midwives, with midwives from forty-six different countries, assembled in London. Interestingly enough (as reported in the *British Medical Journal*, September 18, 1954), "The only countries which refused the invitations sent to them were the Soviet Union and Czechoslovakia." The discussions during the meetings were focused upon such questions as professional responsibilities of the midwife, the midwife's part in reducing maternal and neonatal deaths, and the midwife's training.

I think it might not be too hazardous a statement to declare it probable that in the art of ministering to the needs of a mother about to give birth to a child most midwives are better equipped than most obstetricians. As women, most midwives have that fellow feeling for other women which most obstetricians can so seldom have. This is important, in spite of the fact that in our highly mechanized society we are sometimes inclined to forget the importance of fellow feeling. The midwife is as likely as not to have had children of her own, and in addition to her training will understand what no man will ever understand, namely, what it means to have a child. This is important, in spite of the laughter it may evoke in some quarters. The gentle touch of a woman is to be preferred to the high forceps of the male obstetrician; the only male who should be participating and assisting in the birth process should be the husband. I shall return to this matter in a moment. In fact, the obstetrician should be present at birth only when his emergency services are required, and this, as I have already said, would be in a vanishingly small proportion of cases. The well-trained midwife can do all that is physically necessary that the best-trained and experienced of obstetricians can do, and I have already suggested that she can do more. She will usually have the good sense to refrain from doing all those things which —and I utter the words in tho full consciousness and sense of responsibility of what I am saying—lazy obstetricians often do.

To name but one such practice, there is episiotomy (nicking the vulva to one side) in order to accelerate the birth. And perhaps we may name another, which is even now, when most of the evidence is in, not completely discontinued—the loading of the mother with sedatives which are known to have an asphyxiating effect upon the fetus, and which have almost certainly done more or less severe damage to the brain of many a child living today at a lower mental level than he would had he been deprived of the more than doubtful benefits of heavy sedation.

In difficult labor episiotomy is sometimes indicated, but we may be certain that more often than not it is not indicated. Heavy sedation is rarely indicated. It was, of course, developed with a very good intention, namely, that of rendering the process of birth less painful to the mother. Anesthesia is one of the great boons of medicine to humanity, but every doctor should at this day know that every anesthetic injected into the mother's blood stream or introduced into her body in any other way will reach the fetus in the mother's womb within a few minutes. Well, these are some of the things an old midwife of the last century would have been likely to know—as she was likely to know a good many other things—that are not dreamed of in many a modern physician's philosophy.

Certainly for most normal births the midwife can relieve the obstetrician with every advantage to all concerned—including the obstetrician.

Another objection urged against home births is that the conditions of sepsis and asepsis are dealt with much more efficiently in the hospital than in the home. Pathogenic organisms, it is argued, are much more likely to be encountered in the home than in the hospital, and asepis likely to be at a minimum in the home as compared with the hospital.

In the average American home the exact opposite of this is likely to be true. The danger from pathogenic organisms is less than it is from such organisms in a hospital. For reasons that should be obvious pathogenic organisms are much more likely to be encountered in a hospital than they are in the home. A hospital usually houses a number of persons who have been admitted because they have fallen victim to the invasion of their bodies by such organisms. The fact is that most of the maternal and a large proportion of the infant deaths occurring in hospitals are avoidable deaths. That this is so is borne out by such reports as that from the Seaside Memorial Hospital at Long Beach, California, where out of 14,501 deliveries, Dr. Stirling Pillsbury writes, there was not a single maternal death. This record is attributed to the excellent clinical and administrative arrangements all in the service of the patient. In particular, there is the requirement that physicians obtain written permission for certain types of procedures; thus physicians are prevented from undertaking procedures for which they are not qualified, and at the same time another opinion is provided as to the advisability of the procedure being contemplated.

Drs. Charles M. Steer and Walter P. Kosar of the Sloane Hospital for Women, New York, report on an investigation on fetal mortality during the years from 1940 to 1949. The differences in mortality between the ward and private services were striking.

The differences were all in favor of the private cases, and these are ascribed to the better health and better obstetrical care of the private patients. Drs. Steer and Kosar conclude that up to 60 per cent of the baby deaths were preventable.

A year's experience of the Health Insurance Plan of Greater New York has shown, as reported in 1951 by Drs. George Baehr and Neva R. Deardorff, that under the proper conditions maternal mortality can be reduced to zero, and fetal and newborn deaths can be reduced to a minimum.

The good prenatal, obstetrical, and pediatric care responsible for such reduction in mortality rates simply underscores the necessity of such care for the mother, the fetus in the womb, the newborn, and the infant—a necessity which should be taken as a matter of course, *without the hospital playing any role whatsoever* in these connections. Such care is best given mother and child in the home, in her *normal* environment. Professors Harry and Ruth Bakwin of New York University and Bellevue Hospital, two of America's most distinguished pediatricians, categorically state that "Hospitals are unsuited for the care of the newborn. Physicians and parents who would hesitate to permit an older infant in a hospital ward seem to have no qualms about having newborn babies there, even though obstetrical nurseries are generally more crowded than is the usual ward for infants. Fortunately the newborn is resistant to many of the common infections that beset the older infant. The immunity of the newborn is, however, limited, as is evidenced by the frequency with which diarrhea, pneumonia, sepsis, and other infections occur among them. These conditions are rare in the home, and the baby kept at home is obviously not exposed to nursery epidemics." And the Professors Bakwin tactfully suggest that "some modification of the present system of indiscriminate hospital delivery is indicated."

Cross-infections are the bane of nursery and infant wards. Though they may be mild in themselves, such infections may have the most disastrous results in that the infants tend to stop eating, suffer from diarrhea, lose weight, and die. Such disasters are most unlikely to occur in the home.

Statistics and other data on home as compared with hospital

deliveries are not easy to come by. One of the best sources of such data is the Chicago Maternity Center.[1] The Center is located in the sweltering slums of Chicago just south of the Loop. "Skid Row" is just around the corner. A more depressing and depressed environment could hardly be imagined. Since 1895 the Center has been taking care of deliveries in the homes of the poor. During the years the Center's doctors have delivered over 104,000 babies. For the thirty months ending in August 1954, in more than 8,339 home deliveries *not a single mother had died.* In the best-conducted hospitals this record is seldom equaled, in fact, the maternal death rate for the United States is one per thousand. Of some three hundred cases requiring hospitalization by the Center, only three proved fatal.

It requires to be pointed out that a high percentage of the Center's cases are last-minute calls, where there has been no prenatal visiting, so that practically no sanitary precautions had been taken. These are usually provided by the nurses and physicians forming the delivery team, in the form of newspapers and empty beer bottles. With the bottles for stiffening, newspapers are rolled into bolsters to shield the mother from outside germs. Dr. Harry B. Benaron, the Center's Co-Director, pointed out that while newspapers may not be germ-free, they are certainly cleaner than the sheets found in the average home visited by the Center.

The record of the Chicago Maternity Center is worth all the unsupported objections against home deliveries that have ever been urged.

Another objection that has been urged takes the form of the question, What about prematures? My answer there, too, is that it would have been far better for everyone concerned had most prematures continued to be born in the home rather than in the hospital. Certainly a large number of children now permanently blind would be seeing the world about them as normal persons had they been born at home rather than in the hospital. The disorder known as retrolental fibroplasia (fibrous detachment of the lens) is now known to have been due to the excess oxygen given premature babies while they were in the hospital. This is a

[1] "The Baby Commandos," *Time,* August 2, 1954, p. 46.

fact, and it must be mentioned. It is tragic, and it might be considered by some that it would have been in better taste not to have mentioned it at all. But I am not here concerned with matters of taste. I am concerned with the lives and happiness of human beings and of societies of human beings. Furthermore, this example is but one illustration of the many forms of more subtle damage that is done to child, parents, family, and society by our present hospitalizing procedures.

It is contended by some that the hospital is equipped with all the emergecy materials to take care of the premature weighing under five and a half pounds, whereas the home is not.

What are the facts?

Well, we have one series of studies carried out on an industrial population in the north of England, Newcastle-upon-Tyne, during the three-year period 1945-1947. In this population of 280,000, each year about three hundred prematures are born, somewhat less than one-half of these in the home. A program for home care of prematures was initiated in 1945, with a corps of nurses specially trained, and an ambulance service organized to deliver special beds, blankets, and other equipment to the home. The maximum number of prematures taken care of by one nurse was three. Any doctor could call for assistance by telephoning the hospital.

There being a shortage of nurses, many premature infants born at home could not enjoy the benefits of this service. It is therefore possible to compare not only the results in the home and in the hospital, but also the value of the specialized nursing care over routine care in the home.

During the three-year period, 379 prematures were born at home and 537 in hospitals. It was found that hospital prematures did better than the unattended home prematures, but that the home nurse-attended prematures (159 of them) did at least as well as the hospital group, the mortality rate being the same for each, namely, 19.5 per cent, whereas for the unattended it was 27.2 per cent.

Dr. F. J. W. Miller, who conducted these studies, believes that the indiscriminate hospitalization of prematures weighing under five and a half pounds is unwarranted. From the standpoint of infection he asserts that the home is a safer place than the hospital, that the home attention is more economical, and what is most important, the home birth is wholesome in its effects in promoting family ties and solidarity. Dr. Miller states: "The nurse in her role of teacher and advisor and by her personality mobilizes the family for duties; someone to watch at night; someone to watch during the day; someone, probably a neighbor, to shop; everyone interested is involved and all have a sense of achievement, which gives the child a good start and is far better than if he were taken away to a hospital and returned a month or six weeks later, an unknown infant, feared and strange."

These are, of course, the fundamentally important reasons why children should be born in the home in which they are going to live and of which they are going to form a part. The objections to hospitalization for childbirth are many, the most important of them all being that the hospital tends to dehumanize the mother-child relationship, the very relationship out of which all humanity grows.

The child, in most hospitals—in spite of the advent of rooming-in—is separated from the mother, and the mother from the child *when they most need each other*. Mother and child most need each other during the first forty-eight hours after birth. Let me explain why.

From the standpoint of the newborn who, during the process of getting born has received an enormous number of new stimulations quite unlike those which it experienced during its hibernation in the peaceful environment of the womb, getting born is a comparatively rough experience. The newborn is called upon to make all sorts of adjustments to the new environment into which it is thrust. It must breathe in oxygenated air, its lungs must begin to function, the heart must adapt itself both in position and in function to the new demands which are made upon it, and so on. At this time, more than at any other in its life, it requires every reassurance that all is well and there is promise of good things to come. And this is the very time we choose to separate it from the one person in the world who can give it that reassurance and promise. What the baby needs is the caress of its mother's body and the reassurance which being put to nurse at her breast gives it.

The mother needs the baby almost as much as the baby needs her. The mother is dependent very largely upon the undisturbed relationship with her baby for her own welfare.

Let this be underscored with the facts. When the baby is put to nurse at the mother's breast shortly after birth, not only is the breast stimulated to begin functioning, but, as we have already pointed out in the preceding chapter, three of the great obstetrical problems are in most cases solved virtually at once.

In the hospital the mother is deprived of these benefits, whereas in the home she would be likely to enjoy them. In addition to these physiological benefits there are, of course, the added psychological benefits which accrue both to her and to the baby. The continuity of the relationship between mother and baby should not under normal conditions ever be disturbed. Yet from the moment of birth this relationship is progressively disturbed in the hospital. The routinized procedures of the hospital interfere with the development of the natural functions of both mother and baby. As Professor Harry and Ruth Bakwin point out, "The obstetrical hospital is in good part responsible for the failure of many mothers to breast-feed their babies." More often than not no effort is made to initiate breast-feeding, but instead a bottle formula is prescribed for the baby, and since this satisfies the baby's appetite, the baby is discouraged from sucking at the breast, and the stimulus for the secretion of milk is thus effectively removed. A hard glass lukewarm bottle with a rubber tire at the end of it is not a desirable substitute for the mother's breast.

The feeding demands of the baby do not function by the clock. Yet the practice of bringing the baby to the mother at fixed times and for limited periods, as is done in the hospital, does violence both to the mother's and the baby's needs. We seem to have a genius for starting off on the wrong foot from the moment the human being is born.

The birth of a new member of the family should be a family matter, not a series of problems for comparatively disinterested strangers in the psychologically impersonal environment of the hospital. The father of the child to be born should be a partner in the process of birth. He should be with the mother, his wife, throughout the experience. It is at this time that the firmest psychological bonds between husband and wife are established. As a result of joining in the birth experience *together* each grows to mean more to the other and to their children than could be accomplished by any other means. It is during this period that the wife falls most profoundly in love with her husband, and the husband becomes more deeply involved in his wife and in his family. Instead, under prevailing conditions, where the husband is not permitted to share in the experience, but is caused to wait nervously and expectantly far removed from the one who most needs him, the wife is often left alone, or in charge of a nurse who is busily occupied somewhere else on the floor and occasionally pops her head in to see that things are "all right," or maybe in the presence of a strange young intern, or else holding the hand of her obstetrician upon whom she projects all the love she has to give, and which should properly be received by her husband—and returned by him. At home the husband would be where he belongs, with his wife, and no one should dare keep these two asunder at this most important period in their lives. With the increasing number of "natural childbirths" we have abundant and increasing evidence of the importance and value of the presence of the husband during the birth process. The presence of one husband outweighs in value all the sedatives and medicaments in the world.

If there are any other children in the family they should also be made part of the household that is expecting the new brother or sister. They don't have to be present at the birth itself, but they should be fully prepared as early as possible, and caused to anticipate with all the pleasure possible the new addition to the family. Long before the new baby arrives is the time to anticipate any difficulties which might arise out of sibling rivalry. If the children are properly prepared and made to feel that their bonds with their family will be strengthened by the arrival of the new baby, rather than weakened, much heartache will thus be avoided.

No wonder, under present conditions, when mother goes to the hospital the creature considered responsible for this dastardly separation is the new baby. No wonder the children abandoned at home want to strangle him or gouge his eyes out. For small children this is a much worse experience than it would be for a woman whose husband suddenly appeared, after an appreciable absence, with a beautiful young thing and then announced to his wife, "Mary, this is Gloria, my new co-wife. She will live together with us hereafter and I hope we will all have a jolly old time." It might be less of a shock to some wives than the experience of having the new baby introduced into the household without so much as a by-your-leave is to many children.

The family is a unit, and its unity should never be broken. If that unity must be disturbed it should never be in the manner so customarily and mechanically produced by the obstetrical hospital.

Should babies be born at home? Of course they should, for that is where they belong.

9. The College in the Crosscurrents of Change

IT HAS BEEN JUSTLY SAID that it takes more than science to create moral man and the good society, more than knowledge and its effective application. It also takes, it has been said, "the basic values to which a great college is committed: commitment to responsibility and the striving for excellence."

This is quite so, but we need to ask the questions: Responsibility to whom, and for what? Excellence in and for what? Unless these two questions are unequivocally clearly answered, there is little hope that we shall do more than ritually repeat the confusions of our predecessors. Let us always remember that the meaning of a word is the action it produces. If our colleges are to assist in the process of making responsible men and women whose standard is excellence, it seems to me that a critically important locus is the college—although I would begin much earlier than that, with the nursery school, the kindergarten, the elementary and high schools. The college occupies a critically important place in the life of the individual fortunate enough to attend such an institution. Indeed, it should be for every individual a landmark at the crossroads of his life. For it is at college that such errors as have been committed upon him may be at least partly corrected, and where he may be reconstituted in such a manner that when he leaves college he shall thereafter himself become a diffuser of the good he has there acquired. It is at college that the individual should acquire that glorious contagion which another age called *humanitas*. In

126

an age when the thrust toward science has become the secular religion of the day, in which each day men begin to resemble ever more closely the things and objects that are made by machines, in which instruction is mistaken for education, even in our colleges, it is imperative for the college in the cross-currents of change to ask itself what it is doing.

It seems to me that what most colleges are doing is to instruct —a very different thing from education. What is education? Or rather, what ought education to be? Education should be the nourishing and the causing to grow and develop of the capacity for humanity. And by humanity I mean the ability to relate oneself in a loving, creatively enlarging manner to all other human beings and to oneself. The techniques, the skills, of reading, writing, and arithmetic—all the knowledge that the college takes for its province—should be taught to the highest standards of excellence, but always with reference to, and in the service of, the individuals and the groups: humanity. The techniques of acquiring, utilizing, and communicating knowledge, it seems to me, should always be secondary and instrumental to the development of the individual's capacity to relate himself lovingly toward others. The three R's should not be primary, as they are in our so-called educational institutions today. The education of the moral capacities of the student should not be consigned to something slightingly called "the liberal arts," or to that favored mentor of muscle the athletic coach, or even to chapel. Our colleges must realize that their task is to create human beings who are responsible to themselves and to their fellow men for the harmonious realization of their capacities for loving-kindness, that this must be their principal task and that everything else taught in college must be taught within the ambience of this primary discipline.

The more man advances in science and technology, the more he progresses as a systematist, the more mechanized is his own life and the more stupid he seems to become. Indeed, I can tell you as an anthropological observer, that man has become so stupid that he threatens to stupidify himself out of existence. His right cerebral hemisphere, as it were, knoweth not what the left doeth and vice versa. This is what comes of the one-sided worship of things, of science and technology. Man has become altogether too clever for his own good. The more clever he has become the less intelligent he has grown to be, so that he now threatens himself with his own extinction. Can anything be more cleverly unintelligent than that? Modern man is sick. We must endeavor to restore him to health. What is health? Health is the ability to love and the ability to work.

Our colleges can, if they will, do the major part of the work of restoring man to a sense of responsibility to himself and to others for the realization of his birthright, which is development —development of his capacity to love and work, and development of all other potentialities to the optimum.

Such a viewpoint demands the revaluation of education as conceived at the present time, and it calls for a thorough reorganization of the process of education as it is practiced in our colleges today. The great error increasingly committed by our educational institutions has been the practice of the belief that it is their function to teach subjects to objects, whereas the proper function of an educational institution should be to humanize that most eminently humanizable, that most educable, and most delightfully interesting creature, the learning human being.

I have spoken of the primacy of education in the ability to love. I now wish to speak of the co-related importance of the ability to work.

Just as there may be complete heartlessness behind the show of love, so there may be a fundamental disinterest in work behind the show of busyness for which Americans are so notorious. The habit of work is simply not taught in our educational institutions. The reasons for this would in themselves make a fascinating subject for a discourse. As I see it, the well-meaning desire of parents in America to make things easy for the young, to keep children happy, is fundamentally related both to their lack of discipline and their inability to work. At the college level the training in the incapacity to work is further reinforced by the great number and variety of courses the student is obliged to take which, in addition to leaving him practically no time to think, compels him to concentrate upon too little and to touch upon too much. One of the results is that in any adventitious gathering of men it is scarcely possible to distinguish between the college-educated executive and the high school-educated shoe salesman.

But why work, it may be asked? Shouldn't one have a good time at school and at college? Of course one should enjoy school and college to the limit—much more so than most students do at the present time. I do not believe in work for its own sake. This, however, is the experience of the race: that excellence in anything can only be achieved through work, and that if excellence be granted as a value worth striving for, then work is the principal means by which it can be achieved. Furthermore, not only is work the route to excellence in the acquisition, use, and communication of understanding and knowledge, but it is a major means of self-discipline. Finally, when all else has been said and done, work is the principal source of happiness. If you set out to find happiness it will elude you, for happiness comes to one mainly as a by-product of work.

In a period when we can already foresee increasing days of leisure, and in which leisure is generally interpreted to mean freedom from work, it is most necessary to underscore these points. Just as for too long the idea of liberty was equated with economic libertinism, so it seems to me, the idea of freedom has for too long been equated with doing what one likes. I would suggest, as others before me have done, that freedom does not consist in the liberty to do what one likes, but lies rather in the right to be able to do what one ought. And what one ought to do should be perfectly compatible with doing what one likes.

But what ought one to do? Our colleges should teach the student the answer to that question. But if our colleges are to return a sound answer to that question they stand much in need of revaluing their own values. Colleges, on the whole, reflect the values which prevail in the society of which they are a part. If our colleges persist in teaching those values to their students, then all that they are doing is to maintain the *status quo*. And I submit that far too much of the weal and woe that this world has suffered during the last hundred years has been due to the shortcomings of men educated in our colleges.

The great American idol at the foot of which too many

Americans worship is what William James called the Bitch-Goddess Success—success in terms of material values. There is nothing whatsoever wrong with material values in themselves. It is when they replace the pursuit of humane values that the damage is done. But this is an old story. It seems to me that the challenge is squarely before our colleges to restore a more balanced and humane system of values to its charges. In the final analysis what the college has to convey to its charges is that the greatest gift a man can offer to his fellows is his own character, his personality in all its aspects. For the only true success a man ever achieves is the development of his own character— all other successes are secondary.

Will our colleges make the desired changes? I don't know. We are told that one cannot predict the future. Possibly I have just laid an egg. If so I hope the future will see it hatched. And on this ornithological note I would like to end with a moral.

On the day of their graduation from college two friends vowed that they would return thirty years hence and meet. In the interim one became a missionary in Melanesia, and the other the captain of a merchant vessel. At the prearranged time they met. The missionary made a gift of his favorite talking bird to his old friend, who received it gratefully and introduced it into the cage in which his own talking bird was cockily perched. The missionary bird took one look down the full length of his generous beak at the nautical bird and exclaimed, "What must we do to be saved?" Whereupon the nautical bird replied, "Pump like hell boys, or we'll all go down!"

10. Parents Without Partners

In the united states one out of every three marriages terminates in divorce or separation. Death, and parentage without marriage, are factors which add further to the ranks of the many millions of parents without partners—perhaps the most slighted, most neglected, and virtually abandoned minority group in this country. Indeed, the class of parents without partners has, when it has not been slighted or neglected, been approached with an unrealistic sententiousness or else a maudlin sentimentality that altogether misses both the poignancy and the requirements of the situation. Another widespread attitude is that this is something best not talked about. A divorced person, a widowed member of the family, or one who has become a parent without benefit of clergy is regarded in much the same manner as one used to regard having an idiot in the family, or a returned black sheep, of whom the less that was said and seen the better. Parents without partners have, indeed, for a long time been the displaced persons of our society. And the burdens of displacement have largely fallen upon women.

These archaic attitudes, however prevalent they may be in some of the backwoods of our society, are rapidly giving way to more civilized attitudes. There remains, however, a considerable amount of work to be done before an adequate understanding of these problems and needs of parents without partners becomes more widely diffused.

One thing requires to be underscored at once, because important as the father is, it is a fortunate dispensation that the partner to whom the care of the children usually falls is the mother. I say a fortunate dispensation because by virtue of the fact that she is a mother the mother is generally better equipped to care for the children than is the father. But this fact carries with it an increased responsibility. It is not that the mother has to be both mother and father to the children—which she cannot be—but that she has to be a double parent, as it were. It is obvious that she has to put in a great deal more time being a parent than the parent with a partner. The demands are far greater, and considerably more difficult and complex. The father without a partner is, in general, faced with much less difficult problems than the mother without a partner. In neither the case of the mother nor of the father without a partner has our society exhibited the least consciousness of the peculiarly difficult problems with which they and their children are confronted.

In the United States in particular most individuals have not yet caught up with the fact that within the short period of the last fifty years the structure of the family in this country has undergone a revolutionary change, in short, that the extended family, which has constituted the basic form of the family for millennia, has virtually vanished from among us. Before the advent of the automobile, the customary grouping was the extended family—a family that consisted of one's spouse and children, with the parents of each of the parents living within calling distance of their children, as did uncles, aunts, cousins, and other relatives, as well as close family friends. In such a society father and mother figures were available to fill the void left by the absence of the biological father or mother. Under such conditions the children and their single parent were faced with relatively few of the problems which confront their counterparts in the contemporary atomized family—a family that consists only of the biological parents and their children. In such a family when one of the parents is removed the problems that are thus created are seldom solved, or at least alleviated, as they were within the bosom of the extended family. In whatever manner the singleness of the parent might have come about, there was a great deal more than sympathy given to the widowed parent, and however discomforting the expression of regret, disappointment, and disapproval in the case of divorce, a deep involvement was nevertheless present. Possibly the only person who fares better today is the unmarried mother. We no longer regard the unmarried mother as a disgrace and a pariah. Here there seem to have been many positive gains made, even though the tragedies resulting from the cruelties of customary attitudes are still far too numerous among us.

The ostrich, which is said to hide its head in the sand, does not in fact do so. But our society does in this important matter of the single parent—a most inefficient form of behavior, and disastrous in its consequences for society. For what does not appear to be realized in our society is that not only does the single parent constitute an individual local problem, but that the single parent and the children constitute problems which are also those of society. These are national problems, and they are not problems which can be evaded without the most serious consequences to the society as a whole. For the family is the basis of society, and anything that goes wrong with the family is reflected in many detrimental ways in society. Our society has been evading the problem of the single parent, and the consequences have been and continue to be serious.

Let me refer to some of these consequences for the United States. The United States has the highest divorce and separation rates in the Western world; it has the highest alcoholic rate, the highest violent crime rate, the highest juvenile delinquency rate, the second highest homicide rate, and the fifth highest suicide rate.

These rates are evidences of extreme social disorganization. To this social disorganization "broken homes" have often been accused of contributing. Our society is reasonably well aware of the causes of these conditions, but does virtually nothing by way of prevention, and it is equally delinquent with respect to therapy. Quite clearly there is a great deal of work to be done on the preventive and therapeutic levels.

Many marriages are a mistake—the kind of mistake which the proper future education may reduce to the vanishing point. But while such mistakes continue to be made it is a good thing that they can be corrected by divorce. Often the really first evidence of good sense in a marriage is the decision to divorce. The decision to divorce is frequently evidence of the rejection of false values by at least one of the partners, and hence, constitutes a positive gain. The experience thus gained will undoubtedly have been costly, but it should not be lost upon others. It ought to be made available so that others might in time profit from it. With great insight Ibsen started the process in his play A Doll's House written in 1879. It had a great influence for good, but today we need more systematically gathered material.

There are, of course, many cases in which the divorce was a mistake. This is an area in which we need much more information than is at present available to us.

Prevention is always better than cure. Hence, everything possible must be done to prevent the unhappy marriage that results in a broken home. Or when a marriage is unhappy, whenever possible an attempt should be made to restore it to a happy state. Some may consider that these are neat tricks if they can be accomplished. No one claims that they are easy. But that they can be accomplished there is experience to testify.

When I speak of "prevention" I do not mean the counseling of individuals that they are not suited to each other, that they will not make a success of the contemplated union. I mean something very much more fundamental than that. What I have in mind is the revaluation of the values upon the basis of which most marriages in the Western world are contracted—contracted, in too many cases, like a disease.

When one out of three marriages ends in divorce something is somewhere wrong. And one of the principal things that is surely wrong is the romantic conception of love, that ferment and fret which catches so many in its net. I want to make it quite clear that I am not disparaging the romantic conception of love. What I am criticizing is the romantic conception of love as the only basis for marriage. Romantic love may, if it will, grow out of marriage. Certainly it may be the introduction that eventually leads to marriage, but it should never be the sole basis for marriage. More marriages have, I believe, been wrecked on the treacherous shoals of romantic love than on any of the other isles of illusion. Let me repeat that I consider the idea of romantic love a beautiful one, but not however a realistic foun-

dation for marriage; far better would it be as an outgrowth—
if it grow in that manner—of marriage. A marriage does not
have to be a romance in order to be a happy success. Romances
are novels, works of the imagination, and while there is no reason
why a certain number of marriages should not be a romance, a
work of the imagination, even such marriages have to be a great
deal more than that if they are to be a success. Alas, too many
marriages are entered into with too much imagination and too
little understanding of the realities involved. There is also the
widespread and erroneous identification of sex with love, especially by the male in Western society.

Love, for the male in the Western world, consists largely of a
series of disturbances produced in him by the perception of a
physically attractive female. This is not a good basis upon which
to enter into the marriage relationship for the simple reason
that physical charms have a way of palling after a time, and if
there is not enough else to deepen the involvement of the male,
he is rapidly likely to begin evidencing the symptoms of unin-
volvement.

To the female in the Western world love is a very different
thing. The difference has never been better expressed than by
Byron:

Man's love is of man's life a thing apart
'Tis woman's whole existence.

Let us, without overromanticizing it, say that it is a deep
involvement in the other which, given half a chance, is calculated
to be enduring—for life, and thereafter. That is to put it crassly.
For the female it is usually a great deal more than that. It is the
rather romantically based notion that the male she is going to
marry either is, or will be, a tender, loving, gentle knight, and
everyone will live happily ever after, just as it says in numerous
novels, countless stories and tales, and as our modern trouba-
dours, the crooners, and that greatest of all the obfuscators of
the subject, Hollywood, tell us.

Unfortunately, tenderness, the ability to love, and gentleness
are not qualities which we do very much to encourage in the
males in our society. On the other hand, we place a negative

sanction upon such traits in boys. We bring up our boys to be tough, not tender or gentle. As for the ability to love, that, it is held, is something with which boys should not be concerned. It is not until they marry that males are suddenly called upon to display qualities which virtually everyone has taken considerable pains to see that they do not develop.

This is as unfair to the male who has been so sedulously trained in an incapacity to be what, as soon as he enters upon the married state, he is expected to be, as it is to the female who has been led to expect something quite other than she gets.

In view of these asymmetries in the psychosocial development of the sexes, what is remarkable is not that there are so many divorces but that there are not more. It is this assymmetry in the emotional conditioning of the sexes that, perhaps more than any other factor, is responsible for unsuccessful marriage. If this be so, then it seems to me that this is an area upon which our society needs to focus its attention. This would require something of a revaluation of values, particularly in the area of human relations. It is not parents, not institutions, individuals, or society that are to be blamed for the confusion of ideas with which marriage is regarded. Blaming, in any event, is a folly of immaturity. The fault lies not so much in ourselves as in the values in which most of us are conditioned. Our values are traditionally determined, and we are socialized and conditioned in them long before, if ever, we are capable of taking an objective look at them.

Can there be anyone who will question the statement that the most important of the skills a human being can learn is the art of human relations? Yet this is something we teach by default rather than by design. What little we do teach by design is for the most part unsoundly based and wrong-headed. The value most in need of re-examination in American culture is the value of success, for it is this value by which Americans principally live. Success in terms of material values—this is a theme which has been so often rehearsed that it has become something of a cliché. It is, however, none the less true for all that. It is, I am afraid, very relevant to our discussion. The concentration on material value has progressively reduced the attention given to human relations. Human relations progressively become converted into object relations, so that human beings come to be treated as material objects. Marriages in which even one individual treats the other as an object are not likely to have a happy denouement. Yet such marriages are common.

I think, therefore, that one of the first things we must do is to begin teaching human relations from the nursery school through high school through college. Indeed, I feel that all education worthy of the name is education primarily in human relations, and that all else is instruction. Instruction is important, but it should never be confused with education. Instruction is training, so to say, in the three R's. Such instruction is highly desirable, but it should be secondary, and not primary as it is today. Even the word "primary" does not adequately describe the situation, for instruction is not only placed first in order of importance, but is taken to be the whole of education, and it is, indeed, often all the "education" that is offered. Such instruction prepares the individual to function technically among machines, but does virtually nothing to prepare him in the art of relating himself, not to machines but to human beings. The primary, basic, and essential part of all education should be training in the art of human relations. It is a shocking commentary upon the state of Western civilization that a plea for such a view should be necessary at this late date. Yet until this viewpoint becomes a reality we shall continue to flounder in desperately tragic and uncomprehending confusions.

It is not that we must introduce a course in human relations into our schools, but that the schools must be reformed into institutes of human relations, in which the three R's are taught within the matrix of human relations, in the service principally of the more efficient practice of human relations.

If I am asked how one goes about transforming our educational institutions into schools for the training in human relations, I shall answer that the approaches may be made at many levels and in many ways—assuming, of course, that those who are interested in bringing the change about fully understand what human relations must mean. I suppose that at this point I had better spell out what I understand by human relations.

By human relations I understand the communication to others of a profound sense of involvement and interest in their welfare, a creative relatedness which not only contributes to the harmonic development of the other, but does so in a creatively enlarging manner. It is the art of relating oneself to others in a warm, supportative, and stimulating manner—stimulating of the potentialities of the others to greater realization—and never committing the supreme of all the treasons that human beings so frequently commit against one another, namely, to let them down when they stand in need of you, but to stand by and give them the support and encouragement they need, and in all this, to retain a sense of humor. And this is love. If you can so relate yourself to another, then you can be said to love him. The whole art of human relations consists in this ability to relate oneself to others in a warm, loving manner. As I have already repeatedly said, it is to the teaching of this most important of all the arts that I should like to see our schools increasingly devoting themselves. If this consummation is to be wished, how do we go about devoting ourselves to bringing it to life?

I should say that it would be highly desirable to found one or more schools in which the teaching of human relations is the dominant purpose of the school. I would predict that not only would the graduates of such a school turn out to be rather more satisfactory human beings than the graduates of the traditional schools, but they would also be better educated in the traditional academic sense. The achievement of such a school would provide the greatest incentive to its wider imitation.

Educators within the existing instructional institutions would be interested, even if at first their interest were limited to experimenting with the single classroom, to try something of the same sort in their own schools.

Contributing further toward this end I should like to see the nursery school become part of the public educational system of the land. Several important purposes would in this way be served. The nursery school age is none too early to begin the more formal teaching of human relations—formal only in comparison with the informal teaching that should have been proceeding at home. And the nursery school should bring the parents into the school, in what should be a complementary educational process, in which parents and teacher help each other to help the child. This way everyone involved would be benefited. The father, especially, must be encouraged to participate in such activities with something more than the perfunctorily dutiful manner which is so characteristic of today's much-misunderstood and intimidated father. In this way the parents would not only participate in the education of their children, but would be helped by the school to a more efficient understanding of human relations. What is thus begun in nursery school should be continued through to high school. Were that to be done, I am sure very little, if any, repair work would be required at the college level.

At the college level is the time for thorough resolution and integration of one's comprehension and abilities in the practice of human relations. This, of course, should be concurrent with the study of one's more formal subjects. At college, in order to prepare for a career in the professions, it is taken for granted that years of work will be necessary, but for the important profession of marriage and parentage, the family, we do not consider that any preparation, other than the *ad hoc* variety which, by default rather than by design, the individual is left to pick up as best or worst he may. Surely, we ought to have thoroughly organized courses in marriage, parentage, and the family in our colleges, which everyone should be obliged to take, to study, and be required to show satisfactory proficiency in before being permitted to graduate. The teachers of these subjects should be at least as ably qualified as the teachers of the usual academic subjects.

There are always going to be parents without partners. The understanding of what this, in fact, means should be given to everyone, so that those who will become directly involved shall be better prepared for the contingencies, while those who do not become parents without partners shall better understand the problems of those that do. The time to teach such understanding is in the school and college years. I am not aware that any significant amount of attention is ever devoted in our schools and colleges to this group of human problems. Understanding of these problems could, of course, be taught as part of the course work in marriage and the family.

There is a very real need for basic research into the problems of parents without partners, for these are many and complex, and we should have at our disposal as thorough and reliable a body of knowledge concerning them as possible. If we are to be maximally helpful such a body of knowledge is indispensable. Its acquisition should be encouraged by the setting up of research grants specifically earmarked for such a purpose.

We must also look forward to the development of specialists in this field of parents without partners to whom those in need may go for help with the assurance that they will be receiving it from an expert. Well-meaning advice not based upon a sound understanding of the problems involved must make way for that which is.

Every town of any magnitude should surely have one or more centers devoted to helping parents without partners solve their problems, or such services could be performed by the already existing marriage counseling centers, by the addition of specialists suitably trained.

As soon as the need is properly presented to it, I think we may confidently look forward to a greater interest being shown in the problems of parents without partners by the Department of Health, Education and Welfare. This will be a great help, for with the facilities at the disposal of the Department a great deal of valuable help is bound to be forthcoming.

When we speak of parents there is, of course, the implied relation to children, and it is the problems of children as well as those of the parents without partners that we have in mind when we use that phrase. The children of parents without partners are beset with all sorts of difficult problems. As a one-parent or divided-parent child he feels that he differs from other children. When one parent is gone the child often feels that the other parent may go too. Among other things, this makes for a feeling of considerable insecurity. He is no longer the recipient of undivided attention. The attention he receives is now divided, he may feel, between the outside world to which his parent is giving the attention which should be his, and himself. The child may blame the parent for depriving him of the other parent, for there no longer being a family. He may pick up something of the unquiet desperation, the odd-man-out feeling, the social isolation, the loneliness, the emptiness of entire days that his mother may experience and exhibit. There is the problem of the absent parent who stays absent, and there is the problem of the parent who makes his presence felt rather too much in a variety of ways, though he is physically absent.

These are only a few of the problems of the child of parents without partners. This child is in need of much help, and he seldom receives it. The child of parents without partners must become for us a person of primary concern.

PART III

Images and Identities in American Society

11. Value Determinants and Conflicts in Today's Family

WE BEGIN WITH the axiom that the family is the fundamental and most important institution of society. Fundamental because from it society originates and is perpetually replenished. Important because it is the principal agency for the inculcation and transmission of society's values. It is said that as the family is so will the society be. This is true enough. But is it not also true that as the society is so will the family be? The answer is yes, of course. Both statements are true. Let us examine these matters a little further.

It has become a platitude to say that society is merely the family writ large. Is this true? In a sense, certainly. But might it not, perhaps, be more correctly said that the family is a minusculization of society—that the family is significantly more influenced by the matrix, society, within which it develops than it, the family, influences society? Surely, this is the more correct way of stating the facts. The family does not determine the values of society; but rather it is that society largely determines the values of the family. And the family is, as I have said, the principal agency for the inculcation and transmission of the social values. The very structure as well as the functions of the family are significantly affected by the dominant values of the society.[1] It is true that it is we who make institutions as they are, and if

[1] Arthur W. Calhoun, *A Social History of the American Family From Colonial Times to the Present*, 3 vols. (New York, Barnes and Noble, 1945).

they also begin to make us as they do it is only after the fashion of their creators. Most social scientists, I think, would agree that society, the working system of social values, largely determines the values of the family.

What is the meaning of the qualifying "largely"? Its meaning is that every family more or less contributes some idiosyncratic elements to the determinance of its own value system. This being so, it constitutes a nearer approach to the truth to say that the value system of the family represents the expression of the interaction between the dominance of the social values and the manner in which these are acted upon by the individual family.

It is because of the idiosyncratic character and contribution of the family that social change is possible. This is a fortunate arrangement for the human species, for were it not so, we might all have become as fixed in our responses as the ants who, it is probable, have no juvenile deliquency rates at all, and by the same token, neither have they any potentialities for further development. Among the ants, society is the family writ large. The genotype determines the phenotypic behavior, behavior being fixed and stereotyped. It is, fortunately, not so among human beings, for human beings are characterized by a genotype that is distinguished for the tremendous plasticity of phenotypic behavioral responses that it is capable of making to the environment. It is because of this characteristic of the human species that, within the family, values can be inculcated into its members that differ from those that prevail in the society as a whole. Were it not for this fact, we might all be well advised to pack up as human beings and join the ants. But while there may be a certain safety in not being educable enough to know how to make hydrogen bombs, it must be comparatively really rather dull, and nothing like as exciting to know how to make them, and what is more important, to realize the folly of making them, and to know how to unmake them.

With all these words the point I have thus far been trying to make is that the family dominantly has its values made for it by society, but that the family possesses the capacity to modify and influence those values and also to develop others, and that in virtue of this idiosyncratic capacity of the family there is always some hope, even for a society which, like ours, sometimes seems hopelessly mired in the systematics of its own confusions.

It is often thought that where methods and goals are clear confusion cannot prevail. On the contrary, it is quite possible to go methodically wrong in a systematic manner with the greatest of ease in the attainment of clearly conceived goals—goals which are both unsound and confusing. It is to be feared that this is what too many human beings in our society are habitually engaged in doing. And what is, perhaps, even worse, many people when apprised of the fact that this is what they are doing tend at once to redouble the effort with which they exercise the courage of their confusions. Their clearly conceived but confused goals are powered and implemented by perhaps less clearly conceived though equally confused means.

Americans are quite clear as to their values, their goals, and the means by which they should be achieved. They learn these from both their family and their culture. Since there exists in the family, the culture, and in the world at large considerable conflict among the values, goals, and means that are taught as desirable and permissible, it is not to be wondered at that personal confusion and disorder has become the endemic condition among us.

When mutually irreconcilable goals are pursued by means that are in conflict with one another, confusion and disorder is encouraged. The difficulty is that it is much more difficult to grow out of confusion to order and truth than it is out of simple error. Error can be demonstrated to be wrong, but since confusion is compounded out of a witches' broth of traditional beliefs, myths, half-truths, truths, falsities, and emotional investments of various sorts, they are not as easy to deal with. But they can be dealt with.

As I have already said, the effect of attempting to achieve mutually irreconcilable goals by conflicting means is to produce confusion and disorder in the person and in society. Such persons expend so much energy in attempting to keep themselves from falling apart that well might they exclaim, "All the world's a hospital, and men and women merely patients!" Confusion is not a good teacher, and its fees are excessively heavy.

What are the sources, and what is the nature, of this confusion? This is to ask, in other words, the question implied in
the title of this chapter, "Value Determinants and Conflicts in
Today's Family."

As an anthropologist, and as one who has lived in a number
of different countries, I think it correct to say that America as a
society is characterized by a greater confusion of values than any
other country of which I know. The confusion and conflict of
values is a marked characteristic of American culture—of the
American way of life. Confusions of a similar sort exist in all
societies of the Western world, but, as in so many other respects,
Americans like to do things in a big way—and this appears to
be true of our confusions, which seem to me to be bigger and
more confusing than those of other peoples.

What are the value determinants of American culture as they
are reflected in the American family?

The most dominant value in American culture, as I see it, is
the high premium placed on success. Success in virtually any
shape or form is the basic value. This is not the case in other
countries of the Western world, and in this respect the cultural
difference is marked. In Europe, for example, there are millions
of human beings who have never even thought of success insofar
as it might be achieved by themselves. Success, in the terms in
which Americans are caused to think of it, is something they
know is practicably achievable only by a limited number of
persons. The American, on the other hand, from infancy onward,
is conditioned in the belief that not only *can* he be a success,
but that he *must* be a success. To put it in a phrase, which I
hope will be taken as seriously as it is intended, the American is
taught that in order to succeed he must be a success! It doesn't
too much matter what one succeeds in, as long as enough people
know about it, and the rewards are substantial. There must be
some form of recognition, and there must be some form of profit
realized on the recognition. But the order is not important, for
one may begin with the profit, and the recognition will follow
as a result of having achieved, and perhaps increased, the profit
and all that it enables one to display conspicuously.

The Bitch-Goddess Success runs through virtually every aspect of American culture like a golden thread, leading straight from the idols of the cave to the idols of the market place in which the golden calf is worshiped. "Goodness" becomes early identified with "success," and so do "appropriateness," "fitness," and "adjustment," or "adaptability." I have even found one widely used American dictionary defining "intelligence" as the most successful response to a situation, instead of the most appropriate or fittest. But, of course, it does not have to be pointed out that success in America is held to be a proof of fitness. The Hazen Foundation Study, published under the title *Changing Values in College,* and prepared by Professor Philip E. Jacob, is illuminating in this connection.[2] Among the interesting demonstrations of this important study is the failure of current instruction in the social sciences to influence student attitudes. The majority of American college students set great store by college, but not in terms of the intellectual contribution college can make to them or its nurturing of character and personality, but rather as a vocational preparation and adjuster to the *status quo.*

This was even more devastatingly found to be the attitude of the American adolescent with respect to all education. In the Purdue teen-ager study[3] by Remmers and Radler, no less than 72 per cent of high school students felt that the most important thing young people should get out of high school was "knowing how to get along with people." The teen-ager wants to learn how to conform to the expectations of others, because if you conform you get on, but if you don't, you don't. In the Hazen Foundation Study it was found that the majority of American college students, about 85 per cent of them, believe that "(1) everyone must determine his own destiny, and most of the important things in life are the result of a person's own efforts, rather than of circumstances beyond his control, (2) anyone can succeed by his own hard work (though one in three expect that 'who you know' is also an important ingredient of getting ahead)."[4]

It was further found in this study that, in general, the aspira-

[2] Philip E. Jacob, *Changing Values in College* (New York, Harper, 1958).
[3] H. H. Remmers and D. H. Radler, *The American Teenager* (New York, Bobbs-Merrill, 1957).
[4] Jacob, p. 14.

tion for power or practical material satisfactions predominated over the social values (love and concern for others) or religious values.

At a Quaker college the highest percentage (56 per cent) of freshmen when asked, "What are the two worst things that could justifiably be said about you?" answered, "Personal failure in work and use of talents" (25 per cent), in drive and "success" attitudes (17 per cent), in family relations (14 per cent). Fifty-one per cent thought moral failure equally bad.

Gillespie and Allport, in a comparative study[5] of the outlook of youth on the future in several nations, found the American students pretty much separated from the political and social aspects of their existence, because, as one of the students himself wrote, "We are so busy fulfilling this expectation of success that we have neither time nor energy left for good citizenship." This is the state of mind that has been called "privatism,"[6] the concern with "private" values as distinguished from social, group, political, or religious-moral values, marked by the absorption in private worldly successes.

The pressures towards success, defined as a rich and full personal life, appear to be the dominant ones in the life of the American student.[7] This is, of course, not to be wondered at in a culture in which the symbols of putatively attainable success are held out before everyone like the proverbial carrot before the donkey. In such a culture the pressures are upon outdoing one's competitors. Competition which leads to the concentration on its outcome, on success, as Merton has pointed out, itself leads to anomie, deviant behavior, and the breakdown of the regulatory structure of society.[8] It is not simply that breakdown comes about because of the sin of failure, but the cause of breakdown is due rather more often to the conflicts generated within the person by a socialization process within the family which is productive of anomie, that is, normlessness, personal disorganization, and

[5] James Gillespie and Gordon W. Allport, Youth's Outlook on the Future (New York, Random House, 1955).
[6] Jacob, pp. 24-29.
[7] Otto Butz, The Unsilent Generation (New York, Rinehart, 1958).
[8] Robert K. Merton, "Social Structure and Anomie," American Sociological Review, vol. 3, 1938, p. 680.

demoralization. The intrapersonal inconsistencies produced by this form of socialization are, in my view, one of the principal causes of functionally induced mental illness. Essentially this is the socialization process in which the children, especially the males, are conditioned simultaneously in two conflicting categories of duties and expectations (socialization being the process of learning how to become a functioning human being by learning what one should do for other people, and what one is entitled to expect from them). The conflicting principles of the American socialization process are (1) the principle of goodness, and (2) the principle of success.

The social definition of goals in our society is more or less fully summarized in these two principles, *to be good,* and *to be a success.* As a dominantly Christian society, or one that derives its moral standards from Christianity, we are taught that we ought to love our neighbors as ourselves but at one and the same time to compete with them for the symbols and rewards of success. Putting it in the fewest possible words, our socialization process teaches co-operation and competition at one and the same time. Co-operation means striving *with* others to achieve the same or similar goals. Competition means striving *against* others to achieve the same or similar goals. These two principles are irreconcilable with each other, for they represent contradictions. There are, of course, such forms of behavior as co-operative competition and competitive co-operation, but what I am concerned with in the two principles I have mentioned are co-operative co-operation and competitive competition—and these are contradictories.[9]

The American socialization process teaches the developing person two irreconcilable principles as the means by which to lead a unified and happy life. These principles are resumed on the one hand in the teaching of the Sermon on the Mount, to love your neighbor as yourself, and on the other, to go out and beat your neighbor to the mark in the ruthlessly required manner if one is to be a success. It is this conflicting socialization process that is, in my opinion, largely responsible for the confusion and conflict

[9] Ashley Montagu, *The Direction of Human Development* (New York, Harper, 1955).

that is produced in the individual and in our society. If you teach human beings to become at one and the same time co-operators and competitors, and you make that teaching take the form of co-operation in theory and competition in practice, you create, to put it bluntly, a living lie, a house divided within itself, a divided ego in conflict with itself, a person who, as I have already said, expends so much energy in attempting to hold the conflicting halves of himself together that he becomes inefficient and disordered in the process, with the eventual breakdown of an organism that has been exhausted by the continuous effort to resist the stresses and strains created by a psyche in conflict.

That parents within the family so often fail their children is principally due to the fact that they have themselves been socialized, conditioned, by these conflicting principles and by the consequences that the practice of these principles have had for their own personalities and outlook on life.

The failures and disorders of personality of the parents are visited upon the children. The anomie, the formlessness, the kind of psychic rootlessness into which the parents have been forced by their own conflicts, are bad enough in themselves, but the effects upon the children are rendered grievously more damaging by the attempt of such anomic parents to force the irreconcilable principles of goodness and success upon them. The results are that there are not enough psychiatrists or psychiatric beds available to take care of the innumerable disordered persons we produce in this manner. For a good many years now we have enjoyed the distinction of having the highest juvenile delinquency rate in the whole of the English-speaking world. In 1960 over 700,000 American children were referred to the courts for delinquent acts. We have the highest homicide rate in the world, the highest violent crime rate in the world, the highest alcoholic rate, the highest divorce rate, and because it is not as "successful" a means as these others, we have only the fifth highest suicide rate in the world.

Clearly, America is not a sane society.

Even the concept of goodness in such a society becomes infected by the values of a dominantly commercial-industrial civilization. Goodness, love, become commodities like virtually everything else, which one may use for bargaining and sales purposes. After all, what is good for General Motors is not only good for the country, it is also good for goodness. If you behave yourself according to the rules you may end up driving a General Motors Cadillac, and really demonstrating to the world what a success you have been by the conspicuousness of your car's tail fins.

When you are a child your mother will bargain with you for love and make it conditional upon your being good, according to her lights. Love, which itself becomes identified with a conditional reward for being good, on this superficial level becomes identified with success—the fundamental conflict between the two remains, but it is not consciously perceived at this level as such. If mother gives you her love it is because you have succeeded in being worthy of it. You get love if you are good in terms of your mother's requirements. She withholds love and punishes you when you are bad, and rewards you with love when you are good. It is not, therefore, remarkable that American men—and frequently women—should acquire conspicuously consumable mates on a commodity basis who can be turned in for a new model in a society that has institutionalized sequential polygamy and planned obsolescence. Love is identified with sex, and innumerable women have learned from the model provided by their mothers to make their love or sex a conditional reward for good behavior on the part of their males. The male has, of course, learned from his mother that love is conditional, and has to be purchased with good behavior. This is a condition which I believe to be closely related to the lack of male dominance in the marital relationship in many American families, the subservience of the male to the female which has been commented upon by so many observers, and his inadequacies both as a husband and as a parent. The resulting imbalance in the role played by the mother renders her task a supremely difficult one made all the more complicated by the confused asymmetry of the roles of husband and wife.

With the increasing emancipation of women toward the attainment of formerly masculine freedoms, women, in large numbers, have become confused as to the exact nature of their roles, and so have men. Too many women make the mistake of interpreting equality of rights to mean that they must become men. The conflicts thus engendered in the women—assisted by most of our educational agencies which educate them as if they were men, and give them the aspirations of men—and between wives and husbands in the family, make for a family which is beridden by conflict and confusion. In such a family there is a conflict of interest, with the parents pulling in opposing directions, where discipline is assigned to the mother, with the father frequently disagreeing with his wife's discipline or lack of it, and finally washing his hands of the whole business, in something like a state of suspended animosity. It is not merely that the condition in too many families represents something resembling an armed truce, but too often the state is one of more or less open warfare, with the parents at odds with each other and the children at odds with the parents.

When the family achieves such a pass things are in a pretty bad state, indeed. A society characterized by many such families is in very real danger of breakdown. It were ludicrous beyond words, were it not so tragic, that our leaders should fail to recognize this, and act as if they believed that by the conquest of space or the launching of satellites or the building of intercontinental missiles, we are going to insure our own survival. Never was there so grievous an error. Of what use will be all our external defenses if our inner ones break down? Maginot lines are worse than useless if they do not have the moral support of a people that knows what it wants. It is not enough to know what one does not want. We don't want Communism, of that we are certain. And that is good. What then, if anything, do we want? Clearly we want to be left to pursue the achievement of our creature comforts in terms of our ideal of success. And quite as clearly, to some of us, that way leads straight to disaster.

I mean, in the plainest language I can muster to my purpose, that unless we take a good look at the value determinants which produce the kind of disorganization which is so evident in so many families in our society today, and having taken a good look, do what is necessary, there is a real danger that this society may go the way of the Roman Empire. More than one thinker has remarked the deadly parallel. Rome perished as a consequence of the weakness of its internal defenses while its external ones remained greater and more extended than ever. Every society, it has been remarked, carries within itself the seeds of its own destruction. And every society, in order to survive, must guard itself against the superficial attractions of its deceptively inviting blooms, else it may find itself smothered by a lush overgrowth of orchids.

The picture we see before us is that of *Homo americanus* seated in his ranch-type house, surrounded by all the tangible evidences of the highest standard of physical living in the world, holding an orchid named "success" in his hand while looking out of his picture window at a beautiful prospect, all of which unbeknown to him adds up to a tentative preface to extinction.

But note that it is only a "tentative preface," and not either unavoidable or inevitable. There is nothing either irreversible or irresistible about man's present state. And, in any event, the irresistible is only too often that which no one has troubled to resist. In spite of appearances to the contrary, man is capable of unlearning all the unsound things he has learned and substituting instead the sound ones. In that educability lies the hope not only of Americans, but of all mankind.

If a significant number of us will recognize the state we are in for what it is, and make ourselves clear as to the conditions that have brought us to it, and then each of us resolve to do, and do, what is required, there is more than a hope that we may pull out of the confusion into which we have fallen.

What, then, is it that requires to be done?

We have first to recognize that the person is only as good as his operative values, *not* his covert values, but the values he actually believes in, the values by which he lives. And this is, of course, true also of every society. When I say that the person is only as good as his operative values, the operative word in that declarative statement is "good." I mean something very definite and measurable by this term. By "good" or "goodness" I mean behavior calculated to confer survival benefits in a creatively enlarging manner upon others. Such "good" behavior has the highest adaptive value not merely because it contributes to the greater longev-

THE HUMANIZATION OF MAN

ity of the person, but because it contributes to his optimum development as a healthy human being. A healthy human being is defined as one who is able to love and to work. And "love" is a synonym for "goodness."

How, then, do we produce "healthy," "good," "loving," human beings? (These are all different words for the same thing.) I think the following steps are necessary: first, we must cease raising our children in conflicting systems of values; second, we must raise our children in a positive system of creative values. These values must be based on the understanding of the inbuilt system of values with which every human being is born.[10] This system is comprised of the basic needs of which love, the need to love *and* to be loved, is like the central sun about which the other needs, like the planets of our solar system, revolve. We must understand that the most important of the human being's requirements, the most important of the stimulations he must receive if he is to grow and develop as a healthy human being, is love. The only way one develops the growing human being's capacity for love is by loving him—he grows by what he feeds on—and the most important of all the traits he develops is his capacity to love, to relate himself harmoniously and creatively to others. And this he learns from models who have related themselves harmoniously and creatively to him. It seems to me that the fundamental task we shall always have to attend to before all others in the socialization process is the process of developing the inherent potentialities of the individual to love, for if the individual is not so developed he has been robbed of his birthright and rendered inefficient as a healthy human being; in fact, lack of health has been created in him. We must understand that all other qualities are secondary to this capacity to love, that no matter what the other achievements of a human being may be, if he has been failed in this he has been failed in the development of the principal quality of being human, and that whatever else he may be he has been crippled in his capacity to function as a healthy human being. Such a person being disordered in himself

[10] Ashley Montagu, *On Being Human* (New York, Abelard-Schuman, 1950); Louis O. Kattsoff, *The Design of Human Behavior* (St. Louis, Educational Publishers, 1953).

is likely to make disorder in the world, for man creates his world according to the kingdom that is within him. If we are to make order in the world we must first make order in human beings. And we can best begin the process with ourselves, by first re-ordering some of our own ideas concerning the nature of man, what is wrong with him, and how he may be put right.

We need to reform our ideas concerning the meaning and pur-poses of education, and under education I include the socializa-tion process. We need to understand that the very concept of education requires to be revised in the light of our growing understanding of the nature of human nature, and that what we are doing in the schools must be completely revamped so that they become schools for the teaching not of the three R's as such, but for the teaching of the theory and practice of human rela-tions, and the three R's as skills or techniques in the service of more effective human relations.

Within the family, parents should be equipped with all the attitudes and knowledge necessary to enable them to do the job that requires to be done. I, of course, realize how naively foolish that injunction may sound. But man is an educable creature, he is capable of learning at any age, and while it is easier to make a good parent of him when he is a child than to make a good child-maker out of him when he is a parent, none the less we could do a great deal more in that direction than we are at present doing. Social workers, those angels of mercy, with their ranks increased and their support enlarged, could increase the benefits of their good work both more intensively and extensively than it is possible for them to do at present. The parents must be brought into closer relation with the schools, and this should begin at the nursery school level. Thus, from the earliest school experience the parents should be involved together with the teachers in the complementary task of educating their children. All those involved stand to gain from such an arrangement.

We stand in need of approaches at every possible level, but we must always remember that it is not children who make adults, but adults who make children, and that therefore more of our reformatory efforts must be directed toward adults than toward children. Adults, we must be aware, are mostly deteriorated children, and there is the most pressing need to rescue children from misguided adults by turning the adults into the kinds of persons from whom children do not need to be rescued. Hence, I should like to see our society paying a good deal more attention to preparation for marriage and parentage. And this should be done in the light of the understanding of the newer knowledge concerning the nature of human nature, which it is time we began teaching in our schools.

The American family, like America generally, is so vital an institution, and the desire of parents to do the right thing by their children is so general, that we have great advantages on our side. Americans want badly to be good. Let those of us who are to teach and lead the others learn how to be good ourselves, so that we can properly teach the others.

12. The American Family and American Character

THE FAMILY is the social institution which is developed around the child-mother-father-sibling relationship. Since it is within the organizing field of energies which that institution constitutes that the child first learns to become a human being, a social being, and since as a result of the interaction between himself and the socializing conditions of his particular family the foundations of his character and personality are laid, it should be obvious that if we are to understand that part of the American character which is an expression of the socialization process within the family, it is necessary to understand the structure and functioning of the American family.

At the outset we are confronted with the fact that the American family neither possesses quite the same structure nor functions in quite the same way in different classes. The differences are appreciable and significant, and their effects upon the social development of the person are important. In fact, the effects of these differences play a very considerable role in determining the character and basic personality structure of the person in American society. Bearing this in mind we shall deal, for the purpose of this particular analysis, with the process of socialization in the typical urban middle-class family.

The ethos of the family is determined by the ethos of the society as a whole, and since the socialization of the child within the family is calculated to be a preparation for life in society, it

From *Chicago Jewish Forum*, vol. 20, 1961, pp. 36-40.

is obvious why this should be so. The family is, in a very definite sense, a reflection in minuscule of the aims and ideals of the society of which it is a part. The dominant aims and ideals that prevail in any society are those with which the parents endeavor to equip their children. But we are not so much concerned here with the process of this equipment as with the effects of the actual functioning of the American family upon the development of the character of the American.

In the case of the American family we occupy an enviable position in being able to trace the antecedent conditions which have produced its peculiar structure. The conditions of life in America have uniquely influenced the development of society and the family: the frontier spirit, the spirit of exploration, of adventure, of individualism, the spirit of progress, the measure of a man's worth in terms of achievement, of economic status, the movement onward to better and greater things, the breaking with the past— "the American way." In keeping with this spirit, parenthood in America, as Margaret Mead has pointed out, has become a very special thing: "Parents see themselves not as giving their children final status and place, rooting them firmly for family life in a dependable social structure, but merely as training them for a race which they will run alone."[1]

The American parent is bent on seeing that his children go places and do things, with the difference that his children will go to better places and do bigger things. In no other land do parents do so much to make their children happy and successful as in America. Sensitive foreigners never fail to comment upon the fact that children appear to be so much happier in America than they are in Europe. As compared with Europe there is a greater freedom *from* parental overdiscipline and a much greater freedom *to* behave as a person in one's own right. These forms of behavior are not unrelated.

But let us now briefly consider the structure of the American family. In other societies the family is a common enterprise of mother and father. In America there is an asymmetric segregation of the roles of mother and father in which by far the greater part

[1] Margaret Mead, *And Keep Your Powder Dry* (New York, Morrow, 1942), p. 41.

of the socialization of the child falls to the mother. The father's principal role is extrafamilial; but although his role in the socialization of the children is not, in terms of temporal duration, an extended one, it would be a grievous error to suppose that it is a minor one. The family is very much more than a refuge to him in which his chief purpose is to relax from the rigors of the masculine occupational world; it is that and a great deal more. There is no Western society in which the father is more devoted to his children and kinder to his wife than in America. It is, however, equally true that in no other society is the father so freely willing to make over the greater part of the upbringing of the children to his wife. This is illustrated by the story told of an American who introduced his children to a friend with the remark, "George, meet my wife's children." It was a remark put by a Hollywood script writer into a film. The fact that it was put into a film indicates that it was meant to strike a responsive chord, and it did. Popular recognition of the asymmetric roles played by the mother and father within the family is illustrated by the inquiring remark made by a child to its mother concerning its father, "Mummy, who is that man I see around the house here on week-ends?"

The fact that the father is so much less physically present than the mother, making him the weaker disciplinarian, the weaker socializing agent, has very important implications for the development of the American character. In the first place, the emotional bonds with the mother are generally very much stronger than are the bonds with the father. "Mother's Day" is not merely a tribute to the "weaker sex," for Americans do not believe in a "weaker sex." The peculiar American phenomenon known as "momism," the sentimentalized attachment of the male to "mom," is caricatured by the hulking brute of a boxer who stertorously breathes into the microphone, "Hello, Mom, this is Bruiser. It was a good fight, an' I won. See ya soon Mom." A universally American way of swearing at a man is to call him a "son of a bitch"—an insult directed toward the one to whom the American is emotionally most attached. This oath is so common in America that it has lost a considerable amount of its force, but its original significance should not be overlooked. There is no similar oath involving the father. Jokes, however, in which "father" gets the raw end of the deal are legion.

The attachment to the mother is indicative of the importance of her role in forming the character of the child. This attachment to the mother has one very significant influence upon American character. Through its influence the American develops a certain number of traits which Europeans regard as feminine. Europeans describe these traits collectively under the term "softness," the softness of the female as compared with the "hardness" familiar in European males. The American male tends to be gentle in the feminine sense, to be kindly, to be helpful, to be a "good mixer," generous, and sympathetic. European women who know America agree that American men make the best husbands. They do not consider that American men compare intellectually with European men, but they are convinced that they are easier to live with, that they are more co-operative than European men. In brief, I should say that this difference between American and European men is a function of the difference in the amount and kind, and source, of the love which they receive in childhood. The tenderness of the American male is something of which most American parents are aware. Their anxiety that their boys should not develop too much as their daughters are encouraged to develop is reflected in their overemphasis on "toughness." There is a feeling that a boy ought to be "tough." "Don't be a sisssy" is the kind of thing more often heard in this country than in any other. It is not that parents actually want their boys to be tough, but they distinctly do not want them to be "soft"; and so from early childhood on, there is this double influence on much mothering on the one hand, and on the other, also originating chiefly from the mother, those influences and rewards which are calculated to make Junior a little man. Two forms of socializing reinforcements operate upon Junior—the love of his mother which tends to make him gentle, and her use of her love to help Junior become a man. To return his mother's love Junior soon learns that he must fulfill all the requirements necessary to become a man. Becoming a man, growing up in terms of the American creed, is measured in terms of achievement, and this means competition. You must run better, skate better, play better, get better marks, eat better, get there faster than anyone else. You have got to get ahead. Getting ahead is the great object in life of American Juniors, for Junior's getting ahead is, he learns, the principal means of retaining the love of his parents, particularly his mother. He learns that his parents' love is conditioned upon how he compares, measures up, with others. He must compete and be successful. Becoming a man means being a success; and so the parents and Junior can hardly wait till the time when they can decently put Junior in long pants. America is one of the places in the Western world where boys not yet in their teens wear long pants.

Girls, of course, are also affected by this drive pattern; and by the time the "little women" are halfway through high school, painted fingernails and lips, and most of the other signs of technical adulthood, have been adopted. The female, too, is judged in terms of comparison with other females. The most constant form of conspicuous achievement exhibited by the American female is external attractiveness. The average American middle-class female dresses as well and as expensively as only the members of the upper classes of Europe do. The lower-class American female dresses more attractively than the European middle-class female. In no European land is the principle of conspicuous consumption so significantly symbolized by the mink or sable coat as in America. It is not so much that the male regards his wife as a means by which he can demonstrate to the world his own successful achievement, as that the female uses her husband's money to demonstrate her own successful achievement. To succeed a woman must make herself attractive; and here again the drive is very strong. Hence, in no other land have beauty parlors, Helena Rubinsteins, and Elizabeth Ardens become the kinds of institutions they are in America. Beauty is a big business. The charms of the female are everywhere in the market, but in no other land have they become so aggressively competitive in the open market as in America. It was in America that women first took to "bloomers"; it was in America that women first dared to raise their skirts above the ankle; and it was in America that women first abandoned the "bathing costume" for the kind of beach clothes they wear—or rather, don't wear, but simply affect.

It is not that women are any more sexually endowed in America than they are elsewhere in the world, but simply that the great American spirit of competition has affected them no less than it has the men. The girl must make a better marriage than her mother did; she must move on and ahead. Hollywood interprets the pattern by the time she is old enough to go to the movies.

The women are the most aggressively seductive in the world, and they like their men to be so too. They are contemptuous of the "sissy" who timorously says, "May I?" and they prefer the tornado who descends upon them with a "Pucker up your lips, Babe; I'm coming in on the beam!" A boy like that, they believe, will go places.

To the European, American aggressiveness is puzzling and distasteful, and "the dependence upon externals for the validation of success" (Mead) appears childish. To the European, the American with his tremendous impetus to obtain prestige by achievement, his hunt for status, seems to sell his birthright for a mess of unwholesome prestige.

The American's admiration for big things, for size, magnitude, quantity, the tallest buildings, the largest planes, the longest roads, the most money, and even his love of antiques, reflects the nature of his scale of achievement—he must excel, it is "the American way."

Obviously there is a definite and a clear relationship between the emphasis of the American's socialization process and the nature of his character drives.

Compared with the European father the American father is almost a negative quantity. While the European father may be away from home quite as much as if not more than the American father, the European father is nothing like the *pater absconditas* that the American is. The image of the European father is strong; that of the American comparatively weak. In Europe the mother uses the father as a sort of bogyman with which to threaten the children. "Father won't like that" or "Wait till your father comes home." The father in Europe is feared; one goes in awe and respect of him. The next thing to the power of the deity is the father, and by the middle of his adolescent years an English boy, for example, is referring to his father as " the old man," a phrase which perfectly defines the spirit of all that is patriarchal for the Englishman. And in England there is an appreciable amount of hatred, conscious and unconscious, for the father.[2]

On the other hand, the American father is looked upon as a friend by his children from their earliest years. As a rule he is an interceder who tries to soften the disciplinary behavior of his wife toward the children. His own disciplinary conduct as a parent tends to be kindly. You can argue with Father, and Father will often admit that he was wrong and apologizes to his children. Father gives them an enormous amount of freedom, and everyone knows that Father is a much easier mark than Mother. Nevertheless he can also make things difficult by withholding his approval and his money. But altogether there is a kindly affection associated with him. There is little conflict with him, and he does not constitute a competitor. The Oedipus complex can scarcely be said to exist in Americans. Father is not a rival; he is a friend and you can argue with him. The image of authority is a reasonable one. It is probable that this peculiar child-father relationship explains that striking difference between European and American cultures which can be summed up in the words, "In America you can argue and bawl out the umpire; in Europe you never can." It explains the free relations of American soldiers with their superior officers, and the protective benevolent attitude of officers to their men.

This peculiar attitude toward the image of authority was interestingly exhibited within the first few days following the death of President Roosevelt. Most Americans felt as if they had lost a protecting father. The loss was in many cases felt as keenly as if a member of one's own family had died. The President was not regarded as an awesome unapproachable ruler, but as a kindly, helpful, guiding father, a person upon whom one could rely for a steadying hand, and to whom one could at the same time tell

[2] See the classical study by Edmund Gosse, *Father and Son: A Study of Two Temperaments* (New York, Oxford University Press, 1934).

a joke. In czarist Russia the czar, "batoushka,"[3] (an intimate term for father), was similarly regarded by the peasant, but one could most certainly not "crack" jokes with him; there was enough of a consciousness of his autocratic role effectively to prevent that.[4] The late emperors of Germany and of Austria-Hungary and the kings of Spain and Belgium were not regarded as kindly fathers. In those countries the image of the reigning monarch was patterned on the image of the autocratic father. The American likes his gods, his kings, and his presidents to be good mixers.

Sibling rivalry in the American family is also weak, for as Mead points out, such rivalry is directed outward to success in the outer world, in contradistinction to the European pattern in "which sibling rivalries are directed inwards towards actual personal relationships inside the family group."[5] In the American family one typically gets along well with one's siblings, and generally a great deal of affection exists between them. This ease of sibling relationships may explain the American's easy relationships with strangers, his abilities as "a good mixer." An Englishman will commonly not speak to strangers; to an American a stranger is an immediate stimulus toward the establishment of friendly relations and an exchange of personal and family histories.

The American, compared with the European, is a warmhearted person. He is capable of a good deal of sentiment and affection. These qualities may be attributed to the fact that as a child he receives a great deal more love than European children do. Not all of the love he receives is conditioned upon his successful achievement.

In a sense the American never really grows up; he never grows beyond the ideals which were patterned for him as a child—the male remains an overgrown boy, the female an overgrown girl. The American prolongs his youthful habits and ambitions into middle age. The emphasis in America is positively upon youth.

[3] This term is usually incorrectly translated as "Little Father." My friend, Professor Pitirim Sorokin, tells me that it simply represents a more intimate term for father which, in its ordinary form, is "otietz."
[4] The resemblance between American and Russian family is striking. On the congeniality of the American and Russian personalities see Pitirim Sorokin, *Russia and the United States* (New York, Dutton, 1944), p. 55.
[5] Mead, p. 111.

To remain youthful is itself an ideal to maintain. Hence, in no other land in the world do grandmothers and grandfathers try so consistently to resemble their grandchildren. The American, in short, is in many ways best described as an arrested adolescent, who, therefore, has within him great potentialities for growth and development.

When the ethos of American culture swings away from the overweening emphasis on material achievements to a more balanced view of life, there is a good chance that the American character may yet serve as a guiding light to the rest of the world. And there is good hope of this, for Americans are still in the growing-pains stage of their development.

13. Marriage—The Anthropological Dimension

MARRIAGE MAY BE minimally defined as the socially sanctioned union between a male and a female entered into with the assumption of permanency. Such a minimal definition illustrates the danger of all definition. It says too little. And yet many marriages contracted in the Western world are entered into on a much narrower conception of marriage than is implied in the terms of even this minimal definition. Marriage in the Western world is only too often conceived of as a relationship entered into between two persons, a private affair which concerns the two principals and no one else. This is a thoroughly erroneous idea which can only have come about in the highly sophisticated societies of the Western world in which the fragmentation and atomization of human relationships has proceeded at an accelerating pace.

In some segments of Western societies, and in almost all folk and nonliterate societies, marriage involves multiple and complex relationships with the society as a whole. Marriage in such societies is not merely a complex of customs which relate a male and a female in a bond of union to the beginning new family of which they constitute the procreative elements. It *is* that, but it is also a great deal more. Marriage is an institution, that is to say, a complex of behavior norms upon which the members of a society have in common agreed. Marriage is the institution which defines the roles not only of the mated pair to each other, but also the reciprocal relations between them and their kinsmen, their offspring, the community, and society.

168

In no society is marriage a matter which is exclusively limited to reciprocal involvement between two human beings, and possibly their children, although in some societies of the Western world, as I have already said, many persons behave as if this were in fact the case. Whether some persons act in such a manner because they are neurotic, while others do so because it is the custom in their particular un-neurotic segment of society, are interesting questions which in themselves deserve further exploration. The relatedness of persons to the other members of their society does not cease upon marriage, but becomes more complex and extensive. One marries not only another person but also into another family. One brings two extended families into a new macrofamilial series of relationships in which the married couple become newly involved. This is much more evident in some segments even of our own society than it is in others. And it is uniformly more striking in societies technologically less developed and fragmented than our own.

In a technologically highly developed Western society such as that of the United States, only a small proportion of neurotics come to the attention of physicians, psychologists, and social workers, and we do not know the nature of the marriage relationship in adequate samples of neurotic married couples, still less in the "average" neurotic couple—whatever that might mean.

The fact is that there are many marriages involving persons who could certainly be described as neurotic that are not only enduring but remarkably happy ones. It does not follow that neurotic interaction in marriage must necessarily lead to an unsuccessful or unhappy marriage. On the contrary, it may well lead to a happy denouement when the partners to such a marriage utilize their neurotic conflicts as a basis for mutual self-discovery and understanding, with consequent modification of feeling and conduct. It was in this sense that Balzac remarked that "Marriage is the best school for a man's character that was ever devised." It would be a vast oversimplification to assert that marriages tend to be successful because of the neurotic traits of one or both of the partners. It would equally be an oversimplification to claim, where both partners were in fact neurotic, that it was their neurotic traits which were chiefly responsible for the lack of success in marriage. This would be equivalent to the inference that was drawn by the well-known experimenter who, having got drunk consecutively on whisky and soda, gin and soda, and rum and soda, concluded that since the one constant factor was the soda it was therefore the soda that produced the drunkenness!

Even when a person marries for unconscious psychoneurotic (pathological) reasons, it by no means necessarily follows that such a marriage must end in disaster. Indeed, the success or failure of a marriage may depend not so much upon the unconscious reasons for which the person enters into it as upon his society's conception of the nature of marriage as an institution. There appears to be considerable evidence that the stability of marriage is significantly influenced by the ideas prevailing in any society concerning the meaning of marriage; that where separation and divorce are made easy, marriage and the family become markedly unstable (as the Soviet Russians found to their dismay in their early experimental days), and that where separation and divorce are made difficult, marriage and the family tend to be more stable.

I am not for a moment attempting to equate "stability" with "happiness." But, then, I do not believe that the principal object of marriage is or ought to be happiness. As this may strike some readers as a rather startling statement, I must carefully explain what I mean.

It seems to me a most unfortunate cultural[1] error, particularly characteristic of the Western world, to envisage marriage through the romantic glow of a vision of "happiness" which has very little relation to the realities of life. The "happiness" of those who have "fallen in love" with each other frequently leads to unhappiness in marriage, for the very simple reason that happiness is not the goal of marriage, and that if a person is bent on securing happiness in marriage he will almost certainly fail to find it. For happiness, as in all other connections, will elude one's search if one deliberately sets out to find it, for the reason that

[1] This word is here and elsewhere in this chapter used in its anthropological sense, meaning the particular way of life of a people or the man-made part of a people's environment.

genuine happiness is a by-product of other things, and principally of work.

In marriage this amounts to an *interanimating* mutual growth and development of the marriage partners.

In Western cultures there is a widespread and deeply entrenched belief that at marriage the person has truly arrived at a state of maturity and responsibility, and that thereafter he settles down and raises a family. The growth and development of the newly married couple having come to an end, it now falls to their lot to attend to the growth and development of the new generation which they will have procreated, all this being achieved in a state of more or less roseate bliss. The conception of marriage as a new and demandingly responsible further phase of the continuum of interpersonal growth and development is conspicuously rare in our culture. And yet the ability to grow and develop, to change, to adjust, to modify, to adapt, to give and take, all these and more are the traits which marriage as an interpersonal relationship most imperatively demands.

The adjustive process for which marriage calls is not only possible for many neurotic persons, but has in innumerable cases served as a most effective action therapy. Marriage is by no means a cure for all neurotics, but at the same time it should be understood that marriage between two neurotics does not constitute an automatic bar to a successful and happy marriage. Marriage is a relationship at which one has to work, and if one works at it to make a success of it, then happiness in marriage can be achieved. But if one works merely at achieving happiness in marriage, without first working at making it a success, it is much more doubtful that either one or the other will be achieved.

It was Lord Acton who said that "Liberty is not the power of doing what we like, but the right of being able to do what we ought." In no relationship is this principle more applicable than in marriage. And what "ought" the married couple do? They ought to think of each other's welfare, of their children's welfare, of the welfare of the family. For the welfare of the family is the principal aim and purpose of marriage—and not a puerile conception of "happiness," based on pseudo-emotional rationalizations and unanalyzed systems of value.

In our culture we do not sufficiently emphasize the adjustive relationship that marriage constitutes, that it is something in which one grows and develops, that it is something one must cultivate and work at if it is to succeed, that it is not something that grows and develops of itself, but something that calls for the exercise of one's best qualities as a human being.

Were such an attitude toward marriage more sedulously cultivated in our society many a neurotic, not to mention many a healthier-minded person, would stand a greater chance in succeeding in marriage than he does with his present typically atomized attitudes.

It is not neurotic interaction alone which is the responsible factor in rendering so many marriages unsuccessful, though no doubt there are some in which this is well-nigh the principal factor, but in most cases we must look to neurosis as but one of the factors or conditions in which there are one or more other conditions which together constitute the sufficient cause. Causes are rarely constituted by a single condition. There are surely such things as non-neurotic incompatibilities between persons which are discovered only after marriage, and which are often sufficient to increase the fragility of the relationship.

It cannot be too emphatically stated that the cultural factor in marriage is in all societies a most important one in contributing toward the manner in which a marriage will function. Even in our own culture attitudes toward marriage, the understanding of the meaning of marriage, and even the reasons and purposes for which marriages are entered into vary with the different cultural segments of the United States. Marriages of convenience are still to be encountered more frequently in the upper than in the lower classes. And in Hollywood, on the whole, it remains true to say that marriage seems to constitute little more than a circumspect genuflection before the altar of respectability. Marriages are contracted on the implicit understanding that they are not necessarily "forever." Since film stars represent the royalty of the United States to the youth of America, the example of this celluloid royalty may not be lightly discounted as a factor in conditioning the attitudes of young Americans to marriage.

In the United States, which has the highest divorce rate in the world, almost one out of every three marriages ends in divorce. Where divorce is as easy as it is in the United States divorce presents itself as an ever-ready solution to marital problems that might otherwise be solved by other means. Hence, the very ease of divorce must be regarded as a contributory factor to the instability of marriage in the United States. It is an interesting fact that the lower classes, consisting mainly of semiskilled and unskilled workers, tend to have higher divorce and separation rates than the middle and upper classes.[2] Mental illness rates are also highly correlated with the class structure in our society.[3] The distributions are, however, too complex to deal with here. Mental illness and marital status are also correlated. From Malzberg's study, for example, of first admissions to the New York State civil hospitals[4] it appears that the admission rates for unmarried schizophrenics and manic-depressives is significantly greater than for the married, and that the admission rates for the divorced is much higher than it is for the married (see Table 2). Whether there is some selective factor at work here or whether marriage tends to reduce the number of schizophrenic and manic-depressive breakdowns is a moot point.

The important point that we need to bear in mind is that there are cultural factors involved in every marriage which play a far more significant role in determining its development than is frequently allowed. Such knowledge, in the sense that it recognizes the importance of cultural factors, is enshrined in many folk sayings, as, for example, "One should never marry a horse from another stable" (Russian); "Never marry anybody outside the sound of your parish bells" (English); "Near marriage and distant service are the best" (German). Burgess and Cottrell, among American students of marriage, have been among the most convincing in drawing attention to what they call "The

[2] Mabel A. Elliott, *Social Disorganization*, 3rd ed. (New York, Harper, 1950), pp. 444-445.
[3] August B. Hollingshead and Frederick C. Redlich, "Social Stratification and Psychiatric Disorders," *American Sociological Review*, vol. 28, 1953, pp. 163-169; S. Kirson Weinberg, *Society and Personality Disorders* (New York, Prentice-Hall, 1952).
[4] Benjamin Malzberg, *Social and Biological Aspects of Mental Disease* (Utica, New York, State Hospitals Press, 1940).

TABLE 2

Comparative Standardized Average Annual Rates of First Admissions of Manic-Depressives and Schizophrenics to All Institutions for Mental Disease in New York State 1929-31, by Marital Status*

Marital Status†	Schizophrenia			Manic Depression		
	Male	Female	Total	Male	Female	Total
Single	64.9 ± 1.3	46.9 ± 1.2	55.4 ± 0.9	15.3 ± 0.6	19.5 ± 0.8	17.2 ± 0.5
Married	11.9 ± 0.4	19.3 ± 0.6	15.4 ± 0.4	7.7 ± 0.4	15.7 ± 0.5	11.7 ± 0.3
Widowed	43.1 ± 3.2	26.2 ± 1.5	34.4 ± 1.5	24.3 ± 2.4	15.1 ± 1.1	19.5 ± 1.1
Divorced	49.0 ± 10.0	54.6 ± 9.0	51.3 ± 6.7	27.0 ± 7.5	42.8 ± 8.0	34.8 ± 5.5

* Data from Benjamin Malzberg, *Social and Biological Aspects of Mental Disease*, pp. 127, 128.
† By standardized rate is meant the proportion per 100,000 of the general population of the same marital status 15 years of age and over.

MARRIAGE—THE ANTHROPOLOGICAL DIMENSION 175

Impress of Cultural Backgrounds" as being among the most important.[5] The attitudes and values of husbands and wives are largely determined by the cultural backgrounds of the families in which they were reared and the environments in which they were educated. It is the general finding that those couples with the most similar cultural backgrounds exhibit a correspondingly satisfactory adjustment in marriage, whereas those with strikingly dissimilar cultural backgrounds make a relatively poorer adjustment.

Surveying from the anthropological standpoint cultural differences in relation to marriage, one is impressed with the great differences that exist with respect to attitudes toward marriage in different cultures. This subject has been abundantly but by no means exhaustively discussed by Westermarck and others in a notable series of volumes.[6] Nonliterate societies[7] run the whole gamut from great stability to great instability in marriage.

Among the Auen Bushmen of South Africa, a people living at the lower hunter stage of development, divorce is rare,[8] but among the Samoans marriages are easily and frequently terminated.[9] In nonliterate societies marriage is conceived of not so much as directed toward a romantic gratification of the spouses but rather as a means for cementing group alliances between families or clans. In most such societies everything possible is done to maintain the alliances thus established between families or clans, even though one or both of the spouses may through death or divorce bring the marriage to an end. In the first instance the principle of sibling equivalence is applied in the form of the

[5] Ernest W. Burgess and Leonard S. Cottrell, Jr., *Predicting Success or Failure in Marriage* (New York, Prentice-Hall, 1939).
[6] Edward Westermarck, *The History of Human Marriage*, 5th ed., 3 vols. (New York, Allerton Book Company, 1922); *Three Essays on Sex and Marriage* (New York, Macmillan, 1934); *The Future of Marriage in Western Civilization* (New York, Macmillan, 1936). Robert Briffault, *The Mothers* (New York, Macmillan, 1927). Robert Briffault and Bronislaw Malinowski, *Marriage Past and Present* (Boston, Extending Horizons Books, 1956).
[7] Nonliterate meaning societies without a written tradition, to be preferred to the term "primitive societies"—which are usually far from primitive in anything but the technological sense.
[8] Isaac Schapera, *The Khoisan Peoples of South Africa* (London, Routledge, 1930).
[9] Margaret Mead, "Broken Homes," *The Nation*, vol. 128, 1929, pp. 253-255.

institutions of the levirate and sororate. That is, upon the death of his wife a man, under the levirate rule, is required to marry his deceased wife's (usually) younger sister; correspondingly upon the death of her older sister, under the rule of the sororate, a female is required to marry the widowed husband. In this manner an attempt is made to maintain the original alliances by the appropriate substitutions. In the second instance, when marriage terminates by divorce, the children of the marriage usually serve to maintain the alliance of the families and clans that were originally brought together through marriage. In some societies, as among the Trobriand Islanders, where divorce is as easy as moving one's belongings out of the house formerly occupied with one's spouse, divorce constitutes not the least break in either the child's life or that of society, for from birth on, the child's principal male guardian is his mother's brother, while the child's own father stands in the same relation to his sister's children.

Detailed studies of the psychological factors involved in some kinds of marriages are conspicuously few for nonliterate societies. The whole subject, indeed, of mental illness in nonliterate societies is as dark and as obscure as an Egyptian night. There are few studies bearing upon this subject,[10] and none at all concerning neurotic interaction in marriage. The material is insufficient to permit us to speak with any security concerning the relative importance of unconscious factors in relation to the instability of marriage in such societies, for example, as the Trobriand Islanders and the Samoans. The general impression is that such factors play, if any, a comparatively minimal role.

In his study of marriage and the family in the Kgatla of the Bechuanaland Protectorate, South Africa, Schapera has given an account of an African people who have been in contact with whites for more than a century, and whose institutions have undergone and are continuing to undergo transformation. This

[10] B. J. F. Laubscher, *Sex, Custom and Psychopathology* (London, Routledge, 1937); Ralph Linton, *Culture and Mental Disorders* (Springfield, Ill., Thomas, 1956); Isaac Schapera, *Married Life in an African Tribe* (New York, Sheridan House, 1941); J. C. Carothers, "The African Mind in Health and Disease," World Health Organization Monographs, New York, Columbia University Press, 1953.

study is particularly illuminating in the present connection because it exhibits the profound influence of social conditions upon the functioning of marriage. The more social conditions among a formerly nonliterate people come to resemble those of whites, the more unstable do their marriages tend to become.

Before white contact it was the custom among the Kgatla for parents and other senior relatives to arrange the marriage. Procreation, not companionship, was the main object of marriage. Mutual attraction counted for little, and the preferences of the couple were seldom considered. Today, while arranged marriages are still common, most young people choose their own mates because they like each other and feel that they can live happily together.

In the old days the parents would choose a spouse for their offspring specifically for those very qualities which were likely to insure a stable marriage. Today, when the young may choose their own mates, they are mostly influenced by personal attractiveness; their choices are not always sound. If marriage has become much less stable among the Kgatla than it formerly was, it is characterized by a great deal more freedom. Women, especially, have benefited from this fact.

The traditional view of the relation of the sexes among the Kgatla is that "The husband is the god of the wife." Woman is completely subservient to man and leads the life of a dog, according to the traditional view. Today women are less inclined to tolerate such conduct, and there are likely to be quarrels, desertions, and divorces. There are few happy marriages. While today there is not the same separation of the sexes in social life as there was in former times, when it was considered unbecoming for men to associate with women during the day, there is little intimate contact between the spouses in everyday life. Married people seldom live together all the year round. The husband is usually away from home for months at a time, during which he and his wife are separated. The general effect is to widen the gap in sympathies and interests between husband and wife. The wife frequently seeks solace in the arms of a lover—an event which the husband is often forced to condone. The relative freedom from her husband's tyranny creates a habit of freedom which makes the Kgatla wife less ready to submit to her husband's authority. Often while away he fails to send money and the wife is then forced to maintain the family herself, in the course of which she may become very bitter about her husband.

Such are some of the social conditions which clearly make for instability of marriage among the Kgatla. Temperamental and neurotic incompatibilities could only add to that instability, but it is evident that among the Kgatla social conditions constitute a principal factor in contributing to the fragility of marriage.

The suggestion might, indeed, be hazarded that instability of marriage is in large part a reflection of social conditions—not that the society itself is necessarily unstable but that certain conditions within society, altogether apart from idiopathic or idiosyncratic disorders, by and large play a considerable role in determining the very nature of marriage. That unconscious psychological factors have their importance in virtually every marriage is an indisputable fact. This is clearly evident in studies reporting frankly pathological cases,[11] but there can be no doubt of the operation of unconscious factors in marriage in mentally healthy human beings. And such factors are likely to be operative in every human society. We badly need to learn more about them.

Another matter which requires more study is the significant fact that a marriage may be quite satisfactory to one of the spouses while it is most unsatisfactory to the other. In his study of marital happiness Terman found that the happiness of one spouse was to a surprising degree independent of the happiness of the other.[12] This finding, writes Terman, "is significant in the suggestion it carries that the degree of satisfaction which one finds in a marriage depends partly upon one's own characteristic attitudes and temperament and so need not closely parallel the happiness of one's marital partner." This observation is abundantly confirmed by experience, and though it may be true that "it takes two to make a marriage" it is quite clear that it may take only one to keep it going.

[11] Victor W. Eisenstein, ed. *Neurotic Interaction in Marriage* (New York, Basic Books, 1956).
[12] Lewis M. Terman, *Psychological Factors in Marital Happiness* (New York, McGraw-Hill, 1938).

Where one spouse can adjust to the changing moods and behavior of the other the marriage can be satisfactory and enduring. But where one spouse cannot adjust to the other there is little likelihood of either a satisfactory or an enduring marriage.

When one surveys marital relations in nonliterate societies, it is found that while the notion of marriage for love is not unknown it is seldom possible to practice it. Marriages are usually arranged by the elders, and the spouses have to adjust to each other as well as they are able. In many nonliterate societies, as for example, the Australian aborigines and in innumerable African societies, the female may be married at puberty to a male who is old enough to be her grandfather. In India and in many other parts of the world, the girl's husband is often old enough to be her father. Such marriages are frequently notably successful, but we have neither statistical information nor psychological analyses on the frequency of such successful marriages as compared with unsuccessful ones in the same age groups in nonliterate societies. The fact that such successful marriages do occur between spouses of extremely different age groups who have been brought together in an arranged union indicates that adjustment in marriage under quite unpromising conditions is possible. Such marriages have occurred and occur in literate societies, the *marriage à covenance* having been the rule rather than the exception, until very recently, among the upper classes of Europe. Many such marriages were as eminently successful as others were not. We surely need to study successful marriages at least as much as we are inclined to study the unsuccessful ones. It is true that the study of pathological processes often throws light on the functioning of the normal, but it is well to remember that we can learn more about marriage as a going concern from the study of the healthy as well as the disordered or diseased.

Let us remember, also, that of fundamental value for an understanding of the nature of marriage in our own society we need to understand the functioning of marriage in other societies. Above all, that we need to pay more attention to the role of social and cultural factors in marriage.

Let us remember, finally, that neurotic interaction in marriage is, at least in large part, an effect rather than a cause of cultural disorder, and that it is therefore the cultural conditions which are so largely productive of neurotic behavior which will require our most zealous attention.

14. The American Woman

IT IS TRUE that age cannot wither her nor custom stale her infinite variety. Nevertheless, the American woman is under attack. We are told that she is a monster who devours her mate; that she makes a domestic animal of her husband, designing him to her requirements while he lives, and driving him to an early grave wearing himself out in the attempt to maintain her in a manner to which no woman should be accustomed; that she emasculates her male, thus bringing about the peculiarly American phenomenon of the he-woman and the she-man.

America, we are told, is a matriarchy in which women rule and "momism" is a way of life. The greater part of the wealth of the country is in the hands of women. Women run not only the home but every member of the family, and while it is the function of the American wife to maintain her husband in the illusion that he is master of the household, he is, in fact, as everyone knows, nothing more than chairman of the entertainment committee. It is true that American women are physically the most attractive in the world, that they make the best of themselves, but this only goes to show that they are too preoccupied with sex without being sufficiently sexual. American women, we are further informed, suffer from the Puritan blight. They are cold, calculating, and demanding. Women of other countries make better wives. American women are a mess.

And, of course, a great deal else has been said about American women, but the above represents, I believe, a fair digest of the most frequent criticisms that have been leveled at them. What

From *Saturday Review*, vol. 41, 1958, pp. 13-15.

about these criticisms? Well, there is just enough truth in most of them to constitute an inducement to further inquiry, but as truths or constructive criticisms they are just about as valuable as most of the comments that are usually made on the alleged characteristics of any minority group that is seeking to establish its rights and privileges. Were the accusations that are today increasingly being hurled against the American woman not so seriously misunderstanding of the true situation, they could be appropriately dismissed as strictly for the birds. But the misunderstanding is serious and it is worth taking seriously, the more so since there is an element of truth in it.

It may be suggested that what the American woman stands most in need of is not blame but understanding, and this applies, also, to the American male—who is not entirely free of the responsibility for the condition in which both he and his wife find themselves.

And what is that condition? In a few words it is a confusion of roles. Women are no longer clear as to what it is or should be to be a woman, and while men tend to have pretty definite ideas on that subject, they are not altogether clear as to what their own role is or ought to be. How did this state of affairs come about?

In seeking to escape from the oppressive mythology of inequality with which men and the millennia had saddled them, women were forced into the position of having to prove to themselves as well as to men—that they were as good as men. This meant, for many women, that they must prove that they were equal to men, that they must compete with men on their own ground and emerge from the competition at least as well. For many women this meant identification with men, and envy of the masculine roles. For others it meant attempting to achieve what were formerly regarded as male statuses by playing male occupational roles while at the same time attempting to hang onto one's femininity. For still others the inability to play masculine roles, an "impediment" brought about in most cases by marriage and a family, has resulted in a certain amount of chafing at the bit, and left both marriage and the family slightly the worse for wear as a consequence of all the straining after achievement in the masculine world as a validation of the feminine self. The sad thing about all this is that a good many women have paradoxically sought to validate themselves (as persons) not as women but as men. This is a typical minority group reaction. Anything associated with the higher caste is considered desirable, and is by any means worth attaining.

This is a perfectly understandable human response, as is the confusion of values that produces it, but it is none the less a most misguided, unsound, and adaptively inefficient one. Considering, however, the conditions under which responses are made, any other kind is hardly to be expected.

The male of the species, far from being a help in bringing about a more reasonable adjustment, helped on the contrary to produce the very response in the female which, with the logic characteristic of the "masters" in such situations, he now finds so little to his liking. For if men maintained that women were not the equals of men, and were therefore not entitled to equal rights, women understandably but misguidedly felt that in order to attain equal rights they must demonstrate that they are the equals of men, and so they proceeded to make themselves as much like men as possible. Bloomers were developed to replace skirts, masculine attire was imitated, masculine habits such as smoking and drinking were adopted, and such strenuous sports indulged in as were formerly the exclusive preserve of the male. Physical assaults were made on the guardians of law and order, and other evidences of that peculiarly masculine property, brawn, were more and more frequently exhibited by women. And all this in the heroic effort to show men—as well as themselves—that they were equal to anything that men were equal to, and thus to demonstrate their equality.

That political and social equality rests on an ethical principle and not on a biological one or even upon achievement seems to have escaped both men and women in the struggle for women's independence, just as it has escaped most of those who were involved in arguing for and against the racist position. Whether a person is entitled to all the rights and privileges of development and of citizenship in the community of which he is a member depends not upon his biological background as to race or sex, but rests solely upon the consideration that he is a member of the human species and as such is entitled, without discrimination, to all the rights and privileges of his birthright, and his birthright is development.

In the case of the sexes, as in the case of different "races," we have failed to recognize the overriding importance of the ethical principle of equality. We still speak of biological or innate inequalities for achievement, while at the same time failing to understand that if any biological or innate inequalities exist between the sexes, as between the "races," then the best way of bringing them out is to afford the groups involved complete equality of opportunity. Who knows if by bringing about any inequalities that may exist we may find ourselves unexpectedly enriched? To attribute artficially created inequalities to natural or innate causes is one of the most vulgar of errors. In rebelling against the consequences to them of this particular epidemic error, women fall into the opposite one of proving that with the removal of the artificially created handicaps that had impeded their development they could assume virtually every one of the roles traditionally played by the male. The greater the obstacles that men placed in the paths of women the more determined were the women to overcome them. In short, women responded to the challenge which men threw down to them and to the conditions set by the men. These conditions were, in effect, that if women could do as well in any of the roles in which men traditionally excelled, men would, to say the least, be surprised. It was with something more like consternation than surprise that men viewed the response that women made to their implicit challenge.

Women are today engaged in every occupation in which men are employed, and are emerging as significant figures in the arts and sciences. There are few who any longer doubt that women are a great deal brighter and more capable than they were at one time thought to be. That is all to the good. But among the changes that have come about are some that are not thought to be so good. Among these changes is the psychic masculinization which has affected many women, the tendency to identify themselves with males, to think and act like males, and to aspire to masculine roles—with resulting turmoil and confusion all around. As women have become more masculinized men have become more feminized, so that the male is about as confused concerning his own role in the world as the female is befogged about hers. Both sexes feel that something is somewhere out of joint. Both are unhappy about themselves and their relations with each other.

American women, in great numbers, go to their psychotherapist and complain that their husbands are not as they would have them be, he-men. American men visit their therapist and complain that their wives are not as they would have them be, she-women. The women would like to be more like women, and the men would like to be more like men, but by the time they get to the therapist the difficulties to be overcome seem to be insurmountable. And, indeed, the problem is a difficult one. For male and female roles in all cultures are largely a matter of cultural conditioning, a conditioning which is thoroughly completed in our culture by the time the sexes are ready for marriage, or let us say by the end of adolescence. It is never an easy matter to take asunder the elements that have gone into the making of a personality and reconstitute them to the heart's desire. It can be done, and in many cases it can be approximated, but it is far simpler to render altogether unnecessary any later regimen of reconstitution by avoiding the errors in the process of cultural conditioning that later make such therapeutic repairs necessary.

The conditions that have led to the present imbalance in the relationships between the sexes have been indicated: women have put themselves off balance by attempting to assume the roles of men. This is the original mistake. We understand how that imbalance came about, and we can be understanding, but in putting themselves off balance women have put the male out of kilter, too. A restoration to a healthy equilibrium is indicated.

The manner in which we may most helpfully regard the present condition of the relationships between the sexes is that they are in a transitional phase of their development; that in the passage from the "abolition" phase of the woman's movement to the phase of "emancipation" a certain number of predictable errors were committed by both women and men.

The logic of the situation actually led to the most grievous of the errors committed. This was the argument that insofar as political and social rights were concerned women should be judged as persons and not as members of a biological or any other kind of group. As far as it goes this argument is sound enough, but what seems to have been forgotten in the excitement is that women in addition to being persons also belong to a sex different from that of the other gender, and that with the differences in sex are associated important differences in functional and behavioral capacities. Equality of rights did not and does not imply identity of function, yet this is what it was taken to mean by many women and men. And so women began—and in many cases continue—to compete with men as if they were themselves men, instead of realizing and establishing themselves in their own right as persons and as women. Women have so much more to contribute to the world as women than they could ever have as spurious men. And it is the clarification and recognition of what it means to be a woman, of the nature of the potentialities and capacities with which women are biologically endowed, which should make it possible for women to become happily reconciled to, and gratefully accept, themselves as women.

Men have done everything in their power to impede the progress of women, and so women were forced to struggle against them, to compete with them for their rights, for a place in the sun. Under the conditions, jumping the track a bit seems to have been simply unavoidable. But the situation today is somewhat altered. Fortunately the opposition to women's rights is nowhere nearly as great as it was even a generation ago. If women must, to any extent, still compete with men, it is not as imitation men that they should do so, but as genuine women.

Women have great gifts to bring to the world of men; the qualities of love, compassion, and humanity. It is the function of women to humanize, and this by nature endows them with the most important of all adaptive traits, namely, the capacity to love—and this it is their principal function to teach men. There can be no more important function. It could be wished that both men and women understood this. Women in particular need to understand the meaning of this fact. Once they have done so they will realize that no man can ever play as important a role in the life of humanity as a mentally healthy woman. And by mental health I mean the ability to love and the ability to work. Being a good wife, a good mother, in short, a good homemaker, is the most important of all the occupations in the world. It, surely, cannot be too often pointed out that the making of human beings is a far more important vocation than the making of anything else, and that in the formative years of a child's life the mother is best equipped to provide those firm foundations upon which he can subsequently build.

When the male acquires a true understanding of the importance of the mother in the life of the child, especially during the first years, he will realize that it is a principal function of his as a husband and father to enable his wife to perform her maternal roles as happily and as fruitfully as possible. As the child grows older the role of the father in his own right becomes increasingly more important, and that is to serve not merely as an appanage of the female, as a useful household gadget and a good provider, but by his example to help each of the members of the family to develop their potentialities, and to teach them the meaning of freedom, discipline, courage, and independence. It has justly been remarked that fathers are parents too!

The confusion as to the nature of their roles, from which the sexes suffer, is considerably assisted by the manner in which the American woman carries her confusion into the family in her role as both a mother and a wife.

Whether the American woman carries her need to compete into the family in order to prove herself and achieve her ends, I am not sure, but certainly she frequently gives that appearance. For example, a common method of discipline used by American mothers with their children is the method of "conditional love." Mother, in effect, says to her children, "Mother won't love you unless you behave and do as she requires." The one thing in the world that should be unconditional the American mother makes conditional, a commodity for which one bargains, which one hands out on condition that one behaves. The training in "conditional love" thus received by boys and girls has the effect of teaching the female that she can use conditional love as a device for obtaining concessions from the male, and the male learns that "love" is something that one gets from women only if he "behaves." The American male has learned that love (which becomes identified with sex) is something you purchase by agreeing to the conditions set by the female. This puts the male in a weak and frustrating position in relation to the female, engenders hostilities in him toward her in the marital relationship, and further serves to flatten out and debase his conception of love. It is not to be wondered at that the vendors of cheap substitutes are so numerous among us; that sequential polygamy has become a sanctioned form of plural marriage for those who can afford it; that husband and wife only too often find each other inadequate; that women come to be regarded as cool and calculating monsters who devour their husbands, and their husbands come to be regarded as emasculated weaklings.

Observing the marked asymmetry of the roles played by his father and mother in the home, the great power wielded by the mother and the comparative weakness of the role played by the father, the male in America grows up to know where *his* "proper place" is, namely, anywhere but in the home. The "boss" is mother, and if father has been properly brought up he is perfectly willing to grant that, and, in fact, often jocularly—with the jocularity of the jest spoken in truth—refers to his mate as "the Boss." It is not for nothing that the comic strip that has enjoyed perhaps the longest continuous popularity is entitled "Bringing Up Father."

The view of the "proper" relations of the sexes is further reinforced by the manner in which boys are indoctrinated with the idea that females have a right to expect them to be chivalrous, kind, thoughtful, and gentlemanly, and that even in the face of abuse from a woman a male must never respond in kind. In effect this means that women enjoy special privileges denied to the male, and further has the effect of often rendering him helpless, as an adult, in holding his own against the designs of an aggressive woman.

A further shrinkage in the American male's ego is brought about by the fact that since his wife has more time than he does for reading and the enjoyment of various other cultural activities, the American woman generally succeeds in becoming a more cultivated and knowledgeable person than her spouse. This is a fact commented upon by most foreign visitors to America. I have often heard it said by such observers that the only persons worth talking to in America are the women—the men, on the whole, being described as bores. However this may be, the truth is that most men are willing to admit that their wives read more "and keep up with things more" than they do. Such an admission further serves to demote the male in his own self-esteem.

We perceive, then, that women are quite unwittingly serving to increase rather than to diminish the disequilibrium that at present exists between the sexes, and that men, by taking the complaisant position they do—"for the sake of peace," as they so often say—are aiding and abetting the process. It is for this reason that a clear understanding of the conditions that have produced this state is necessary on the part of both men and women if the desirable changes are to be brought about and the relations between the sexes restored to a more balanced and harmonic state.

One of the principal areas in which men combine with women to confuse the roles of the sexes is education. It is through the agency of education, and particularly college education, that women have been especially trained in a confused perception of their roles. The chief error has been to educate women as if they were men. In our schools and colleges there is scarcely any recognition given to the fact that such a difference exists as male and female. In our women's colleges women are educated in precisely the same manner as men are in men's colleges. The effect of such misbegotten and misguided education is that women are encouraged to develop aspirations which were designed exclusively to meet the requirements of men. Our schools and colleges encourage women to go into the world to compete with men as if they—the women—were men. No one has told them what it means to be a woman or what a woman's role should be in the home and in the community. But they have been led to believe that a woman can be an engineer, a doctor, a lawyer, scientist, writer, or anything that she desires to be that a man can be. Of course she can! But she can and ought to be a great deal more. And so, the better educated a woman is the more likely she is to be confused as to her role as a person. She feels frustrated as a homemaker; she has been educated for "better" things. There she is with her B. A. degree and, as it were, nowhere to go with it. She has been expensively prepared to play a role she is prevented from performing by the frustrating and dulling duties which cut her off from that other world of affairs in which she had hoped to play a significant part.

Such women are confused and unhappy. Those who get out of the home and realize their "otherworldly" aspirations are only too frequently equally confused and unhappy, however successful they may be in their careers. Of course there are a good many women who are both good homemakers and happily employed outside the home on full-time jobs, but these are the women who either have no children in the home or whose children are of adolescent age. I put it down as an axiom that no woman with a husband and small children can hold a full-time job and be a good homemaker at one and the same time. The early years of family life constitute a full-time job in themselves, and while a homemaker needs rest, change, and diversion in sufficient frequency to maintain her freshness of interest and enthusiasm for her job, there can be no doubt about the totality of the demand that homemaking in the early years of family life makes upon the homemaker. Hence, any feeling of frustration, of inadequate fulfillment, of dissatisfaction with one's lot, due to the confused understanding of what her lot should in fact be, creates a state of unhappiness. Such a state exhibits itself in the common response to frustration, namely, in aggressive behavior of various kinds. Such aggressive behavior on the part of the married woman may take any number of forms, such as inadequacy as a home-maker, sexual inadequacy, nagging, and the like. The wife may begin to compete with her husband at home by assuming various dominant roles, which in a hundred and one ways subtly undermine the power of the male. Most women are quite unconscious of the fact that they are engaging in such competition with their husbands, and are hurt and bewildered when they are accused of doing so. And this is the tragic element in the situation, for American women mean to be as good wives as women are anywhere, and are resentful and uncomprehending when they are told that they don't make as good wives as European women do.

Comparisons are notoriously odious, but it is quite true that on the whole European women make better wives than American women. Such a statement is no discredit to the American woman. The American woman has had to pass through much more turmoil and change than her European counterpart to attain her present freedoms, while the historical necessities of her development in this country have been quite different from anything that occurred in Europe. I am referring, in particular, to the pioneering spirit which the American woman was called upon to exhibit in common with her husband in the settlement of America and the consequences of this for both sexes. From the first, women played a more dominant role in the family in America than they did in Europe. However this may be, in Europe women can accept the fact that they are women and be glad of it. The European woman is not bedeviled by doubts as to her role; for her it is precisely defined and she suffers from no confusion of goals. Her life is focused principally upon the happiness of her husband and children, and this is likely to be more satisfying to everyone concerned than is the case in America. European women, it has been said, seem to behave as if they loved their husbands; in comparison American women appear to behave toward their husbands as if they merely liked them. This is, no doubt, somewhat off the mark, but there is perhaps just enough of an element of truth in the comment to make it worth thinking about—just as there is sufficient of an element of truth in many other comments that have been made on the American woman to make them worth thinking about.

What the American woman needs is a great deal of sympathetic understanding. But what the American woman needs quite as much as that is a parallel maturation of the American male.

15. Is There a Beat Generation?

IN PREPARING THIS CHAPTER I thought I might begin in something like the following manner: the question is, Is there a Beat Generation? I would ask, How unbeat can you get not to know the answer to a question like that? Clellon Holmes, in an article in *Esquire*—that breviary of the fluctuating bachelor—defined "beat" as being "at the bottom of your personality, looking up." Not to know that there is a Beat Generation and what it is suggests a slightly discreditable concern with one's own problems that disables one from digging the howls of the other cats around one. Such a one, even though he lived in Greenwich Village, might not know that so many other couples living there were really triangles and that there are plenty of squares in the Village besides Washington and Sheridan.

But fearing that I might be thought not to be treating the subject with the seriousness it deserves, I decided to forgo anything in the least suggesting levity, for I would not wish my words to be misunderstood—as may be illuminated by citing the case of the non-beatnik who in exasperation remarked to his beatnik friend, "Do you know what good clean fun is?" And the other beatifically replied, "No. What good is it?"

As an observer of the contemporary scene, I have little doubt of the existence of a Beat Generation. I cannot agree with those who maintain that the term strictly applies to a literary school of which Mr. Kerouac is the godfather if not the father. Certainly the beat writers belong to the Beat Generation, but I rather think that they represent only the most articulate part of it. The beat writers are simply and faithfully writing about themselves and

192

IS THERE A BEAT GENERATION? 193

the others like them. The question is whether the beat writers are describing a genuine and widespread phenomenon which justly depicts a substantial part of a whole generation. My answer to that question is that I think they do. There is a Beat Generation, and numerically it seems to be of sizable dimensions. But quite clearly, not everyone who was born within the last thirty years—give or take five or so years—is a member of the Beat Generation, and there are many who were born before who are quite as clearly beatniks. The term "Beat Generation" at most, then, refers to a segment of a generation most of whose members were born within the last thirty or so years.

I am concerned here to discover the marks by which the run-of-the-mill beatnik may be recognized.

When I think of the type of the beatnik, I think of the late young screen actor James Dean. He was idolized by millions of adolescents for the very reason that he expressed in his appearance, mannerisms, and attitudes toward life what they felt themselves to be. Even the manner of Dean's tragic and gratuitous death was entirely consonant with what the Beat Generation thinks not only of death but of life—that it is a kind of Russian roulette. The gun is loaded with a single bullet, that bullet has someone's number on it, and sooner or later that someone is bound to pull the trigger. Fatalism is not surprisingly one of the distinguishing marks of the beatnik.

Beyond all else, beatniks are characterized by a cultural rootlessness, a detachment from traditional values, and a peculiar alienation from themselves. They have abandoned the old morality in the name of a new morality in the attempt to free themselves from those disorders which traditional morality seems to them to have produced in the world—the world of moral chaos, the world they never made—a world that continuously threatens collective annihilation, and in which intimations of impending doom are an everyday experience, the unremitting stresses of which produce the human exhaustion that is the apathy of the contemporary adult. The Beat Generation will have no part of this. Apathy is strictly for the squares. The only conformity is to nonconformity. Hence, to be beat is to be extremely individualistic and bent on discovering the world for oneself, in a manner which constitutes impressive testimony to the profundity of the moral breakdown that has occurred in the West.

In his autobiographical novel *The Subterraneans,* Mr. Kerouac puts it all very touchingly when he writes

> . . . it was just another big downcrashing in the night and all for nothing . . . waking up, I, in the morning with the final hangover that said to me, "Too late"—and got up and staggered to the door through the debris, and opened it, and went home. . . . and at home I wandered around, couldn't stay in the house, couldn't stop, had to walk, as if someone was going to die soon, as if I could smell the flowers of death in the air, and I went in the South San Francisco railyard and cried.

In short, these are the children who were failed by their elders. In England they become Teddy Boys and Angry Young Men. Here they become beatniks.

It will, of course, be the common response of those who produced the Beat Generation to deny responsibility for them, and self-righteously to condemn the members of that generation for being what they have caused them to become—a generation of confused children wandering in the night helplessly crying in the wilderness their elders created. As Mr. Kerouac puts it, "deep in the dark pit of the night under the stars of the world you are lost, poor, no one cares."

What I am trying to say is that it is not condemnation or contempt that is called for but compassion and understanding, that the Beat Generation is not something either to bemoan or disown, but a suffering confusion of human beings crying out for sympathetic understanding.

The Beat Generation represents the ultimate expression of a civilization whose moral values have broken down, and in many ways, what is even worse, a civilization with little faith or conviction in the values it professes to believe. Its *ideal* values are one thing, but its *real* values, the values by which it lives, are quite another. Our ideal and our real values are in conflict. The Sermon on the Mount and the principle of competition are simply not compatible with each another, and this fact gives rise to the great hypocrisy of a society that preaches the one and lives by the other, and it gives rise, among other things, to a demoralization of the sort which results in beatniks.

Human beings living in a society in which such mutually irreconcilable, such conflicting and false values are dominant, are likely to be confused and confusing. Those who subscribe to them damage not only themselves but wreak havoc upon their children, many of whom constitute members of the Beat Generation.

The beatniks know that there is too much that is wrong with the non-beatniks, but they are thoroughly confused as to why it is that what is wrong is wrong. Their cult of "unthink" is of no help. Nor is resort to esoteric cults and Eastern religion. Whatever it is they are in revolt against, we must take care that the anarchy that is so apparent in the Beat Generation is not mistaken for anything other than it is, namely, a signal of distress, a cry for love, a refusal to accept defeat at the hands of the unloving lovers who made them what they are. We owe a debt of gratitude to the beat writers for so forcefully articulating what the less vocal members of this generation feel and think . . . or "unthink."

16. Selling America Short—

Our Failure in

Human Relations

AT AN INTERNATIONAL MEETING which I recently attended, a member of our State Department reported on the views which people of other countries hold concerning America. The picture was not a pretty one. Polls had shown that foreigners think of us as materialistic, technical, and moneytheistic. We were lacking in spirituality, we were arrogant and egocentric, and we were poor sports. A very large number of people didn't like us.

There are people who seem to think that this attitude toward Americans is something new in the world. It is not. Nor was our State Department official unaware of this, for he mentioned the fact that when he was a Rhodes scholar at Oxford the subject debated at one of the Oxford Union's meetings was whether it was true that America constituted an example of a society which had progressed from barbarism to decadence without the intervening benefits of civilization. One has but to read Mrs. Trollope, Charles Dickens, Matthew Arnold, and numerous other nineteenth-century writers who had visited these shores to realize that the low esteem in which Americans are held abroad is by no means a new phenomenon. What is perhaps new is the greater extension and the increase in the intensity of this dislike.

Is not this dislike strange? Why should *we* be disliked—we who helped liberate Europe, we who have poured so many

From *Saturday Review*, vol. 35, 1952, pp. 22-23.

millions into Europe, sent grain to India, and established peace in Greece. Where would the French and English be today had it not been for our gifts and our loans? And yet, there are millions of Frenchmen, Englishmen, and others who do not like us. Why?

Our State Department official suggested that if only we had a thousand Albert Schweitzers at our disposal we could send them out as missionaries to the rest of the world charged with the task of explaining Americans and America. There are many other naive things which our State Department official said, and I am afraid that though he was well-meaning he had nothing of value to contribute either as to the reasons why we are disliked abroad or what could be done by way of changing this attitude toward us.

Perhaps, as one who was born abroad and spent the first half of his life living abroad, and the second half living as an American citizen in the United States, and also as one who has visited various parts of Europe often during the last thirty years, I think I can offer some reasons for this dislike, which are based on numerous experiences and exchanges with Europeans, high and low.

In the first place, it does not appear to be too commonly realized in the United States that there is a long European tradition concerning America. This tradition is probably largely of English origin, and seems to have been gradually diffused throughout Europe to become, in the course of time, independently confirmed by that unique of all American exports, the American tourist. In a capsule, the tradition may be stated as follows: Americans are ill-bred, vulgar, illiterate, uncultivated, and materialistic. This tradition was reinforced by numerous eminent visitors to these shores, who, adept at both pen and persiflage, returned to their homelands and there enlightened their countrymen as to what Americans were really like. What these eminent visitors mostly saw were the superficial things, but they also saw some of the deeper sources of American traits, sources which many Americans were not sufficiently distantly removed from to be able to perceive as clearly as their foreign evaluators and critics. And because the picture that these foreign visitors drew of them appeared to be so much out of focus, with the emphasis on little and unimportant things, they rejected as hostile these caricatures of themselves. A peculiar state of mind has resulted from this. It is that foreigners don't and won't ever understand us. And yet there are no people in the world who want to be as much liked as Americans do. Every visitor to these shores from abroad will tell you that the question he is most frequently asked is, "How do you like America?" And most visitors from abroad, and most permanent residents of foreign birth in the United States, will tell you that no people are more kind or more hospitable than Americans. And yet these very same visitors will often agree more or less wholly with the criticisms of America and Americans which have been made ever since America came into being.

Most persons are not able to stand personal criticism of themselves, especially when it emanates from strangers, but criticism of one's country, particularly, it appears, if one is an American, is even less tolerable than criticism of oneself. Americans, more than any other people, seem to feel that a criticism of any of their country's institutions or ways constitutes a criticism of and an insult to themselves. A psychologist cannot help wondering whether this sensitivity does not betray a rather deep-seated insecurity which causes most Americans to respond in this way to such criticisms. When one is secure in oneself criticism of oneself is accepted for what it is worth, and usually gratefully received. When one is insecure in oneself one cannot tolerate criticism simply because it adds to one's insecurity and increases one's anxiety.

One of the most important things that Americans have to learn and accept about themselves is that they are an extremely insecure people—individually and collectively. This individual and mass insecurity explains a great many things about Americans which foreigners see but which many Americans are so frequently unwilling to face. What looks to the foreigner like arrogance and conceit are simply the overcompensatory devices by means of which the American is trying to cope with his feeling of inadequacy and show that he is a "success." It is only in his franker moments that he will be willing to admit that there may be something in this interpretation of his behavior, but in the everyday workaday world Americans do not see themselves as either arrogant or conceited, and, of course, not all Americans are— but the latter are not the kinds of Americans who are very visible or very noisy, and so, for the most part, they go unnoticed. The stereotyped picture of the American which Europeans and other peoples have is, however, frequent enough to constitute a very serious reality which not only Americans must begin to take seriously, but which the rest of the world simply cannot fail to if it is to survive.

America today is the most powerful nation in the world. Most of the remainder of the world's nations are by comparison weak. The relation of America's power to the rest of the world's weakness constitutes not only a grave problem for America, but even more importantly—and Americans would be wise to recognize this as quickly as possible—for the whole of the rest of the world. Because of its great power foreigners are today more than ever interested in America and in Americans—and more distrustful of them—for as a result of World War II many foreigners saw Americans in the flesh for the first time. Observing them, with all the willingness in the world to like them, most foreigners were sorrowfully forced to conclude that Americans were not likeable people. Let us go over some of the reasons for this widespread and very serious conclusion.

The chief ambassador from the American people to Europe was the American GI. The general feeling about the American GI in England was summed up in the refrain "Overdecorated, Oversexed, and Over Here." That was what was wrong with the American GI. Because he was also overpaid he enjoyed a distinct advantage over the British Tommy with the girls. The lack of courtesy, the frequent absence of the ordinary forms of politeness, the general crudity of behavior, the forwardness, and the high frequency of criminal behavior among American troops had a devastating effect. Add to this the racism and exceedingly unsportsmanlike attitude of many American soldiers toward Negro soldiers, and the general feeling exemplified in the village publican's notice "Only Coloured American Soldiers Wanted Here" may be understood. I am speaking about the over-all impression. There were many other villages whose people will never forget the kindness of American GIs. I think, particularly, of one village in which the GIs stationed there saved up for many months all the candy and other things they could buy at their PX store, and then at Christmas made a present of all this to the children and their parents. More good was done in that one village for Anglo-American relations than one could conceive being achieved by any other means. But under siege and in the large towns where hundreds of thousands of soldiers may be on leave for a few days the psychology of the soldier is likely to be somewhat different. At any cost he is out to have a good time.

In France, as in England, the French were appalled by the brutishness of so many American soldiers. One of the phrases I heard most frequently applied to the American GI by towns-people was "sexual beasts." One would encounter, in mock grudging admiration, the following kind of remark: "A European soldier when he steals will steal a package or even a carton of cigarettes. But Americans . . . nothing but a whole train with all its contents will do; They will steal a whole train and sell not only its contents, but the train, too! Now, there's imagination and breadth of vision for you! You, see, Americans always do things in a big way. It's always on the biggest scale." And amid guffaws of laughter the punch line would follow: "And you think it is just ordinary soldiers who are involved in this? No, my friend, non-commissioned officers and regular officers all the way up to colonels. And if you think they are all men, you would be mistaken. . . . There are women, too . . . officers of the women's corps, they are as big thieves as the men."

There is much else along similar lines, but the above should do as a sample. What about the "higher ups," the "liberators" of Europe? As everyone knows, the incoming American forces were greeted throughout the length and breadth of Europe as the liberators of mankind. No foreign army had ever been greeted with a deeper feeling of gratitude and welcome than the Americans. And, then, what happened? Instead of removing the Nazis and Fascists and other undesirable elements, the Americans maintained them in office and even dragged many out of hiding and put them into office over the heads of the men and women who had sacrificed virtually everything to keep the flame of decency alive during the "Terror." What kind of "liberation" was this?

Whose side were the Americans really on? Well, nearly twenty years after the "liberation" the Europeans know. Their conclusion is unequivocally that the Americans are on no one's side but their own. Whether this is a correct conclusion or not, that is what the Europeans believe. Americans, it is generally believed, are so afraid of the Russians that they will do anything to keep that bogey from their door. Europeans, in general, rightly or wrongly believe that the Russians do not want a war, that they want to fight a cold war, not a hot one. It is for these reasons, so it is held, that the Americans behave as they do in Europe and elsewhere, and it is this reason which causes so many Europeans to disapprove so violently and fundamentally of American foreign policy and American political conduct in the occupied areas of Europe and elsewhere in the world. Why did the Americans back Chiang Kai-shek when they could have backed the democratic elements in China and saved the 450,-000,000 Chinese people from going Communist? Why did the Americans support and force the monarchy upon the democratic people of Greece? And, today, why, in the name of democracy, are the Americans dealing with Franco?

All that the Europeans can see is that if there is a war between America and Russia it will be the Americans who have forced it upon the world, for the Russians, they believe, want to avoid war since with the aid of American foreign policy they can make all the gains they wish without war. In such a war, the Europeans feel they would be crushed beyond recovery. At the very best, whoever won, they feel they would lose.

The Marshall Plan, ECA, and other assistances of a similar kind have done a great deal of good, but the Europeans feel that it would have been so much more effective if these benisons had been given with more humility. As it is, many of them feel that these aids simply represent so many attempts by the Americans to hold the frontiers in Europe while America prepares to wage the war which by this very preparation the Americans are making inevitable. Europeans cannot feel either grateful to or fond of Americans while believing this. Are Europeans right or are they wrong in holding such a belief? How many well-informed Americans can there be found today who would claim that they are wrong?

So many Americans take it for granted that they are disliked by Europeans, as well as by other peoples, that they have become calloused to what others think of them, and have fallen out of sympathy with the unappreciative attitude of these peoples, and are no longer alive to the seriousness of what they think or even care. These "calloused" Americans are, perhaps, in the minority. But those Americans who do care are gravely concerned, and some of them want to send a thousand Albert Schweitzers out as apostles to the gentiles. But the gentiles will not be convinced by what the apostles *say*. What they will be and are convinced by is by what Americans *do*. No matter what the apostles might say nor how successful their efforts, the delay in granting a visa to one Graham Greene on the ground that he was a Communist in his youth will do more irreparable damage than can be corrected by a hundred thousand apostles preaching the good sense and good intentions of Americans.

Unfortunately the true apostles and molders of public opinion abroad are the players on the tennis teams who behave in a manner considered unsportsmanlike by those who have a nobler conception of the game than Americans seem to have; they are the GIs, the consuls and vice-consuls and their families; the tourists who overtip and don't say "Please" or "Thank you"; the occupation officials who makes speeches about democracy and behave in an undemocratic manner and institute undemocratic regulations; the movies we export; and the grain we delay sending to the starving Indians while Congress bargains—and the Russians exploit the opportunity by sending the grain without asking any concessions.

And speaking of the Russians and Indians, our State Department official told us that the most successful propaganda job done by the Russians in India has been to convince the Indians that the Americans are not interested in dealing on a basis of equality with the colored "races" of the world. To support their claims they print photographs for those who are unable to read showing race riots and lynchings in the United States, while for those who are able to read they quote chapter and verse proving that these things actually occur in the United States. When our State Department official referred to these photographs he said that they "purported" to be of race riots and lynchings. Indeed, throughout his whole talk there was a tendency to play down the faults from which we Americans are alleged to suffer. This tendency to play down, explain away, and even deny some of our worst faults is another of our traits which people abroad do not like about us. It is foolish to speak of "purported" photographs of race riots and lynchings when almost every American has seen photographs of, and thousands have participated in, the real thing, and numerous others have quietly acquiesced. If we really want to make friends and influence people abroad we should let them know the whole truth about ourselves. The truth about ourselves will be much more sympathetically received than the unconvincing glosses. Race riots and lynchings have occurred in the United States for many years—we should admit this freely, and we should deplore with all the feeling that is within us the occurrence of such tragic disasters. We should explain to those who are genuinely interested in an explanation the reason for such ghastly occurrences, and we should set out some of the great gains which have been made, especially in the recent period, in the realm of race relations, and we should also make clear some of the reasons why greater progress has not been made. We may legitimately point with some satisfaction to the states and towns and villages and institutions which have abolished all discriminatory racial laws and practices, and instituted laws and procedures calculated to make all discrimination on such grounds illegal.

In the eyes of the rest of the world we Americans are particularly vulnerable in this matter of race; it is therefore incumbent upon us to handle intelligently the task of enabling those abroad who wish to understand us to do so successfully. Race riots and lynchings are as shocking to most Americans as they are to anyone else, and this is what we ought to let the rest of the world know; for the rest of the world, and particularly the colored world, is interested in our race riots and lynchings as an index of our probable attitudes toward them. What the colored peoples of the world want to know is whether we Americans are interested in dealing with them on a basis of equality or on a basis of skin color. Looking at race relations in America at the present time through the alembic of foreign propaganda they have no doubt as to the answer. These peoples need to be told that for forty years the Congress of the United States refused to grant statehood to its own territories of Alaska and Hawaii, largely because there were politicians who feared the potentially incoming votes would favor the advancement of civil rights— especially for its colored citizens. But by 1960 Alaska and Hawaii became the forty-ninth and fiftieth states of the Union.

Europeans, quite often, feel that Europe has not only become a dependency of the United States, but that the government of the United States is using its money to influence and shape the foreign policies of their own countries. This feeling I encountered not only in the man in the street but also among several European political figures. One of them said to me, "We have become a nation of lickspittles. No one may dare voice a criticism of the United States. We are told to be quiet, for we must on no account offend the Americans. We need dollars." I was given many examples of this attitude in high political circles. One significant example will, perhaps, suffice. In keeping with the policy of quietism, jokes about Americans are discouraged on the stage, and in one case, so I was informed, the management of a private theatrical group running a play which had several jokes about Americans was heavily penalized on the charge that they had admitted a nonmember who paid at the door. A month earlier, so the story went, on a similar charge another theatrical group had been merely nominally fined. There were no jokes about Americans in *their* play. That an able and intelligent member of a European legislative body could seriously tell such a story and believe it to be true would be merely amusing were it not for the fact that millions of other Europeans believe much the same things.

Among many other Europeans there is the strong feeling that America needs Europe vastly more than Europe needs America, and their attitude is: "Certainly we shall be willing to help the

Americans with any reasonable request they may make—but they must permit us to run our own affairs our own way. Advice and suggestions will be welcome, but we don't want to be told what to do. We want to co-operate, but we don't want to be coerced or compelled. We don't want to be pushed around, and if the Americans won't do anything about it, we shall have to tell them that we shall have to do without them."

That such views can be held by Europeans suggests that something is somewhere wrong. Whatever the truth may be, it would appear that we have not done a very good job of human relations. The fault may not be altogether our own, but that it is partly so I think there can be little doubt. We have tried to "sell" ourselves and we've sold ourselves short. We might try giving up the values and the practices of the market place, and instead of attempting to "sell" ourselves take a good look at ourselves and attempt to see ourselves as others see us, for what we are is not what we think we are but the appearance we present to the world. We might also attempt to take a look at others in terms of *their* needs as well as our own.

The Europeans and other peoples want to like us, and *we* want genuinely to like them. The only way one ever gets to be liked is by liking others. Apparently we have not succeeded in conveying our liking for them to the peoples of the rest of the world, and until we learn how to do so we shall never be understood by them, and they will continue to think as they do of us.

Liking other peoples consists in making them feel that we are genuinely interested in their welfare, and that we are not helping them for exclusively selfish interests of our own. Since much of our motivation is already of this kind this task should not prove too difficult.

PART IV

Humanity and Equality:
Problems in Society

17. The Negro's Problem:
The White Man

To EXTERNALIZE A CONFLICT within oneself by projecting it upon another person is a common device of the mentally sick. That perhaps is why the white man talks of "the Negro problem" when what he really means is "the white problem"—the problem of himself in a frustrating hostile world. So far as I have been able to discover there is no Negro problem. Negroes do not create problems in interpersonal relations, but whites do, and It is the peculiar character of white logic in these matters to assert that it is Negroes who create such problems. What the Negro wants, and what the Negro has always wanted, could never under any commonly decent circumstances give rise to problems in ethnic or interpersonal relations. The Negro wants the right, in common with all sober human beings, to live and to realize the best that is within him. Is that a criminal desire? Is that a claim which is unreasonable? Is that elementary wish one which should give rise to problems in human equity? All decent men know the answer, for that is all one needs to be to know the true answer—simply a decent human being. While the facts of science in this field are all on the side of decency, they are irrelevant so far as the argument of humanity is concerned, and that, where human relations are involved, must and will always remain the final argument.

What the Negro wants is to have the opportunity shared by all other men to be treated as a human being who is neither better nor worse than other men. Is such a wish asking for too much,

From *The Negro History Bulletin*, vol. 8, 1945, pp. 177-179, 188.

for something unjustified? Should it lead to any problem? Should the right to be heard, to free speech, a free press, the right to vote, the right to receive a fair return for one's labor, the right to work, the right to a fair hearing and trial, the right to just redress for wrongs committed against one, the right, in short, to live as a citizen of the country with all the rights, privileges, and duties granted and demanded of all other citizens without discrimination of any kind—should any of these rights entail the least problem among ordinarily decent human beings? The answer is in no doubt. These rights, privileges, and duties are guaranteed to the citizen of these United States by the Constitution. Why is it, then, that one particular group of citizens in these states is to varying degrees forcibly deprived of and forbidden these elementary rights? Who is it under such conditions that creates the problem, the victim or the oppressor? There are no problems of this sort where all men are free to be good citizens; it is only when one group of the citizenry deprives another of its freedom and frustrates it at every turn that problems are created. So far as the world is concerned, and particularly so far as the Negro is concerned, it is the white man who creates those problems—not the black. The world's problem is the white man, not the black man. Men of every complexion today have a problem, and that problem is the white man, in fact their greatest problem, for the white man is mentally very sick indeed. Very fortunately not all white men are sick—there are many who are not—and among those there are some who have been able to diagnose the white man's sickness fairly clearly. It may be that these physicians will be able to direct mankind toward the cure of the white man's present sickness, a sickness which the world has seen realized in its extremest form in the theory and practice of Nazism.

In common with all other minority groups the Negro's problem is the gentile white man—the man who professes to be a Christian living by the religion of Christ in a land where the principles of democracy are said to be most fully realized. How is it that a person raised in such a faith can in his conduct be so unchristian and so frightfully tyrannical and authoritarian? In the answer to that question lies the explanation of the white man's sickness.

It is important for the Negro to understand why the white man is sick and what the exact nature of his sickness is. The white man is not suffering from dislike of the Negro, but from dislike of himself. The white man is afraid, not of the Negro, nor of himself, but of the world in which he finds himself. He is insecure, not because the Negro constitutes any kind, the very least kind, of a threat to him, but he has been made insecure by the processes of socialization to which he had been exposed, the process, in other words, which makes a human being in society what he is. In the kind of society in which the white man is socialized the Negro happens to be the most highly visible minority group upon which the aggressiveness of his accumulated frustrations may be profitably expended. There is, of course, more in it than that. The point I wish to make is that the Negro in America serves as the principal scapegoat not because he is recognized to be particularly awful or dangerous, but merely because he is the most convenient object for such scapegoatism. I am speaking now of the masses of whites in their relation to the Negro, for it must be clearly understood that the relations of whites to Negroes are very different in the different social classes. The upper classes are generally "very friendly" in their relations with Negroes; they have little of the dislike so openly shown by the middle and lower classes. The reason for this is that their relation to the Negro is not one in which they believe him in any way to constitute a threat or a challenge to their security, but rather they look upon him as a valuable tool in maintaining the type of social and industrial economy which is to their interest. For them the Negro is a kind of puppet who does what his masters desire him to do. When it serves his masters to use them as pincushions into which the frustrated members of the white working classes may stick the barbs of their unexpended aggressiveness, the Negro is offered up as an easy mark. Should one wish to obtain votes, then all one has to do is to assure the white electorate that if they do not vote for you the Negroes will be strengthened—and you can be sure which way the votes will go. If you wish to distract the attention of the people from important issues, all that needs to be done is to start a campaign against the Negroes. Why among white men it is easy to do this will become apparent shortly, but is it not clear that in Europe the pattern was precisely the same, except that the absence of Negroes in Europe has traditionally simply made it necessary to deal with such minority groups as were available, and as everybody knows the most widely distributed minority group in Europe are the Jews. If there had been no Negroes in the United States the Jews would have served as the principal scapegoat instead. And had there been no ethnic, religious, or cultural minority groups there can be no question that some section of the lower classes would have become the scapegoat.

It is important to understand that "race prejudice" is really but another name for "class prejudice." The mechanism of both is almost precisely the same, one group considering itself biologically and socially superior to the other (lower class) group.

The only difference between the class prejudice that prevailed in Europe and the race prejudice as exhibited by whites in America toward the Negro is that the Negro is treated as belonging to a distinctively separate caste rather than class. As a member of a class one *can* migrate into the upper classes; as a member of a caste only very rarely can one do so, and not at all if one is a Negro.

It is important to understand that the attitude of the upper classes toward the Negro is very different in certain respects from that of the lower classes. There is more hatred for the Negro among the lower classes because they consider him an economic threat to their own security, at least they have been taught so to consider him. The somewhat differing attitudes toward the Negro appear to be based on motives having a large part of their origin in economic factors. And this is true, but because the Negro supports the upper classes economically they feel quite benevolently toward him, while the lower classes, who live in a more or less constant state of economic insecurity, have been taught to regard the Negro as one of the chief reasons for their own depressed insecure condition; therefore the Negro becomes a frustrating object to the member of the lower classes and thus becomes the proper object of his resulting aggression. Among the upper classes, there is, in fact, normally no hostility for the Negro. The Negro is simply regarded as a useful domestic animal whose usefulness is greatest when he loyally does as he is told. As long as he is content to serve in such a capacity he will be treated as well as any domestic animal has ever been treated, even better upon occasion, and one can have the same friendly feelings toward him as one has to one's horse.

It is the age-old attempt of this class to maintain itself in its special privileges at the expense of other human beings which is responsible for the "white problem," and for racism everywhere.

It is the attitudes toward other human beings held by persons in positions of social power which determine what interpersonal relations will be like in any given community, for it is the socially powerful persons in a community who determine the pattern of that community's conduct.

In a society in which great emphasis is placed on the possession of money as a necessary means of getting as much out of life as possible, those who have acquired this necessary means are understandably interested in maintaining the conditions which make possible the continuance of its enjoyment. If the oppression—horrid word—of any minority group is involved in this process, it may at once be justified on the grounds of a thousand and one rationalizations which have in common the fact that they are all calculated to show that some people are biologically inferior to others, and it is to the advantage of the biologically inferior to be controlled by the biologically superior. This is the so-called "white man's burden." But the white man's burden is something quite other than this; it is his sick mind— a mind which enables him to live by the suffering and human disenfranchisement of others.

It is not necessarily a lack of human sympathy which enables a member of the upper classes to maintain such an attitude toward other human beings. This is probably a factor in some cases but not in most. In most cases a tradition of ideas is simply being perpetuated, a tradition of ideas which has it that such things as the place of the Negro in society and of the classes are naturally ordained. This is the disease which afflicts the upper classes, who are the chief purveyors of "racism." "Racism" is a disease. It is a malfunctioning of the mind which endangers human relations, a disease due to the infection of the mind by false ideas concerning the status of other groups of human beings. In much the same way as organs become diseased as a result of the action of germs, so minds become diseased as the result of the action of wrong ideas. Racism is a disease which is endemic among the upper classes and is transmitted by them from generation to generation. Whenever these classes feel that their position is endangered, they have but to release some of the racist germs among the discontented population, and the latter at once begin to exhibit the symptoms of an acute attack of racism.

Most members of the upper classes believe that the classes and castes of modern Western society arrange themselves into naturally determined biological strata, and in the course of several generations they have succeeded in building up—with the assistance of their less scrupulous fellows engaged in the enter-prise of imperialism—a bastion of rationalizations and myths which fully convinces them of the justice of their position. The ruling classes everywhere in relation to their subject peoples are full of such ideas. It is only the rare exception who knows that what he is doing is unjust, but even he may have his ex-cuses. In pre-independence days I heard highly civilized English-men say, "I know we shouldn't be in India, but if the continuance of English culture depends upon our being there, then I'll fight to the death to hold onto India." The error here was, of course, to assume that the continuance of English culture depended upon the oppression of a single being, let alone four hundred million Indians. It was not English culture but colossal English fortunes which were dependent upon the British maintaining their grip on India.

What can one do with such members of the ruling classes? Is it possible to cure them of their disease? In some individual cases, yes; as a class, no. The only form of re-education which they would understand would be a reorganization of society along lines which would eliminate all possibility of one person or group advancing themselves at the expense of another. The achievement of such a state of human relations is what such persons and groups have from the very beginning fought against. The "white problem" will be solved when the white man learns to co-operate with rather than to rule his fellow men. The imperialist exploitative form of society could never be a co-operative society. Speaking in terms of the long view, the cure of the white man's sickness lies in freeing him from the effects of an economic organization of society which looks upon men as commodities, which is productive of interpersonal conflict, of chronic social disorganization, and of the brutalization of man. So much for the sickness of the upper classes in whom, under a socially stratified form of society which is dependent upon the exploitation of masses of men, the disease of racism finds its focal point.

Among the lower classes the personal instability, insecurity, and frustrations of life which result from such a form of social organization give rise to a permanent anxiety state—a state of fear and scarcely subdued hostility of man for man. The frustrations which pile up in the course of such a normal lifetime give rise to an enormous amount of aggressiveness which finds a ready outlet in the great American scapegoat, the American Negro, and in any other convenient minority group. In our society every man fights his own battle for survival alone. He cannot pause to consider the other fellow. If he does so he has good reason to believe that he is lost. The struggle for existence is hard. Life for the common man in our society is frustrating, disappointing, and productive of seething aggressiveness. We are all too familiar with the personality which develops under such conditions—it is the personality of the white man. This is not alone the Negro's problem, but the problem of us all. It is well for those who are the principal victims of the white man's disorder to recognize the cause of the disease from which they are in turn made to suffer.

The reorganization of society which will result in the cure of the white man's sickness will take a long time to achieve. What, meanwhile, is the Negro to do?

Above all else I believe the Negro must concentrate on securing his rights as a free citizen of the United States. The abolition of every device of discrimination and restriction must be secured. The Negro must assert his right to be treated as a human being. The great majority of Negroes will not, for some time to come, be in a position to do these things, but their leaders and educators must set them the example. I am no starry idealist. I have more than a faint notion of the awful conditions under which millions of Negroes are forced to spend their lives in this country. I know how helpless they are. But remember, so were the Irish for five hundred years, and the peoples of India for over two hundred years, under British rule; so were the Negroes of the Caribbean for three hundred years, and think back upon the position of the Negro in this country less than a hundred years ago. Progress *has* been made, and it will, in future, proceed at an accelerated pace. In regulating that pace, the Negro himself must play a prominent role. He will have to do it with discretion—a discretion which is, however, coupled with moral heroism guided by intelligence and planning. Science, truth, and humanity are on the Negro's side. The white man is a sick man, and the Negro must learn to deal with him as such and not to hate him. The passion he engenders must be turned into a creative force, the organized force to secure by legislative means in the first place the righting of wrongs. Jim Crow laws must be abolished, education must be more equitably available, housing conditions must be improved, and a thousand other things must be done. Finally, the Negro must realize that he has many friends among the whites who are with him, that he is not alone, and that they will go on helping him to solve new problems as Granville Sharp, William Wilberforce, Thomas Clarkson, and Abraham Lincoln helped toward the solution of older ones.

18. Some Psychodynamic Factors
in Race Prejudice

THE WORD "race," once a respectable scientific term, today stands for something very different from what it originally meant. Originally used in a strictly biological sense to embrace geographic varieties of the same species, the term today, particularly in relation to men, has assumed social, political, and emotional connotations which have no connection with scientific realities but belong rather to the field of pathognomic mythology.[1]

A myth is not less real because it is based on emotion than is a belief which is based on scientifically demonstrated fact. Indeed, to the person holding it, the myth may be and usually is more acceptable than the facts, for the simple reason that the myth is more satisfactorily integrated into the personality structure of many persons than are the facts. Myths, in such instances, pay much higher emotional dividends than do the facts. Emotionally insecure persons are largely interested in such emotional dividends, hence, the widespread presence of myths.

Dr. Read Bain has pointed out[2] that "The myth emerges from the uncritical verbalization of hopes and fears. It flourishes by repetition and authoritarian tradition, is sustained by coercive control, and finally dies out when science and common sense demonstrate its absurdity and harmfulness."

From *The Journal of Social Psychology*, vol. 30, 1949, pp. 175-187.
[1] M. J. Tumin, "The Idea of 'Race' Dies Hard," *Commentary*, vol. 8, 1949, pp. 80-85.
[2] Read Bain, "Man, the Myth-Maker," *The Scientific Monthly*, vol. 65, 1947, pp. 61-69.

Is it not possible that this view of the nature of myth overlooks the more profound realities of the situation? Myths surely, as Nicholas Calas has put it, are idealized forms of social conditions, so that when inequality becomes very obvious the main function of myths is to explain the origin of differences in a manner which will satisfy the needs of a given group. Insofar as a myth accounts for social differences it corresponds to a legal fiction; but insofar as it attempts to justify in legal terms the *status quo* it serves a historical function.[3]

Surely it is a piece of naïveté to suggest that the myth eventually dies out when science and common sense demonstrate its absurdity and harmfulness. As long ago as 1848 Renan already knew better than that.[4]

Myths, sacred and profane, secular and even "scientific," persist in spite of the demonstrations of science and common sense. Indeed, the conjunction of science and common sense is in reality often represented by *dis*-junction, in which the one stands in contradiction to the other. Common sense is what the myth-maker most often appeals to, and such phrases as "It stands to reason," "The facts show," "Some of my best friends . . . ," and the like, are most often upon his lips. Not only this, the myth-maker, if he is schooled enough, will frequently appeal to "science" to support his views, and, indeed, the myth-maker may himself be a scientist whose emotional drives bear a close family resemblance to those of the allegedly more emotional bigot. The facts of such a scientist may be objectively the same as those of any other scientist, but the interpretation which he puts upon them will, so far as it is possible, incline in the direction which he favors. It has been shown, for example, that there is a strong tendency for scientists who are Republicans to come to very different conclusions on such a matter as the relative importance of heredity and environment from scientists who are Socialists or Democrats. I need not, perhaps, say that the Republicans usually plumb for heredity while the Socialists and Democrats hitch their wagon to environment. It is not without interest to note that when the Socialist or Democrat becomes a Tory or

[3] Nicholas Calas, "Myth and Initiation," *Chimera*, vol. 4, 1946, pp. 21-24.
[4] E. Renan, *The Future of Science* (London, Chapman and Hall, 1891).

Republican, he usually switches from favoring environment to the celebration of the virtues of heredity.[5] Scientists as well as laymen often mistake the prejudices of their social group for the laws of nature.

As we shall see, myths are idealized forms of social conditions —social conditions which, so the myth-maker thinks, would satisfy his needs.

Since the problem of race constitutes what I have elsewhere called man's most dangerous myth,[6] it is imperative that we be quite clear as to the nature of the phenomenon with which we are dealing, so that we may the better be able to handle it.

Let me say at once that I do not think that the teaching of the scientifically established facts about race or the teaching of the equality of man would alone be sufficient to solve this problem. I believe that one could talk and write oneself blue in the face on all the scientific facts until doomsday without in any way satisfactorily solving this problem. Many persons are, of course, assisted to look upon the problem more intelligently, but many others are not, and it is these many others who principally constitute the race problem. It is the discriminators, not the discriminated, the prejudiced, not those against whom the prejudice is exhibited, who are the problem. Since the racist beliefs and conduct of such persons are generally motivated by traits of personality of which they are themselves unaware, it is impossible to influence them substantially by exposing them to the facts of science and so-called common sense—impossible because their ego structure will permit the integration of nothing within it which is opposed to the satisfaction of its needs. And this is the fact with which we have to reckon.

[5] See the works of Nicholas Pastore: "Nature-Nurture Controversy: A Sociological Approach," *School and Society*, vol. 57, 1943, pp. 373-377; "Social Rôle of Heredity," *Education Administration and Supervision*, vol. 30, 1944, pp. 218-224; "Social Approach to William McDougall," *Journal of Social Forces*, vol. 23, 1944, pp. 148-152; "Social Influences Upon Psychological Trends," *Journal of General Psychology*, vol. 38, 1948, pp. 15-29; *The Nature-Nurture Controversy* (New York, King's Crown Press, Columbia University, 1949).

[6] Ashley Montagu, *Man's Most Dangerous Myth: The Fallacy of Race*, 3rd ed. (New York, Harper, 1952).

The race problem is not a problem of the facts of biology, of scientific data thoroughly analyzed and systematically taught. It is first and foremost a social problem which can be satisfactorily dealt with by social means of a kind which will require important revisions of some of our present ideas. For until the psychological disturbances which are created in the person by our processes of socialization are modified, the race problem will continue to plague us. Hence, the importance of inquiring into the nature of these processes and the effects which they produce upon behavior.

Before proceeding to the further discussion of these matters, let me say that in view of the fact that the word "race" has become so emotionally muddied, so injected with false meanings, some scientists in speaking of human breeding groups which are or have been geographically and therefore reproductively isolated from other such groups, prefer to speak of them as "ethnic groups" rather than races. In the biological and genetic sense races of man do exist. Such races are distinguishable from one another by the possession of different frequencies of certain genes and by certain visible physical characters. But many groups called races are not races at all, being either national, linguistic, or mixed populations; and none of the biological or miscalled sociological races, in spite of innumerable investigations calculated to show that they do, are known to differ in their mental potentialities from one another.

The racist, on the other hand, maintains that racial physical traits are linked with particular mental traits. This is demonstrably untrue, for physical characters in men are known to be independent in their inheritance of mental potentialities, and under opportunities and conditions which are equal for all, men of all ethnic groups are known to be equally capable in all mental respects within the normal range of variation for any group of men anywhere.

Professor Dobzhansky and I have shown that natural selection, during the evolution of man, has probably placed the greatest premium upon educability—plasticity or adaptability of behavior to changing conditions—that it was this trait rather than the development of special abilities which must have been most highly favored, and that in this respect the evolution of all men must have been similar. The effect of natural selection in man has probably been to render genotypic differences in personality traits, as between individuals and particularly as between races, relatively unimportant compared to their phenotypic plasticity.[7] Hence the mental potentialities of mankind must be regarded as potentially similar. This does not eliminate the possibility that there exist genuine differences in the gene frequency distributions of genes which exercise limiting effects upon some mental potentialities. It would be surprising, however, if these differences proved to be anything more than differences in the *frequency* with which genes occur in such groups, genes which are *common* to *all* mankind. The evidence, as we know it, indicates that all human groups possess all the gene potentialities that all other human groups possess, but that there are differences between groups in the manner in which such genes or potentialities are both distributed and environmentally conditioned. If genetic differences exist, and we are far from certain that they do, then as between one group and another they must be very small and insignificant indeed. It must be remembered that genes determine not characters but the responses of the developing organism to the environment, that as Confucius put it, twenty-five hundred years ago, "Men's natures are alike; it is their habits that carry them far apart."

As I have already indicated, the biological facts have nothing to do with the social realities. The biological facts are available, but the racists do not choose to accept them because they are emotionally unacceptable to them. Why? This is the question we must now seek to answer. When we have done so we shall perhaps be in a better position to see how the solution to the problem of race may be approached.

The one thing clear concerning "racial" hostility and prejudice is the ease with which persons are led to exhibit it. There are very few persons in our society who have not, at one time or another, exhibited evidence of "racial" prejudice; and it would seem clear that most persons are capable of being brought to a

[7] Theodosius Dobzhansky and Ashley Montagu, "Natural Selection and the Mental Characters of Mankind," *Science*, vol. 105, 1947, pp. 587-590.

state of mind in which they are really glad of the opportunity of freely releasing their feelings against some group or person representing such a group. When society as a whole sanctions the attachment of such feelings to any group, the free exercise of "racial" intolerance is enjoyed as a happy release for feelings which are ever ready to find expression. Now, it is in the nature of such feelings, the character of which we shall presently discuss, that they can be suitably directed against some person or particular group of persons, and it is for this reason that they can be so easily directed to the support and maintenance of "race" prejudices. The person exhibits "race" prejudice because it affords him a means of easing certain tensions within himself, because he is happiest when he is most freely able to release those tensions. As far as the person is concerned, the prejudice itself is unimportant, it merely provides the channel through which his feelings are allowed necessary expression. Such feelings should, and for the sake of the health of the person must, find expression. As I have already said, such feelings will attach themselves to the most suitable object offered, whatever it may be. Such feelings are *not* feelings of "race" prejudice, or any other kind of prejudice; and they are not inborn. On the contrary, such feelings are to a very large extent generated during the early childhood development of almost every person. There can, however, be little doubt that the elementary forms of these affective states in their undifferentiated condition are physiologically determined.[8] The manner in which such feelings are generated has been discussed in great detail by the psychoanalysts and others. I shall here briefly review the process involved in these dynamisms.

The aggressiveness which adults exhibit in the form of "race" hatred would appear to have universally the same origin. That is to say, the aggressiveness, not the "race" hatred, has the same

---

[8] F. Fremont-Smith, "The Physiological Basis of Aggression," *Child Study*, vol. 15, 1938, pp. 1-8, and "The Influence of Emotional Factors Upon Physiological and Pathological Processes," *Bulletin of New York Academy of Medicine*, vol. 15, 1939, 560-569; H. Jost, "Some Physiological Changes During Frustration," *Child Development*, vol. 12, 1941, pp. 9-15; M. J. Muste and D. F. Sharpe, "Some Influential Factors in the Determination of Aggressive Behavior in Preschool Children," *Child Development*, vol. 18, 1947, pp. 11-28.

origin universally and this aggressiveness is later merely arbitrarily directed, in some societies, against certain groups. Under other conditions this same aggressiveness could be directed against numerous different objects, either real or imagined. The object against which aggressiveness is directed is determined by particular conditions, and these we shall later briefly consider.

If it be agreed that in "racial" intolerance and prejudice a certain amount of aggressiveness is always displayed, we must ask and answer two question: (1) Where does this aggressiveness originate, and (2) Why is it exhibited?

Briefly, it is here suggested that a considerable amount of the aggressiveness which adults exhibit is originally produced during childhood by parents, nurses, teachers, or whoever else participates in the process of socializing the child. By depriving the infant, and later the child, of all the means of satisfaction which it seeks—the nipple, the mother's body, uncontrolled freedom to excrete and to suck, the freedom to cry at will, to scream and shout, to stay up as late as one wishes, to do the thousand and one things that are forbidden—expected satisfactions are thwarted and frustration upon frustration is piled up within the child. Such frustrations lead to resentment, to fear, to hatred, and to aggressiveness. In childhood this aggressiveness or resentment is displayed in "bad temper" and in general "naughtiness." Such conduct almost invariably results in further frustration, in punishment. At this stage of his development the child finds himself in a state of severe conflict. He must either control the expression of his aggressiveness or else suffer the punishment and the loss of love which his aggressiveness provokes. Such conflicts are usually resolved by excluding the painful situation from consciousness and direct motor expression, in short, by the repression of one's aggressive energies. These are rarely ever completely repressed, but only insofar as they permit a resolution of the original conflict situation, and the farther the original derivatives of what was primarily repressed become removed from these energies, the more freely do they gain access to consciousness and the more available for use do they become. The evidence renders it overwhelmingly clear that these energies are never to any extent destroyed or exhausted. Being a part of the total organism, they must, in one way or another, find expression, and the ways in which they can find expression are innumerable. "Race" hatred and prejudice merely represent familiar patterns of the manner in which aggressiveness may express itself.[9]

Fear of those who have frustrated one in childhood, and anxiety concerning the outcome of the situation thus produced, lead to the repression of aggression against the original frustrators and thereby to the *conditioning* of an emotional association between certain kinds of frustrative or fear situations and aggressive feelings. As a result of such conditioning, any object even remotely suggesting such fear and frustrative situations provokes the aggressive behavior with which such fears and frustrations have become associated.

It must again be emphasized that the aggressiveness which is more or less common to all human beings is not a cause of "race" prejudice, but merely represents a motive force or affective energy which can be attached, among other things, to the notion that other groups or "races" are hateful and may thus serve to keep such ideas supplied with the emotional force necessary to keep them going. Under such conditions, "race" becomes important, not as a biological description or ethnic classification, but as the expression of an unconscious conflict.

Since the infliction of mental, and even physical, pain, as well as the frustration and depreciation of others, is involved in the process of "race" prejudice, and since much of the aggressiveness of the person owes its existence to early experience of a similar sort, it is perhaps not difficult to understand why it is that most persons are so ready to participate in the exercise of "race" prejudice. By so doing they are able to find an object for their aggressiveness which most satisfactorily permits the free expression of aggressiveness by means almost identically resembling those which in childhood were indulged in against them. In this way is the person, as an adult, enabled to pay off, quite unconsciously, an old score of childhood frustration. The later very appreciable frustrations suffered in adolescence and adult life

[9] John Dollard and others, *Frustration and Aggression* (New Haven, Yale University Press, 1939); E. F. M. Durbin and John Bowlby, *Personal Aggressiveness and War* (New York, Columbia University Press, 1939).

naturally add to the store and complexity of aggressiveness, with the resulting increase in the already formidable pressure of aggression.[10] Aggression is very easily displaced, that is to say, shifted from one object as outlet to another, and it is also very easily projected; feelings and impulses associated with hostility and aggression in oneself which have been refused conscious recognition are projected or attributed to others.

As illustrative of these points I should like to refer to some recent studies which were instituted in order to discover what kind of persons adopt and become active carriers of, for example, anti-Semitic ideas, why they so readily become "scapegoat addicts," and what function, if any, anti-Semitism has in their personality structure.

With these purposes in view Frenkel-Brunswik and Sanford[11] investigated a group of approximately one hundred state university students, seventy-six being women. Subjects giving evidence of a high degree of anti-Semitism were classified as "high extremes," those showing the contrary tendency were classified as "low extremes," and those with in-between attitudes, as "intermediate."

The high extremes were found to be conservative in their attitudes, automatically tending to support the *status quo;* they were generally Republicans, although they showed few signs of having developed an organized sociopolitical outlook, and there was a tendency to hold their own ethnic or social group in high esteem, to keep it unmixed and pure, and to reject everything that differed from it. The father's income was higher than that of the father of the average intermediate or low extreme subjects, and the appearance of the high extreme girl was in the best middle-class tradition of good grooming (almost all subjects were members of the middle class), very different from that of the low extreme girl. On the surface these anti-Semitic girls appeared composed and untroubled. They seemed to have little

[10] T. Parsons, "Certain Primary Sources and Patterns of Aggression in the Social Structure of the Western World, *Psychiatry,* vol. 10, 1947, pp. 167-181.

[11] E. Frenkel-Brunswik and R. N. Sanford, "The Anti-Semitic Personality," in Ernest Simmel, ed., *Anti-Semitism: A Social Disease* (New York, International University Press, 1946).

familiarity with their inner lives, but were characterized rather by a generally externalized orientation. They were sensitive to any encroachment from the outside. On the surface they showed an uncritical devotion and obedience to their parents, and to authority in general. They were mostly interested in social standing, and in making an appropriate marriage.

The low extremes, on all these points, contrasted sharply with the high extremes, being nondescript in appearance, less at ease socially, possessed of varied interests, quite willing to talk about themselves and their situations, and able to make critical appraisals of their parents.

Examination of the results of tests and interviews revealed the fact that the high extremes are markedly characterized by unconscious aggressive drives of a destructive nature, the repression of basic impulses, ambivalent attitudes of love and hate toward their parents, basic insecurity. Both sexes in the high extreme group tend to be more hypochondriacal. Analysis of the content of their responses suggests that their aggressive attitudes toward out-groups stems from frustration received (mainly at the hands of the mother) in childhood, frustrations which appear to have produced definite inferiority feelings.

The rigidity with which the high extreme girl adheres to her conventional values or stereotypes of behavior, and the anxiety which she exhibits in the presence of opposite tendencies, affords the clue to the sources of her behavior. Insecurity is the condition with which such girls are struggling. The fear of losing status is associated with the fear that they will be tempted to release their inhibited tendencies in the way they believe Jews and proletarians do. Anti-Semitism thus helps them to maintain their identification with the group to which they belong and to ward off anxiety.

What is clearly awry here is not so much the middle-class values of the group but rather the rigidity with which they are enforced and adhered to. As Frenkel-Brunswik and Sanford suggest, the rigidity with which the person adheres to these values seems to be a result of the manner in which they have been inculcated in the developing person.

The mischief is done when those trends which are taboo according to the class standards become repressed, and hence, no longer susceptible to modification or control. This is most likely to happen when parents are too concerned and too insistent with respect to their positive aims for the child and too threatening and coercive with respect to the "bad" things. The child is thus taught to view behavior in terms of black and white, "good" and "evil"; and the "evil" is made to appear so terrible that he cannot think of it as something in himself which needs to be modified or controlled, but as something that exists in other "bad" people and needs to be stamped out completely.[12]

Evidently, then, parental-child relationships need to undergo a substantial change in the direction of greater understanding and sympathy on the part of parents, in the dropping of "either-or" attitudes, since disjunctive commands give rise to disjunctive personalities, and there must be a development of a greater and more sensitive awareness of the meaning of the whole process of socialization. As Frenkel-Brunswik and Sanford say, if the kind of repression which they have uncovered in their high extreme girls, and its consequences, are to be prevented "there must be less fear of impulses on the part of parents. The parental attitude toward children must be more tolerant and permissive. Parents must learn that the 'bad' impulses can be modified and controlled and that it is of crucial importance to invite the child's participation in these processes." Parents must learn how to give their children the maximum degree of security consonant with the ideal of a socially fully integrated personality. In this task teachers as well as parents must play their role.[13]

Ackerman and Jahoda have made available the results of a study[14] calculated to reveal the dynamic basis of anti-Semitic attitudes in a number of persons who have experienced psychoanalytic therapy. The material was collected from about thirty

[12] *Ibid*, p. 122-123.
[13] Ashley Montagu, *Education and Human Relations* (New York, Grove Press, 1958).
[14] N. W. Ackerman and M. Jahoda, "Toward a Dynamic Interpretation of Anti-Semitic Attitudes," *American Journal of Orthopsychiatry*, vol. 18, 1948, pp. 163-167.

accredited psychoanalysts, and the conclusions both enlarge and confirm those of Frenkel-Brunswik and Sanford as well as those of other investigators.

Two extreme types of anti-Semitic types were theoretically set up by the authors. The one is the anti-Semite whose attitude seems to be one of superficial conformity to the values, in this respect, of the dominant group; the other is the anti-Semite whose hostility derives from some definite disorder in his own personality structure to which his anti-Semitism has a specific relation. All the cases encountered fell between the two extremes, presenting both elements in varying proportions.

All the patients suffered from anxiety. They were insecure in their group membership. They had a basic feeling of rejection by the world, a feeling of not belonging. They failed to form safe and secure personal attachments. They felt a continuous apprehension of injury to their integrity as individuals. They frequently suffered from an exaggerated sense of vulnerability. They do not seem able to derive support from their own identity as persons. Because of their insecurity, their confused and unstable image of themselves, they lack direction and make erratic shifts in their group associations. Fundamentally they are weak, immature, passive, dependent, with the desire to control unrealized in the normal channels of constructive social action. They endeavor to deny to consciousness the image of themselves as inferior and crippled.

> Overtly they have the urge to conform but unconsciously they resent the compulsory submission and react with destructive rebellion. At the unconscious level they have no hope of being able to repair their damaged identity as persons; basically they accept it as irreversible. However, this basic despair is concealed from consciousness, where they behave in exactly the opposite manner. The core of these character traits is the weak identity, the immaturity, the unconscious passivity, the intense sense of vulnerability to social injury—all of which are denied in consciousness where they are replaced by aggression.

In relation to such a syndrome anti-Semitism plays a functionally well-defined role. It is a defense against self-hate, a displacement of the self-destroying trends of the character structure described. At the psychic level anti-Semitism here assumes the function of a profound though irrational effort to restore the crippled self, and at the social level it constitutes a pattern producing secondary emotional gain. Were the anti-Semite to permit his internal conflict, between what he *is* unconsciously and what he thinks of himself as being consciously, to proceed to its logical conclusion, he would find the consequences unbearable. And so he escapes the dilemma by preoccupation with external events, thus achieving a spurious relief from tensions and the bogus satisfaction of being a member of a powerful, united group, an in-group in whose program of action he can join. Nevertheless, the central conflict continues with unabated intensity.

To summarize: the prejudice pattern is created through the mobilization of the following series of mechanisms: (*a*) by denial of anxiety and substitution of aggression; (*b*) by an effort to reinforce affiliation with dominant social groups; (*c*) by the elaboration of a variety of reaction formations and compensatory emotional drives; (*d*) by renunciation of parts of the person's image of self and the concomitant substitution of a borrowed identity. Associated with this there is a suppression and repression of anxiety-ridden impulses.

Having submissively renounced parts of their own individuality they feel deep resentment against anyone who does not do likewise. They demand that other people should conform to the same restrictions. The demand for conformity is thus a result of partial self-renunciation. The person who is forced to renounce his real self as the price of social acceptance is doubly sensitive to others who do not conform. Here lies the root of the excessive reaction to difference which characterizes our anti-Semitic patients. Every sign of non-conformity in another person is, as it were, an unwelcome reminder of the painful sacrifice that the prejudiced person has made by renouncing part of his self in the vain hope of achieving group identification. The fear of the "different" is hence not in proportion to the extent of objective, measurable differences; rather it grows in proportion to the implied ego threat, in other words, to the degree to which the difference symbolizes the fruitless suppression of the self. All prejudiced people insist on conformity to the extent of trying to destroy the non-conformist. Since conformity connotes surrender of the individuality, a person who is "different" symbolizes non-surrender, and therefore, an individual who is strong, mature, independent, superior, able to stand up against others with his differences. The prejudiced person cannot bear the implied comparison. Because of the inherent weakness of his own self-image, the "different" person represents a potential menace to his own integrity as an individual or whatever there is left of it. The inevitable response is to attack the menace, the person who symbolizes difference.

The elaborated and highly inconsistent picture of the stereotype Jew forms a perfect projective screen for the anti-Semite's irreconcilable impulses. The Jew is at once successful and low class; capitalist and communist; clannish and an intruder into other people's society; highly moral and spiritual and given to low forms of behavior such as greed, sharp business practices, and is also dirty; magically omnipotent and omniscient, and incredibly helpless and defenseless and therefore readily destroyed.

What any individual projects upon the Jew invariably represents unacceptable components of the self or components envied in others, at least unacceptable on the conscious level though unconsciously such attributes form an active part of the person's psychic drives.[15] Hence what is consciously rejected, the rejection of the Jew may, at the unconscious level, be represented by a strong identification with him. This identification, because of the symbolic aspect of the Jew's weakness, his crippled, defenseless position, cannot be admitted, because to do so would be to endanger the person's ego and social position. It is therefore denied and in its place there is substituted an identification with the attacker, in order to avoid being victimized and also to draw strength through identification. Thus, as Ackerman and Jahoda state:

> . . . the Jew at one and the same time stands for the weakness or strength of the self; for conscience, for those parts of the person which blame and accuse the weakness of the self, and also for

[15] N. W. Ackerman, "Anti-Semitic Motivation in a Psychopathic Personality," *Psychoanalytic Review*, vol. 34, 1947, pp. 76-101.

those primitive appetites and aggressions which must be denied as the price of social acceptance.

It may be objected that inferences based on data obtained from patients who have been psychoanalytically treated cannot be justly applied to the analysis of the behavior of normal persons. To this objection several replies may be made. First, it is very doubtful whether normal persons are ever anti-Semitic in the disordered sense here described, and since a very large proportion of persons give evidence of disordered character structure it is very likely that the observations made and the conclusions drawn from them are valid for a great segment of the population of anti-Semites. Second, the inability to pay the fees of a psychoanalyst is no mark of normality, and third, in any event the study of the pathological is still the best way of learning to understand the nature of the pathological, and anti-Semitism is a pathological disorder of society.

Anti-Semitism is, of course, only one form of group prejudice, as is race prejudice in general. Other kinds of group prejudice, such as religious prejudices, national prejudices, sex prejudices (in the nineteenth century women were the "natives," the inferior group),[16] class prejudices, and the like, are merely special forms of the same general phenomenon of group prejudice. As soon as one becomes aware of group membership and identifies oneself with that group the ground is laid for the development of group prejudice in some particular form. The prejudice may be of the most benign kind and socially not make for the least disharmony. On the other hand it may develop under certain conditions in so disoperatively strong a manner as to threaten the very existence of the society in which it appears. This happens to be the case in the United States as well as in some other lands. Awareness of this fact together with our understanding of the psychodynamics of the development of such forms of behavior suggests the immediate necessity of reconsidering our processes of socializing children in relation to the health of the social structure as a whole.

[16] Ashley Montagu, *Man's Most Dangerous Myth.*

From what has already been said it should be obvious why the teaching of the facts about race or race prejudice will not be adequate to solve the problem. The roots of prejudice are woven into the very psychic structure of the person, and unless we attend to the soil from which they draw nourishment it will not help either the resulting plant or ourselves if we attempt to cure its sickness by lopping off the ailing leaves. The soil in which race prejudice grows is the social experience to which the developing person is exposed, and it is to this that we must attend if we are to be saved from the sickness which is "race."

Let us never forget that race prejudice is at its strongest where social maturity is at its weakest.

19. The Nature of Race Relations

WHEN WE SPEAK OF "race relations" what do we mean? I think it will be agreed that it is not always clear what we mean, and that a great deal in this phrase is taken for granted which requires more explicit definition than it usually receives.

"Race relations" represent a form of interaction between certain social groups. In order to clarify the nature of these relations we have to ask and attempt to answer two questions: (1) In what way are the social groups involved in "race relations" distinguished as social groups, and (2) What are the determinants and what is the nature of the specific types of interaction between so-called "racial" groups?

In response to the first question the answer is usually returned that the social groups involved in "race relations" are distinguished by the fact that they belong to recognizable and distinct "races." It is at this point and in virtue of this type of answer that the first and principal element of confusion is introduced into the subject. Implicit in this type of answer is the belief that biological differences exist between certain groups, called "races," and that these biological differences to a large extent determine the types of interaction which occur in "race relations." As illustrative of this point we may quote Sir Arthur Keith, the distinguished morphologist. He writes, "prejudices are inborn; are part of the birthright of every child." These prejudices "have been grafted in our natures for a special purpose—an evolutionary purpose. . . . They are essential parts of the evolutionary machinery which Nature employed throughout eons of time to

From *Social Forces*, vol. 25, 1947, 336-342.

secure the separation of man into permanent groups and thus to attain production of new and improved races of Mankind. . . . Nature endowed her tribal teams with the spirit of antagonism for her own purposes. It has come down to us and creeps out from our modern life in many shapes, as national rivalries and jealousies and as racial hatreds. The modern name for this spirit of antagonism is race-prejudice."[1]

This view has it that "races" exist in order that prejudices shall operate among human groups to produce conflicts between them. In this way, it is alleged, by "competition" between such groups Nature (spelled with a capital "N") secures the survival of the fittest, and the perpetuation of "new and improved races of man-kind." In the name of such a view of "race relations," the ex-termination, suppression, disenfranchisement, segregation of, and discrimination against other racial groups is held to be not only permissible but even necessary and obligatory. And this is called "competition" between such groups—a kind of competition which in the modern world amounts to tying the hands and feet of your "competitor" and then giving the verdict against him for losing the race which he has been prevented from running.

The biologistic bias which is associated with the term "race" is implicit in the thinking of most persons about "race relations." Their "race" stereotype, as Walter Lippmann has quoted William James on stereotypes in general, is "a way of substituting order for the great blooming, buzzing confusion of reality."[2] But what the "biologistic-race" stereotype, in fact, succeeds in doing is to introduce disorder under the guise of "order," an "order" which leads to disordered conduct and thinking. His belief in the biological foundations of "race prejudice" and in the biological differences between what he esteems to be racial groups gives the ordinary man a mandate for acting perfectly self-righteously as he does. For is it not "natural" so to act? In fact, for the

---

[1] Arthur Keith, *The Place of Prejudice in Modern Civilization* (New York, John Day, 1931). These views are repeated in Keith's book *Evolution and Ethics* (New York, Putnam, 1947).
[2] Walter Lippmann, *Public Opinion* (New York, Penguin Books, 1946), p. 96.

ordinary man, though he may never have analyzed them so explicitly, "race relations" mean much the same things as they mean for Sir Arthur Keith.[3] In America it is part of the overt cultural pattern for such views to be implemented every day in the firm belief that "races" are unequal and that the "inferior races" must be kept in their place. *That* might, in fact, serve as a summary definition of the ordinary man's conception of the nature of "race relations," so charmingly expressed by many Southerners in the phrase "The nigrah's all right—so long as he keeps in his place," or by other all over America, "Some of my best friends are Jews, but look what happens to real-estate values as soon as you let one settle in your neighborhood."

Persons socialized in an environment in which the emotional and intellectual consequences of such a belief are seen in the everyday behavior of the members of their own group scarcely ever entertain a doubt as to the soundness of the view they thus come to acquire. They function as if nothing could be sounder than their "race" prejudices as guides to their conduct in their relations with certain other persons or groups. There are vast numbers of such people, particularly in the United States, who for the most part are unaware of the fact that there exists or could possibly exist any serious challenge to their views, and, as I can testify from my own experience, it comes as a genuine surprise to many otherwise tolerably well-educated persons to learn that some of their most cherished beliefs concerning the alleged differences which are supposed to exist between various "races" do not have a leg to stand upon.

Whether they are consciously aware of it or not, most Christian whites in their relations with members of other "races" act toward them not only as if they were different but also as if they were inferior. Whether they ever consciously formulate it or not they act as if they believe the difference and the inferiority to be innately determined. The fact that in many cases there do exist certain obvious biologically determined physical

[3] For a fuller account and critical examination of Keith's views see Ashley Montagu, *Man's Most Dangerous Myth: The Fallacy of Race*, 3rd ed. (New York, Harper, 1952).

differences renders it very easy to assume that all other observed differences are similarly biologically determined. In this way, a natural justification, as it were, is found for social behavior in "race relations." The inferior must not be allowed to drag down the superior. The member of the "inferior race" must be "kept in his place."

The manner, then, in which socially recognized groups are distinguished from other types of social groups, is, for the racist, that they are biologically characterized, that is to say, endowed with biological qualities which are said to distinguish each of them in more or less unique ways. The Negro, for example, has a black skin, kinky hair, thick lips, a low intelligence, and tends to be lazy—all traits which are considered undesirable and against which barriers must be erected to prevent their dissemination within the white group. Jews have a white though sallow oily skin, a hooked nose, curly hair (these, of course, are the stereotypes), gesticulate, are very aggressive, unscrupulous in business dealings, and have shrewder or sharper (not "better") brains than gentiles. Hence, barriers must be erected against them because everyone else is at a disadvantage in competition with them and because their social traits are objectionable. Variations upon these two themes of too little and too much are utilized by racists everywhere as providing a basis for the social control of other groups.

It would be a mistake to assume that such a system of beliefs represents nothing more than a notable talent for self-deception, nothing but a system of rationalizations. Many persons, who are not altogether unaware of what they are doing, do indulge in such elaborate rationalizations. But it is important to realize that there are a large number of persons who honestly believe that their racist views are unquestionably sound.

Whether rationalized or otherwise, most of us know how fatally strong and dangerous such beliefs are. Those of us who have devoted some time to the study of the "race" problem know that there is no ground for believing that there exist any significant biologically determined behavioral differences or capacities for performance as between the so-called "races" of man. The evidence points, on the other hand, very strongly to the fact that the very real behavioral differences which exist are socially, *not* biologically determined.[4]

A consideration of the evidence strongly suggests that under the conditions of socialization in which all vertebrate groups develop—I am deliberately avoiding the suggestion that it is inherent in such groups—identification with the group of which one is a member is an inevitable process. Children, even at the pre-nursery school age, are already making this identification and distinguishing between persons who belong to their group and those who do not.[5] The existence of groups is founded upon group solidarity, which is in itself based upon a consciousness of kind or identification, and certain feelings of tension and insecurity in the presence of other groups are, at least in human societies, under the usual conditions of social development, inevitable. Human beings grow to be dependent upon the familiar and tend to feel insecure in the presence of the unfamiliar, the strange, and the unlike. That is basically why men tend to cling to their own group. Membership in a group ministers to man's basic need for security; it satisfies his dependency needs. In that respect his own group is superior to all others, and the existence of other groups which may impinge upon the integrity of his own is taken to be, at least, a potential threat to his own security. The very fact that another group differs from his own is often, in the presence of such a group, sufficient to engender a feeling of insecurity in the individual. Such feelings are easily turned into anxiety and hostility toward the out-group, and where the devices which may serve as the vehicles for such hostility are already at hand they are easily turned into group prejudice. "Differences are emphasized because they offer the readiest rationalization for defense against real or fancied dangers. It is easiest to detect the enemy when certain qualitative differences mark him; it is easier to attack him when these differences are readily pointed out."[6]

Now, the point I wish to make here is that in the development

[4] *Ibid.*, pp. 8-16.
[5] Ruth Horowitz, "Racial Aspects of Self Identification in Nursery School Children," *Journal of Psychology*, vol. 7, 1939, pp. 91-99.
[6] Fred Brown, "A Socio-psychological Analysis of Race Prejudice," *Journal of Abnormal and Social Psychology*, vol. 27, 1932-33, pp. 364-374, 394.

of such group prejudices there is nothing inherent. There is no such thing in man as biologically determined group antagonism, or in terms of popular belief, there is no instinctual basis for such prejudices, and under a sensible socialization process such prejudices need never appear. These prejudices do, in fact, appear because human beings are taught group exclusivity, because they are taught by the continuous reinforcement of example and precept that they belong to a group which is both different and superior to others. They are taught to take pride in their own group, to regard themselves as members of an in-group. Under such conditions group prejudice is inevitable. Group prejudice becomes a culturally sanctioned force, handed on from one generation to another, specifically directed against members of out-groups physically or culturally different. Such group prejudice represents a biased nonlogical attitude based on erroneous judgments and held as final by the subject.

Realizing and understanding this we may perceive that it would be quite possible in the socialization of the person to produce a sympathetic appreciation of the value of other groups and to eliminate all feelings of insecurity and anxiety in the presence of such groups. This appears to have been achieved in Brazil.[7] There is no reason to think that it could not be achieved everywhere else in the world were the will to do so but present. It is a job that enlightened educators must in increasing numbers take in hand.

Another important aspect of "race relations" to which I should like to draw attention, is that "race relations" are essentially of the nature of class and caste relations, a special case of so-called "race relations."

In lands, for example, in which class distinctions are well marked and there exist no significantly large ethnic groups other than the dominant national population, group prejudice assumes the form of class prejudice. There is hardly any difference between class prejudice and race prejudice. Almost every condition found in the one is to be encountered in the other, even down to the imputed biological differences.[8] The upper class make

[7] D. Pierson, *Negroes in Brazil* (Chicago, University of Chicago Press, 1942).
[8] For a brilliant discussion of this subject see Lancelot Hogben's chapter

THE NATURE OF RACE RELATIONS 239

much of "breeding," of "good stock" or "birth" or "ancestry," and will not generally marry out of their class or "quality." To marry out of one's class is to lose caste, not only socially but also "biologically," for such a person's children can belong only to the class of the "inferior" parent. There are, of course, exceptions, but this is the rule, a rule which is strictly applied to women, but much less strictly to men. The upper-class male generally elevates the woman he chooses to marry to his own class; the lower-class male generally reduces his wife and children to his own class. The "biology" and stratification of the classes are patrilineally determined, that is to say, they operate through and in favor of the male line. This is not the case where ethnic crossing is concerned, and it constitutes one of the few differences between the workings of class and "race" prejudice. Thus, for example, should an upper-class white male marry a Negroid female, the offspring will, in the United States, at least, belong to the class of the mother, not to that of the father's family.

It should be clear that in societies in which there is an extreme division of men into classes whose interests are necessarily opposed and in which the means of earning a living—the economic system—is organized upon an extremely competitive basis, there will be abundant opportunities for class or "race" antagonisms.

It is methodologically and from the practical viewpoint useful to understand that "race" prejudice is, in fact, a special case of class prejudice, a prejudice that will be developed under certain conditions where different ethnic groups are thrown together in significant numbers. In the absence of such conditions or in the absence of a variety of ethnic groups the prejudices of the upper classes against all members of the lower classes and their conduct toward the members of all such classes will, in almost every respect, take the form which is usually associated with "race" prejudice. Wherever classes exist, there exists class prejudice. In socially stratified class societies the shift from class

"Race and Prejudice" in his *Dangerous Thoughts* (New York, Norton, 1940), pp. 44-58. See also Richard H. Tawney, *Equality* (New York, Harcourt, Brace, 1931).

prejudice to "race" prejudice is very easily achieved and, in fact, amounts to little more than the change of names, for the "race" against which prejudice is now especially focused is but another class or caste, even though it may be regarded as something substantially different.

A class differs from a caste in that a greater degree of social mobility is, in all respects, permitted between the members of the upper and the lower social classes than is permitted between castes. The class is dynamic, the caste static. A caste is a specific, socially limited status group. The function of the limiting factors of caste are, in effect, primarily to create barriers against sexual relations between members of the hegemonic caste and those of the "inferior castes," and, secondarily, to regulate the social status, privileges, and social mobility of the members of the "inferior castes."

A writer has attempted to show that "race relations" are not caste relations, and for this purpose he assumes that Brahminic-Indian society represents the only developed caste system in the world.[9] This seems to me an extraordinarily wrongheaded view to take and nothing short of astonishing when the author declares that he does not know of any sociologist who relies, for his criteria of caste relationship, on any other than the Brahminic-Indian caste system. On the other hand, I don't know of any sociologist who does! The criteria which most sociologists take for the recognition of caste relationships are those which I have stated in the definition given above. No one, so far as I know, ever intended to say that the details of caste relations in the United States, for example, operate exactly as they do in India. In point of fact there is a very close similarity, but there are very definite differences in detail. The caste system in India represents but one form of caste relations; other forms of caste relations prevail elsewhere in the world, and it only adds to the confusion to make such arbitrary claims as that the Indian caste system is the type which must be exemplified by all other caste systems if these latter are to be recognized at all.

Mr. Cox, the writer referred to, notes that "caste has reference

[9] Oliver C. Cox, "Race and Caste: A Distinction," *American Journal of Sociology*, vol. 50, 1945, pp. 360-368.

to the internal order of a society; race suggests a whole people, wherever found about the globe."[10] Is that, indeed, all that "race" suggests? I rather think that it suggests a great deal more. Does it not also suggest a mode of behavior toward that people wherever it may be found upon the earth? Whenever the internal order of one group enters into interaction with another, are not such forms of behavior likely to be essentially of the nature of caste relations? Mr. Cox goes on to say, "A people in actual world dispersion will not conceive of themselves as members of a caste."[11]

That is precisely where Mr. Cox demonstrates the fallacy of his argument, and he does so in other places at greater length. He feels that unless caste behavior is actually explicitly recognized and structured within a society, given definite names, and fully recognized for what it is, then a caste system does not exist. In that sense we certainly do not have a caste system in the United States, but in the light of actual social functioning between different ethnic groups we most certainly do have a caste system in the United States, even though it may overtly go unrecognized as such. We simply call our caste system, which is made up for the most part of our fears and anxieties, "race relations." The rigidity of our caste system varies from virtual completeness in the South to a somewhat looser organization in the North and elsewhere, but the assignment of roles and the maintenance of endogamous barriers tends to be as strongly enforced as it is in India.[12]

The point surely is that certain so-called minority groups, particularly the Negro in the United States, are treated as if they were members of an inferior caste, and in their particular case "race" is made a basis for the distinction. Germans, Frenchmen, Spaniards, Scandinavians, and others are erroneously conceived to be "races," but members of these nations or so-called "races" are rarely treated as if they were members of an inferior caste.[13]

[10] *Ibid.*, p. 363.
[11] *Ibid.*, p. 363.
[12] For a criticism of Mr. Cox's views see Norman D. Humphrey, "American Race Relations and the Caste System," *Psychiatry*, vol. 8, 1945, pp. 379-381.
[13] Except in certain local areas, but not throughout the United States as a whole, as is the case with the Negro.

The fact is that Negroes are so treated. I think it is a clarification, not an obfuscation, of the nature of "race relations" to recognize that fact. It is certainly not that Negroes regard themselves as members of a caste, but that from the point of view of other social groups they are so regarded in terms of the conduct and controls which are exhibited in relation to them.

Furthermore, in terms of social relations there can be only class and/or caste relations. "Race" can serve only as a sign, within any given society, for the exhibition of certain forms of behavior. Whatever one may call this behavior it is certainly not race behavior in the sense in which "race" is commonly understood. There is no biological determinant in it of any kind, and it is the nature of that implication concerning which it is desirable to be clear, and in its unclear form to avoid when considering the nature of "race relations." And where such relations are actually in the nature of caste relations that fact should be clearly and explicitly recognized. "Race," let us remember, in the words of the late unlamented Benito Mussolini, in his pre-racist days, "is a feeling, not a reality." And if groups are treated *as if* they were castes let us clearly recognize that fact whether or not such castes correspond to some paradigmatic form or not.

The important point to grasp, and this cannot be too often or too emphatically repeated, is that "race relations" are not biological relations but social relations. The so-called race problem is not a biological problem, it is a social problem, and as such it does not even present any socially relevant biological problems. "Race" is a term for a state of mind which is created by certain types of special social conditions, and it is most definitely not a state of mind created by the fact that some persons have white skins while others have black. It is rather that under certain social conditions skin color becomes a socially relevant fact.[14] It is that a socially determined state of mind under certain unfortunate conditions gives rise to social relations between ethnic or so-called minority groups and certain more powerful groups, which are essentially of the nature of caste relations.

[14] R. D. G. Simons, *The Colour of the Skin in Human Relations* (Princeton, Elsevier, 1961).

In the social context of America, to take a familiar example, those groups which are referred to as "races" are usually treated as if they were castes. Negroes, Jews, Mongoloids, and Indians are in actual practice treated by the dominant white groups as if they were members of specific lower castes. A more or less distinct caste order is even recognizable, Negroes being at the bottom of the caste system ("The white man's floor is the Negro's ceiling") while Mongoloids and Indians stand somewhere between these and the Jews, with the Christian whites arranging themselves in a variety of superior castes, based for the most part on lineage or family, religion, generations of inherited wealth, fame, influence, and similar factors. Compared to the Brahminic-Indian caste system, that which exists in the United States is somewhat less rigidly organized, but that it exists there cannot be the least doubt.

To our first question, then, we may reply that the social groups involved in "race relations" are distinguished as such in that they are treated as if they were more or less distinctively recognized as having a specific caste status.

To our second question we may reply that the determinants and nature of the specific types of interaction between so-called racial groups are entirely social in nature and have nothing whatever to do with biological factors of any kind.

When men wish to exploit the members of certain other groups they can justify the implementation of their desires by calling the groups they exploit "inferior." And they can do so in what they believe to be perfectly good faith and reason.

To my mind the outstanding example of this type is represented by the late Professor Karl Pearson. Pearson was a man of great distinction of mind, unusual breadth of learning, and considerable humanity. He was one of the greatest scientists of our time. Nevertheless, in his great book *The Grammar of Science,* he could write at the beginning of this century in the following terms: "It is a false view of human solidarity, a weak humanitarianism, not a true humanism, which regrets that a capable and stalwart race of white men should replace a dark-skinned tribe which can neither utilize its land for the full benefit of mankind, nor contribute its quota to the common stock of human knowledge." And in a footnote to this Pearson adds, "This sentence must not be taken to justify a brutalizing destruction of human life. The anti-social effects of accelerating the survival of the fittest may go far to destroy the preponderating fitness of the survivor. At the same time there is cause for human satisfaction in the replacement of the aborigines throughout America and Australia by white races of far higher civilization."[15] Well might Alice James, in 1890, remark upon "the profound irreconcilable conviction" of the English "that outlying regions are their preserves, for they alone of human races massacre savages out of pure virtue."[16]

If racism had not already existed, the age of imperialism would have been forced to invent it.[17] When certain social groups feel obliged to behave toward certain groups of men in a manner which their moral teaching forbids, they can—and do—easily say that such human beings do not really belong to the class of mankind to which such teachings apply. As Professor Howard W. Odum has recently pointed out, the Southern view with respect to the Negro may be summed up in the statement that the Negro's place is outside the common brotherhood of mankind.[18] When the pro-slavers had quoted at them the text from *Exodus* 21:15, "And he that stealeth a man, and selleth him, or if he be found in his hand, he shall surely be put to death," and many others like it, it provoked the reply that the Negro was not a man from the standpoint of those who wished to maintain the slave trade and the institution of slavery. Or, granting that he was a man, he was an inferior type of man whose proper place

[15] Karl Pearson, *The Grammar of Science* (New York, Everyman's Library, Dutton, 1937), p. 310.
[16] *Alice James.* A. R. Burr, ed. (New York, Dodd, Mead, 1934), p. 138.
[17] Hannah Arendt, "Race-Thinking Before Racism," *Review of Politics*, vol. 6, 1944, pp. 36-73; Richard Hofstadter, *Social Darwinism in American Thought 1860–1915* (Philadelphia, University of Pennsylvania Press, 1944).
[18] "Why was southern conduct, then [in the year 1942-43] so contrary to all preaching and principles which, without a peradventure of doubt, were sincere? Why didn't the tenets of fellowship and Christian religion hold here? The only answer was that the Negro did not come within the framework of human brotherhood." Howard W. Odum, *Race and Rumors of Race* (Chapel Hill, University of North Carolina Press, 1943), p. 23.

in relation to the white man was one of subordination. The doctrine of white supremacy was a deliberate invention; it has become for many an article of faith, and it had been generalized to involve other ethnic and minority groups all over the world. Such views are social in origin and social in their consequences, and what is more they have, in the United States at least, become institutionalized in that definite forms of behavior are prescribed in relation to such ethnic and minority groups. In thirty out of the fifty states of this great Union marriage between Negroes and whites is illegal.[19] In the state of Mississippi it is a punishable offense to publish any statement to the effect that the Negro is or should be the social equal of the white.[20] No Negro in the United States is free to live or work as the white man is. The white man's floor, it is held, must remain the Negro's ceiling. Possessed of all the necessary qualifications, very few Negroes are free to enter any institution of learning which is open to whites. In many parts of the land Negroes may not enter hotels, restaurants, places of amusement, public vehicles, and so on, either at all or except under very definite restrictions. As one Negro leader put it:

We are the unwanted people and I mean practically every Negro is unwanted practically everywhere. Most of the good things that are said and done in America are not meant for us Negroes. Thousands of preachers talk of brotherhood, but they don't mean brotherhood with Negroes—not in most churches. Orators say all men are created equal, but they don't mean equality in houses, jobs, schools, or transportation for Negroes . . . the more the Negro tries to rise and be a good useful American, the more he is pushed down.[21]

[19] Ashley Montagu, Man's Most Dangerous Myth, pp. 302-308.
[20] Mississippi, 1930 Code Ann., sec. 1103: "Any person, firm or corporation who shall be guilty of printing, publishing or circulating printed, typewritten or written matter urging or presenting for public acceptance or general information, arguments or suggestions in favor of social equality or of intermarriage between whites and negroes, shall be guilty of a misdemeanour and subject to a fine not exceeding five hundred dollars or imprisonment not exceeding six months or both fine and imprisonment in the discretion of the court."
[21] Reported in The Christian Science Monitor, 2nd ed., June 12, 1945, p. 11.

And yet there are some who assert that the Negro is not treated as if he were a member of a caste, that he does not belong to a distinct and inferior caste in America.

It is not organic conditions which make whites behave in this way toward Negroes, but social conditions. In all so-called "race relations" the relations are determined by social not by organic conditions, and that is, of course, where the very real hope lies for the future. What is produced by social conditions can be changed by socially instrumental conditions, and if only a sufficient number of us keep working away at it I am confident that "racism" will one day be regarded as one of the major aberrations of an early stage in our social development. As a reviewer of my book on race has put it:

> My own guess is that posterity will view the racism of our time much as we view the witchcraft of the seventeenth century. Then there were many who blindly believed in witchcraft, and others who felt that there must be at least something to cause such widespread belief. It was hard then for men to believe that all this was pure error; just as it is hard now for men to believe that about racism. But I can see no essential differences between witchcraft and racism as nonsense.[22]

Early conditioning in infancy and childhood, frustrations suffered at all ages, the development of basic insecurities which our society is so fertile in producing, the need to find some outlet for unexpended aggression, scapegoatism, economic insecurity and rivalry, political and industrial exploitation, the American credo of successful achievement in terms of material values, and the essential lack of maturity which characterizes the American adult personality are conditions which not only determine the relations between different groups but also between different persons of the same group. All these conditions are sources of interpersonal conflict and of group hostilities, and until they are replaced by functionally more equilibrated forms of motivation we shall never be rid of such conflicts and hostilities.

[22] Bookwright, in review of *Man's Most Dangerous Myth: The Fallacy of Race*, *New York Herald Tribune Book Review*, August 12, 1945, p. 6.

20. Social Problems of an Aging Population

THE AVERAGE EXPECTANCY of life of a male child at birth in the United States is sixty-nine years, of a female child seventy-five years. The population of persons of both sexes over the age of sixty-five years in the United States at the present time is in the vicinity of twelve million. Within another generation it is estimated that this number will have passed the twenty-five million mark. Never before in the history of mankind has a population had so many older people as the United States. In less than a generation more than one-eighth of the total population of the United States will be over the age of sixty-five years. This fact has consequences which we would do well to forsee and prepare for, if we would have our society function as happily and as efficiently as possible.

The changes which have taken place in relation to the problems of age have been so many and have occurred so rapidly that most of us have not quite caught up with them. Most of us have a feeling that something has changed about age, and many of us who have turned the corner of middle age have become more than ever conscious of the fact that life no longer begins at forty but at fifty. Indeed, it was not so long ago that a person aged fifty was considered to be old. What used to be called "the prime of life"—a phrase, interestingly enough, little used in our time—centered about thirty-five years of age. It is still true

From *Journal of the National Medical Association*, vol. 52, 1960, pp. 338-342.

that at thirty-five a person is likely to be in better physical shape than at forty-five, but there can be little doubt that the additional ten years gives him the advantage of greater maturity, and that by and large his accumulated experience and judgment are likely to be socially more valuable than those of the person a decade younger. The bureaucratic rubber-stamp conception of aging must make way for one more in keeping with the realities. Business no longer considers the man past forty a poor risk; on the other hand, he is more likely to be preferred because of his greater maturity of judgment and experience.

There has, in fact, been a definite cultural change in our attitudes toward age which we have scarcely yet recognized, and this may be briefly summarized in the statement that insofar as age is concerned we tend to judge people not so much, as it were, by the calendar as by the barometer. Many people are gradually and rightly coming to the conclusion that the important thing about age is not measured by the clock but by *the actual state of being of the person no matter what his chronologic age may be.* This is the distinction required by the human biologist in the terms *chronologic* as compared with *physiologic* age. What a person is in reality is what he is physiologically so far as his physical age is concerned, and not what he is arbitrarily considered to be within the framework of chronologic or calendric time into which he has been forced. A person may be thirty years of age chronologically, but physiologically he may be considerably less than the norm which the majority of people approach at that age, or he may be considerably older. That is to say while he may be thirty years of age by the mechanized clock he is not thirty years of age by the true clock, the clock of his own developmental rate in terms of physiology. We all know of people, some of whom look much younger and act much younger than their age, while others look much older and act much older than their age. We also know some people who look much younger than their chronologic age but who act much older, and some of us know some persons who look much older and act much younger than the norm for their chronologic age.

This is where the concept of psychologic age enters. The true age of a social human being is essentially more accurately expressed by his psychological age. This is not the same thing as the psychologist's mental age or intelligence quotient; it is much broader than both of these. What I mean by psychologic age is not only the degree of intellectual development of the person, but also the degree of his environmental development together with the harmonic blendings of these two aspects of mind to form a personality well-balanced, sound and mature in judgment and humane in feeling. People may be quite advanced in chronologic and physiologic age but they may be quite retarded in psychologic age, or vice versa. Hence, in addition to being a most inadequate measure of physiologic age, chronologic age is also a poor measure of psychologic age.

But, perhaps an even more important concept than any of these is what I shall call *social age*. By social age I mean the measure of a person's ability to behave in a mature manner in relation to his fellow men and their institutions. If chronologic age is a poor measure of psychologic age, it is an even poorer measure of social age. Hence, in view of all these factors we shall have to deepen our understandings of the meaning of age and revise our traditional conceptions of it. This seems to me an area in which much re-education is necessary if we are to develop a true understanding of the meaning of age and utilize the resources of age which we at present still tend to neglect.

In other words we need to take a more intelligent, a more realistic, view of age, and perhaps we ought to accustom ourselves to speaking of *aging* rather than of *age,* since aging is a process, a dynamic process, rather than a static condition. We have tended so much in the past, and still continue to do so in the present, to think in terms of age grades or statuses that we have, as it were, ossified the concept of aging and broken it up into a number of grades. This is a way of looking at aging which we have inherited from the remote past, and while for legalistic purposes there may be some value in it. It is an unsatisfactory and inefficient way of dealing with the process of aging unless its arbitrary nature is fully recognized.

If we can once get our categories or functions of chronologic, physiologic, psychologic, and social age clear, we may then begin to understand that aging is properly regarded as a process of growth, a process of growth which may reach different levels of development in the same person as between each of these functions. The practical consequence of this understanding is the appreciation of the important fact that when we speak of age we are speaking of a complex of conditions each of which may be proceeding in development at very different rates and have reached different degrees of differentiation. For example, of a person aged sixty years we would correctly conclude that his chronologic age is sixty years by our reckoning, but we could not take it for granted that he is either physically or constitutionally on the decline, nor would we be right in assuming that he had stopped growing physically, and certainly we would not be right in assuming that he had stopped growing psychologically or socially. Indeed, we now know that in all these connections human beings possess remarkable capacities for growth no matter to what advanced chronologic age they may live. Hence, when anyone speaks of "old age" we ought no longer to take it for granted that the user knows what he means or that what he means is correct, but we should hang a question mark on the term every time it is used and see to it that our questions are answered, for while high walls may not a prison make, our traditional prejudices do. We would do well not to lose sight of the head for the gray hairs. We must drop our "race" prejudice against "age," and judge each person for himself, as a whole and as a person of parts. So far as his place in the community is concerned each person is called upon to play certain roles (the dynamic aspects of his various statuses) and to perform certain tasks. His capacity for those roles and tasks should not be judged by some arbitrary standard of age, but by his ability to perform those roles and tasks. This is the only sound way to evaluate a person, and the only efficient and just way. Furthermore, this is the manner in which we must learn to evaluate the aging population if we are to plan and achieve a happy solution to the social problems of an aging population.

In contrast to the attitudes of the past, present trends are much more enlightened, but the enlightenment needs to be more widely diffused. With the formal initiation in the second half of the twentieth century of the scientific study of aging (gerontology) and the development of a new branch of medicine devoted to the process of aging and the treatment of the aged (geriatrics), there has for the first time become possible the development of a body of knowledge which may be constructively utilized to make the process of aging, from every point of view, a happier one. Not only this, as a consequence of the growing interest in aging it is highly probable that medicine as a whole will be substantially influenced to pay more attention to the conditions contributing toward the maintenance of health. Our medicine today is largely a medicine of disease, and this has been especially true of the practice of medicine with respect to the aged. Present trends indicate an increasing interest in the preventive medical aspects of aging. This is an area of geriatrics which is ready for very considerable advances. I believe that in this area one can best begin not with the old but with the young.

The time to prepare human beings for "old age" is not when they have reached or are about to reach it, but long before they have entered upon it. Everyone will agree that preparation for old age is a psychologically necessary preparation for the individual, and an extremely important step socially for the community. Hence, one of the objectives we should aim to achieve is the institution in our schools of courses on "Growing Up," and such a course should form part of the general education of every high school and college student. It is in such a course that the future citizen and future aging person can be made to understand the problems of aging and be prepared to meet them satisfactorily in others and eventually in himself. Such a course will dwell not only upon the problems and solutions of aging, but upon the whole process of growth and development in relation to which the process of aging will receive its proper but not undue emphasis.

In addition to producing a change in the attitude toward aging on the part of others, we need to produce a change in the attitude toward aging on the part of the aging themselves. For as is well known, the aging—as a result of the culturally determined attitudes of the society into which they are born—in our culture have tended to feel that they are not only the forgotten ones but also the unwanted ones, the superfluous ones, the dispensable ones, the displaced persons of our culture. Such a feeling makes, of course, for a most unhappy psychological state. There are other cultures in which the old are simply abandoned and left to die, and some in which they are killed. In our culture we have had more refined ways of achieving the same ends. We who talk so much of our national resources have done what we could to abandon and kill off one of the greatest, if not the greatest, of our national resources, the know-how, the experience, and the wisdom of those who have lived long enough to acquire them. In enlightened circles the trend is away from such social errors, but the need is, as I have already stated, to diffuse that enlightenment much more widely. The apathy and despondency from which so many aging people suffer in our culture is as tragic as it is wholly unnecessary and wasteful. The cash cost is enormous enough, and the toll in human misery is frightful. It is not only the psychological unhappiness which is so great but there is also a great toll in the organic disorders, the diseases which accompany the conditions of apathy, despondency, and the feeling of not being wanted. The psychosomatic illnesses of the aging would to a large extent be reduced were the aging but made to feel, as they should be, that there is an honored place for them in their society among their fellow men, each according to their ability and willingness to work.

The greatest emphasis must be placed on the psychological health of the aging, for this is the foundation upon which the development of progressive attitudes toward and by the aging must be built. The psychological health of the aging must be the first and paramount consideration in looking forward to a harmonic and creative restoration of the aging to their proper place in society. Present trends in this direction are already evident, and it is clear that a great deal of fundamental and pioneer work needs to be done in this area.

The climate of cultural opinion in relation to the aging is at the present time highly favorable and is likely to continue and become increasingly more favorable. This is extremely fortunate and encouraging because the social problems associated with an increasingly larger aging population press close upon us.

A considerable cultural change in our way of life which has

occurred and hardly been noticed is that increasingly large numbers of parents no longer expect at any time to live with their married or unmarried older children. Not only this, there is an increasing geographic mobility, so that as soon as the children become independent they are increasingly more likely to become geographically separated from their parents; they move to different towns or different states or to different parts of the same town. In any case, parents approaching the sixties are increasingly likely to find themselves with only themselves to take care of, and what it is important to observe, no one but themselves to take care of them. These are important changes; the days of domestic servants seem to be well-nigh over for most people, and this fact is already producing considerable social changes. For example, a style of house construction is spreading widely, and sensibly, of the ranch house or single ground-floor type, which eliminates staircases and other unnecessary and expensive taxes upon the strength of the aging. Houses are being built more compactly and more economically, and above all more intelligently. The increasingly aging population will increasingly continue to demand such housing, and a great part of the rural and suburban population is likely to be influenced by the advantages of this style of housing.

While we are on this topic it needs to be stressed that to inhabit their own home or apartment, to live apart from their children, does not mean that the older parental generation ceases to live in the environment of younger people or that it is any hardship upon them when they do. In any community they are likely to encounter and see the normal number of younger people, and it is highly desirable that they do, both for their own sake and the sake of the younger people. For their intimate friends most older people prefer persons of their own generation and they should, of course, enjoy adequate opportunities for being with them.

I think it highly undesirable for us ever to think in terms of setting up communities or any kind of other residential institution for the "care" of the aging. We should avoid the institutionalizing of aging, and we should avoid repeating those ghastly iniquities of a more openly sadistic age, such as "The Home for Incurables" or the "Insane Asylum." I suggest that "Homes for the Aged" are much more undesirable than "Homes for the Incurable" and "Insane Asylums." We should avoid any form of deliberate segregation of the aging, and concentrate rather upon enabling them to adjust themselves to whatever environment or environments they wish to inhabit. Aging is something we should recognize for what it is, and not prejudge it for what it isn't. We should behave toward the aging as persons and not as members of a rubber-stamped group. This does not, of course, mean that we should ignore the realities of aging; it *does* mean that we should not make a disorder or a problem of aging. Aging is not a pathological process nor is it a social offense, yet there have, in the past, been strong tendencies to regard it as both. This is an attitude which we need to relegate to the Museum of Hoary Errors. We need in short to develop healthier attitudes toward aging, and this is essentially a matter of education, a matter of disseminating the facts about aging and dissolving the myths that have grown up about it.

Let us consider some of the most widely held of these myths. Perhaps the most entrenched of these myths is that which is enshrined in the saying, "You can't teach an old dog new tricks," the notion that older people can no longer learn. This is utterly untrue; human beings are capable of learning to the last days of their lives; the difference in favor of younger people is that they learn more rapidly. So far as mental processes are concerned anything that younger people can learn older persons can learn also. Another myth is that on the whole younger people tend to be brighter than older persons. What this belief in fact means is that younger people are as a rule "quicker on the trigger" than older persons, but on the whole that would tend to mean that they are in fact less intelligent, for intelligence requires the proper weighing and evaluation of the evidence, the ability to say, "Let me think this over," the ability to inhibit. Being "quick on the trigger" is often equivalent to "going off half-cocked." The major responses of the young are almost always faster than those of the old, and this is important when such fastness of response is of value, but this does not mean that an older person cannot drive a car with equal if not greater safety than a younger person. On this matter, indeed, the evidence is in favor of the aging, for per capita of the driving population the percentage of accidents is much higher among younger drivers than among the older ones. And this lends greater force to the fact that it isn't the heat that matters so much as the humility. The young, being insufficiently experienced, being comparatively less wise than the aging, tend to take chances whereas the aging tend to be more careful. However, in our desire to do justice to the aging do not let us fall into the error of undervaluing or denigrating the young. The young have a way of growing into the aging, and it should be an important function of the aging to teach the young how to do so gracefully and with as little trauma as possible.

With increased understanding of aging the probabilities are high that there will develop an increasing respect for what the aging have to offer, and it may be that the unique phenomenon, in our culture, will be observed: the young taking the advice of the aging! At any rate, with the improved understanding of aging there can be little doubt that one of its consequences will be an improvement in human relations.

Another widespread myth is the belief that aging persons are physically weak. As a group it is true that the aging are not as physically strong as the young, but again, with respect to physical strength as to everything else, aging persons should be evaluated as persons and not as members of an age class, for the fact is that numerous aging persons retain their strength till quite an advanced age. A great many aging persons, on the basis of this myth are denied employment to which they could do full justice. I am not suggesting that aging persons would do well as stevedores or weightlifters; I am referring to ordinary employment in stores and offices and other such places in which an ordinary and not an extraordinary amount of physical strength is called for.

Again, in disposing of the myths relating to aging we must not neglect to give proper emphasis to the facts. These facts should be well and thoroughly understood. The process of aging, especially of later aging, is physically one of breaking down and slowing down, but psychologically and socially it can and should be a process of building up and consolidation of gains. It would be wrong to emphasize the one and not give due emphasis to the other. The effect, indeed, of emphasizing the physical running down of the organism in later aging has been to produce a psychological running down in older persons which is often taken for an inevitable accompaniment of the process of aging, whereas it is in fact usually an effect produced by our traditional attitudes toward aging. Once more the proper educational approaches are necessary.

I have already emphasized the necessity of such education in the schools and colleges. The trend in this direction is already under way in some colleges, and these are chiefly medical. This trend will undoubtedly develop into a normal part of the education of every medical student. Education in the data of gerontology and the practice of geriatrics should form as indispensable and fundamental a part of the training of every physician as pediatrics does at the present time. Many medical schools do not yet give courses in these subjects, but there can be little doubt that it will not be long before all of them do. Meanwhile, every encouragement should be given medical schools to found a Department of Gerontology and Geriatrics.

In addition to physicians all nurses should receive a training in the facts of gerontology and the practice of geriatrics, as should also social workers. In fact, almost everyone who has anything to do with human beings should be fully apprized of the facts of gerontology. In this connection it is of great interest to note that many women's clubs in the United States have organized gerontology sections—which is in keeping with the great tradition of foresight, intelligence, and social interest of perhaps the most progressive element in the world today—American women.

The direction of the trend of the cultural changes in our attitudes toward aging is toward a clearer recognition of the great riches which the aging have to contribute to our society and the betterment of mankind.

21. The Bomb

IN MID-AUGUST 1953, apparently irritated by the repeated news of Chinese Communist prisoner atrocities and obstructionist tactics, a United States Senator, in most unladylike fashion proposed that the United States use the atom bomb to end our frustrations in the Far East. "If the current negotiations don't produce peace, but do break down and the war is resumed," she said, "then drop the atomic bomb on these barbarians who obviously in their past atrocities have proved that they have no concept of a desire for decency."

For their conduct toward so many of the soldiers of the United Nations the Chinese Communists stood condemned before the bar of humanity. We can agree with the honorable Senator that this was barbaric, but should it be the way of a Christian nation to meet barbarism with barbarism? Surely the road to peace lies through putting the principles enshrined in the Sermon on the Mount into practice not only among ourselves but among people everywhere. We must not give up. Resorting to the atom bomb would be an admission that we had.

Dropping the atomic bomb has become a sort of swear word every time the Communists begin acting up. It is not only in Washington that one hears this form of swearing, but as one travels across the country one hears the suggestion often expressed that we ought to use the atom bomb against the Communists before they use it against us. I am quite sure that this is not the opinion of most Americans. Most Americans want peace and would do everything in their power to secure it. But those Americans who seem to have forgotten or who never knew

257

what the effects of an atom bomb are upon human beings need perhaps to have the facts brought to their attention. I had almost said "brought home to them." That might have been the more appropriate phrase, for I propose here to give an account of what has actually happened to Americans *in the United States* who have been exposed to atomic radiation. I am doing so in the hope that an account of the effects of such radiation upon human beings who were good, healthy, loyal Americans, working in their own way in the interests of peace, will shock those Americans who need to be shocked into an understanding of something of the meaning of this terrible weapon, and why it and other such weapons, such as the hydrogen bomb, should be outlawed by the whole of humanity.

During work on the atom bomb in laboratories in the United States there have been several accidental releases of nuclear reactions which have produced the kind of ionizing radiation which was responsible for some 5 to 15 per cent of the casualties in the outlying districts of the bombed areas at Nagasaki and Hiroshima. The Japanese casualties have been reported in some detail, but we seem to have forgotten them pretty quickly. The American casualties do not seem to have made any great impress upon the press. They have been described only in the medical literature, and there figured in all their gruesome detail. The illustrations accompanying the medical reports are not intended for the squeamish or for those who desire to engage in undisturbed sleep.

I shall here tell the story of what happened to one young American who was exposed to atomic radiation.

A young American male, aged twenty-six, was working with some fissionable material when a nuclear chain reaction occurred. The chain reaction was identical with that which takes place in the explosion of an atomic bomb. The reaction was immediately stopped, but not before the young man had received a large dose of radiation. He was at once rushed to hospital, and was admitted twenty-five minutes after the accident. At that time he complained of a numbness and tingling of both hands. His right hand, which had been in contact with the material, was already diffusely and tensely swollen; his left hand was also swollen but less so than the right. An hour and a half following exposure he developed a severe gastric distress in the form of nausea and repeated episodes of retching and vomiting. These episodes occurred throughout the first twenty-four hours and persisted into the second day. Although he no longer vomited, he had prolonged periods of hiccoughing. The swelling of the hands increased rapidly and involved both of the arms and legs. Numbness was gradually replaced by increasing pain, and pain remained the dominant symptom throughout the first week. The very slightest exertion caused shortness of breath and a feeling of faintness.

Everything medically and humanly possible was done to relieve the patient from his distress.

On the sixth day a general poisoning developed and the patient became steadily worse thereafter. By the tenth day a "canker sore" had developed on the patient's tongue, and he became nauseated after eating. Cramps and generalized abdominal pain appeared, accompanied by swelling of the liver and other organs. Shortly afterward the whole mouth became inflamed, and a thick gray-white membrane covered the whole mucous membrane and the edges of the tongue. The lips were swollen, cracked, and bleeding. The mouth was extremely sore. In addition there was a paralytic obstruction of the bowel accompanied by diarrhea. The inflammation of the mouth terminated in destructive ulcerations.

There were prolonged periods of mental confusion. On the seventeenth day the heart sac showed signs of inflammation. The swelling and blistering of the extremities proceeded at a rapid rate, and by the end of the second week the fingers were in various stages of dry gangrene. The abdominal skin, which had begun to redden on the third day, and that of the lower chest was wholly destroyed, the destruction being most severe and painful in the groin. The hair on the head began to fall out on the nineteenth day, and by the time of death, five days later, was almost completely lost.

Progressive destruction occurred of the blood. Two weeks

after exposure the patient became irrational, and falling into a coma was mercifully released from his sufferings by death on the twenty-fourth day after his exposure to radiation.

Thus died a young American from the accidental release of atomic energy on American soil. He will not have died in vain if from his death a sufficient number of us will have been deeply enough impressed to see to it that the threat of the deliberate release of atomic energy for destructive purposes is removed forever from this earth.

22. Living in an
Atom Bomb World

GENERALLY UNKNOWN is the fact that when the atom bomb was put together by those scientists who made it, they unanimously agreed to petition the President of the United States not to use it as a destructive weapon. They strongly urged that the Japanese government should be informed of its existence and that the United States government would be willing to release it over any uninhabited Japanese territory specified by the Japanese government. For reasons best known to himself, the President declined to act upon this suggestion, and the world witnessed the spectacle of a civilized nation taking upon itself the moral responsibility of destroying two Japanese cities, and killing and maiming several hundred thousand human beings.

That any other nation would have done the same may or may not be true. Certainly no nation that has been Westernized to an appreciable extent would have desisted. Western man has become so calloused to the meaning of life that he has virtually lost respect for it. Some men even talk of wars less intelligently than they do of the common cold. To avoid the latter they will take some precautions, but to avoid the former they do nothing. They blandly believe that wars are inevitable, that wars are as natural as fighting between animals, that the impulse to make war is inborn, and that there is nothing to be done about it. Nothing could be further from the truth. Wars are fought for artificial reasons and arise from artificial causes. They are fought

From *Technology Review*, vol. 52, 1950, pp. 205-206, 228-229.

with artificial devices, and they are as stupid as they are unnatural.

Man is, by nature, a peace-loving creature. It is through education, by the processes which are borne in upon him in the
course of his transformation into a human being, that he becomes
aggressive and sympathetic to any and all belligerent invitations
which are extended to him. The Eskimos do not understand the
meaning of war; neither do the Australian aborigines; nor do
the nonliterate peoples of Siberia—the Chuckchi, the Yokut. All
of these peoples are characterized by cultures in which the idea
of war is nonexistent. War is simply *not* one of the ways in which
these people solve problems which Western nations are accustomed to put to the arbitrament of war.

If we do not solve the problem of the atom bomb, these people
might well survive us. The atom bomb will not see the end of
the human species. We can be quite sure about that. But do we
want the atom bomb to be the end of our civilization? Of ourselves? Of our posterity? It is not sensible to answer, "We do
not," for what we wish, and hope, and believe is not what we
say, but what we do. If we are to evaluate the answer in terms
of what we do, rather than what we say, the logical conclusion
is that we do wish to see the end of ourselves, and of our children and their children.

Most people have been frightened by the atom bomb; it might
be dropped on them. They are not, however, averse to dropping
it on others. As long as people continue to think and act in that
way, there can be no hope whatever that we shall be spared the
treatment we accord to others.

What we have most to fear is not any new means of destruction, but simply ourselves. The atom bomb is just another instrument of mass destruction. We, who created it, can help to outlaw
it. But that will do us little good until it is possible to outlaw
that thinking which makes it possible to use such destructive
instruments against our fellow men. So long as anyone maintains
overt or covert hostility toward human beings because they are
in some way different, war and destructive weapons will be
employed.

So long as we continue to think that we are in competition

with other human beings, we shall continue to compete with them. Friendly competition may act as a spur or stimulant, but hostile competition too often leads to the use of force. So believing in the use of force, we shall segregate potential competitors whenever we can, so that they may be handicapped in the race with us.

A Living Brotherhood

Mouthing beautiful Christian sentiments about loving others as ourselves and of brotherly love, we shall discriminate against others because they are of another skin color, or religion, or culture, or nation. We shall oppress, coerce and exploit, fear and hate, and these things shall become so habitual to us that we shall scarcely, if ever, be aware of our crimes against our fellows. To prevent the danger of becoming conscious of such things, we shall build up a system of rationalization about the inferiorities of other peoples and convert our prejudices into laws of nature, which have but to be taken for granted to be lived with a more or less easy conscience. So to live is to live ever nearer the brink of inevitable disaster. There is only one thing that can save us, and that is to stop talking about brotherhood and to live it.

> No man is an *Iland*, intire of it selfe; every man is a peece of the *Continent*, a part of the *maine;* if a *Clod* bee washed away by the *Sea, Europe* is the lesse, as well as if a *Promontorie* were, as well as if a *Mannor* of thy *friends* or of *thine owne* were; any mans *death* diminishes *me*, because I am involved in *Mankinde;* And therefore never send to know for whom the *bell* tolls; It tolls for *thee.*

Written in 1624, John Donne's beautiful words express the eternal truth by which men must live if they are ever to live happily together. Whether anyone likes it or not, one world is today already a functional reality. The voice of man can travel to any part of the earth within a fraction of a second. Communication on the physical plane is now possible between all the peoples of the earth, and most human beings want to communicate with us, not only physically, but socially. They want us to be as actively interested in them as human beings as they are interested in us. They want to learn from us, and they want us to help them, as many of them have taught and helped us.

To us, who are so sophisticated, the nonliterate peoples appear as humble and rather undeveloped members of the human family. Yet, humble and technologically undeveloped as they may be, they are often the bearers of spiritual riches and ways of life from which we could both learn and gain much.

We of the Western world have been too vain and egotistical, too prideful and patronizing to notice the riches which those, whom we had condemned to an inferior status, had to offer. We have already brought the atom bomb to the peace-loving people of the Bikini atoll. We have made their immemorial home uninhabitable, and not one of us protested against this outrage. We believed that the atom bomb had to be tested, and we blandly consented. The people of Bikini had solved the problem of living together. We haven't. The problem of living in the modern world will have to be solved by the peoples of the Western world—the peoples, in effect, who created the atom bomb.

As James F. Byrnes, former Secretary of State, has put it: "We live in one world, and in this atomic age regional isolationism is even more dangerous than is national isolationism. . . . Today the world must take its choice. There must be one world for all of us or there will be no world for any of us."

Indeed, as the Federation of American Scientists has declared, no nation can, in this new age, feel secure until the problem of the control of atomic power is solved on a world level. That solution can only be a moral and political one. It is a solution which cannot come from one people, one nation, but must come from all peoples, all nations; and the solution can and must come in the same manner as the bomb was created, that is, by cooperation between nations. The atom bomb was made possible by the work of Mendeleev, a Russian; of Thompson, Rutherford, and Chadwick, Englishmen; Einstein and Hahn, Germans; Bohr, Danish; Meitner, Austrian; the Curies and Joliot-Curies, Poles and French men and women; Fermi, Italian; Anderson, American; and Yukawa, Japanese.

By putting together the ideas developed, and the discoveries made, by all these scientists, the atom bomb was produced. Why can't we put the ideas and discoveries for the maintenance of man's life in peace and universal amity to work in the same way? The answer is that we can and must. Another war will mean the suicide of Western man. The destiny of Western man is being decided now, at this moment, by each and every one of us. Each of us, as a citizen, is a possessor of great potential power. Each of us can play a most important part in seeing to it that the the right decision is made about the atom bomb.

It should have been obvious all along that atomic "secrets" could not be kept for more than a few years by any nation or small group of nations, and that there can be no assurance that peace will be maintained as long as any nation has the sovereign right to decide questions of war and peace for itself. Peace is not merely the absence of war but the presence of justice, law, order —in short, of government.

A World Law

World peace can be created and maintained only under world law, universal and strong enough to establish justice and prevent armed conflict between nations. The only way by which a people can assure its survival and preserve its liberties is to unite with other peoples for the creation of a world government to which shall be delegated the powers necessary to maintain the general peace of the world based on law and justice.

As now constituted, the United Nations is a league of sovereign states bound together by treaty, not by world law. As such, it is not a world government and, therefore, cannot by law prevent armed conflict between nations and establish justice and security. Nevertheless, it is the greatest step yet taken by mankind toward world peace. Since the charter provides for amendments, every effort should be made to transform the United Nations into a world government.

Such objectives cannot be reached overnight; but, despite all difficulties, these objectives can, nay must, be accomplished. We must help build support for world government, and we must start now. The time is short. We must convince our friends, and get them to convince theirs, of the urgency and manner in which they may work to make world government a reality. In the first place, we must become clearly aware of the issues involved, and these may be summarized as follows:

1. There is absolutely no defense against the atom bomb.
2. No system of inspection could prevent its secret manufacture.
3. No law-enforcing authority could prevent its secret manufacture.

It is only by the creation of a concert of nations, all of whom will work in harmony with one another in a common world government, that any nation can be assured against the use of the atom bomb. To this end, therefore, it should be sought to introduce the following proposals to the United Nations:

1. That the United Nations be transformed from a league of sovereign states into a government deriving its specific powers from the peoples of the world;
2. That the General Assembly be reconstituted as the legislative branch of the world government in which the citizens of the member states are represented on an equitable basis.
3. That the General Assembly, in addition to its present functions shall have the power:
   (a) to make laws prohibiting, or otherwise controlling, weapons of mass destruction and, so far as necessary for that purpose, regulating the uses of atomic energy;
   (b) to make laws providing for such inspection as is necessary or appropriate to the execution of the foregoing powers;
   (c) to provide for appropriate civil and criminal sanctions for the laws enacted pursuant to the foregoing powers;
   (d) to provide and maintain such police forces as are necessary for law enforcement.
4. That independent judicial tribunals be created with jurisdiction over cases and controversies arising under laws enacted by the General Assembly or involving questions concerning the interpretation of the charter of the United Nations.

5. That a Bill of Rights be designed for the protection of persons affected by laws enacted by the General Assembly.
6. That the Security Council be reconstituted as the executive branch of the world government with the power:
   (a) to administer and insure the enforcement of the laws; and
   (b) under the direction of the General Assembly, to perform its present functions as defined in the charter.
7. That the powers not delegated to the General Assembly be reserved to the member states.

These proposals and objectives represent the essence of the best thought upon the subject, and are, in fact, the proposals and objectives drawn up by the Rollins College Conference on World Government. They represent the minimum requirements necessary for the creation of a world government capable of averting the catastrophe of another war in the atomic era.

Congress Awaits

Since the first reaction to the consequences of the atom bomb has gradually died down and been replaced by a concentration on a possible war with Russia, the situation of mankind has become more dangerous than ever. Congress is waiting for the people to tell it what to do. If we raise our voices, we shall be heard. If all of us join our voices together, what we have to say will prevail. There is very little time left. Here is what we can do:

1. We can make our Congressmen aware of the reasons for the necessity of world government, and can urge them to make their influence felt on the subject.
2. We can urge the United Nations to adopt the above proposals.
3. We can support all organizations having world government as their objective.
4. We can organize a world-government group in our neighborhoods if one does not already exist there.
5. World government implies co-operation, not competition, between the peoples of the earth. One of the things we can do immediately is to cast our vote for peace by beginning to live co-operatively. The only defense against the atom bomb is the

moral aspiration of people to live in peace with one another in a united world under a common world government.

Freed from the menace of war, atomic energy can be, for all of us, in all nations, the great cohesive force which makes one world possible. To assist us toward realizing this aim, we have today at our disposal the philosophy, firmly based in science and in religious teaching, of the unity of all mankind; a philosophy which creates emotional force as well as intellectual conviction; a philosophy which creates the consciousness of a common purpose in mankind, which at once establishes the principle of the right to cultural self-determination and the international co-operation of all mankind.

The scientists who created the atom bomb have themselves set us the pattern by means of which this purpose can be realized; for, into the creation of the atom bomb went the genius of many nations. The free and untrammeled co-operative labors of the scientists of the whole world contributed to the discovery of atomic energy. Without world co-operation of scientists, that discovery would have been quite impossible. We knew that atomic energy was a real and not an imaginary thing before we discovered how to release it. We have now to conquer it. Similarly, scientists know that mankind is one, and are in process of discovering the means of releasing those energies which will make all the world believe it. But the task is far more difficult than that of the nuclear physicist, far more difficult and far more complex. Thousands of us will have to be engaged upon a thousand different fronts in order to solve our problem; and, we can solve it only as the nuclear physicists solved theirs: by co-operation. In co-operation, and in unity on a world scale, lie the strength which will make humanity safe for mankind. Now is the time for clear and careful thought implemented by resolute action. Unless we act with intelligence and resoluteness now, we may never have another chance.

PART V

Man Red in Tooth and Claw: The Menace and the Misconception

23. Social Instincts

> Now this is the Law of the Jungle—as old and as true as the sky;
> And the Wolf that shall keep it may prosper, but the Wolf that
> shall break it must die.
> . . . the strength of the Pack is the Wolf, and the strength of the
> Wolf is the Pack.
> —RUDYARD KIPLING

IT IS CURIOUS that generally "the law of the jungle" has come to
have an entirely different meaning from the one Kipling suggested. Most people would say that the rule of the jungle is: kill
or be killed. Rugged individualism, aggressiveness, warfare—
these have been thought to be the natural tendencies throughout
the animal kingdom. Kipling's sentimental verses suggest that, on
the contrary, the law of the jungle is not the law of tooth and
claw but the very opposite—co-operation. And strangely enough
a great deal of modern research in various sciences indicates that
Kipling was right. Through many laboratory experiments and
observations in the field we are being shown that we have been
close to 100 per cent wrong in thinking of animal life as a dog-
eat-dog existence. The truth seems to be that nature adheres to
the principles of the highest ethics: the Golden Rule is sound
biology.

Examples of co-operation in the animal world are not at all
difficult to find, and they turn up in the most surprising places.
Take the case of African elephants, which are notoriously savage
and resistant to taming. Hunters in Africa have seen elephants
stop beside a wounded comrade and laboriously lift him with

From *Scientific American*, vol. 182, 1950, pp. 54-56.

their trunks and tusks, when the so-called law of self-preservation should have made them run to safety. The noted explorer Carl E. Akeley several times saw threatened herds of elephants gather in a ring, with the younger and huskier beasts forming the outer circle to protect the older ones.

Or consider chimpanzees, traditionally regarded as self-centered little creatures. Workers at Yale University's Yerkes Laboratory of Primate Biology in Florida have seen chimps helping each other carry loads and even passing food to one another through the bars of their cages.

Even so lowly a mammal as the mouse is known to co-operate with its fellows. A Polish experimenter named T. Vetulani found that white mice isolated in separate cages failed to grow as fast as those that were grouped two, three, or four in a cage. The grouped mice huddled together and kept each other warm, thus conserving energy for growth, and they also healed one another's sores by licking.

At the University of Chicago the zoologist W. C. Allee and his co-workers have discovered tendencies toward mutualism among goldfish. For example, a young goldfish will grow more rapidly in water that has previously been inhabited by another goldfish than in clean, uncontaminated water. The reason is that the second fish feeds on food regurgitated by the first.

Allee made a systematic investigation to determine whether animals survive a catastrophe better in a group than singly. The most interesting of several experiments on this problem involved planarian worms. The catastrophe was ultraviolet radiation, which is deadly to these animals. The worms were arranged in Petri dishes, the experimental animals being crowded twenty to a dish and the control animals isolated one to a dish. The worms were then irradiated. All the worms died eventually—but the crowded worms hung onto life much longer. In one test they lived an average of 517 minutes after radiation, while isolated worms lived only 41 minutes.

One possible explanation is that the crowded worms tended to shade one another from the lethal radiation. But that is not the whole story, as was proved by another experiment. This time all the worms were irradiated in groups of twenty; none was isolated until after the damage had been done. Then ten worms were taken from each group and placed singly in separate dishes, while the other ten were left together. Again the grouped worms lived much longer than the isolated ones, surviving an average of 148 minutes to the latter's 78. The worms that were together somehow lent strength to one another. How? Whatever the factor is, it has not yet been identified.

Allee and other investigators have found that this rule of strength in numbers holds true practically everywhere they have looked. For example, a sea gull breeds more young when it lives in a large flock than in a small one. A salamander tadpole whose tail has been cut off will regenerate it more rapidly when other tadpoles are in the tank than when it is alone; the probable explanation is that the presence of several tadpoles raises the salt content of the water to approximately that of the cut surface and thus favors growth. An ant digging a nest moves more dirt when it works in the company of other ants than when it works alone. The spermatozoa of the sea urchin retain their ability to fertilize eggs much longer in a heavy concentration than in a diluted one. And so on; the examples can be multiplied.

But all these examples deal only with co-operation among animals of the same species. What of the so-called warfare between different species? Lions kill zebras—no question about that. But the lions do it only for food. This type of aggression can no more be considered war than man can be said to war on oysters and chickens. Lions do not kill for sport or out of blood lust; they kill only when hungry. African explorers have seen them trot through herds of easy game without making the slightest attempt to attack.

Surely cats and rats are instinctive enemies! Actually they are not: a cat has to learn to kill rats. A Chinese investigator named Zing Y. Kuo raised three groups of kittens under different conditions. Group A were left with their mothers, and from the first days of life saw how rats were killed. Group B were not allowed to see killing until they were several months old. Group C never saw killing at any time, and were raised in the same cage with baby rats. The upshot was that in Group A 85 per cent of the kittens became rat killers; in Group B only 45 per cent killed rats; in Group C the kittens lived in peace with their rat cage mates and all other rats of the same species. Kuo concluded: "If one insists that the cat has an instinct to kill the rat, I must add that it has an instinct to love the rat, too."

The traditional belief in "hereditary enemies" among animals is constantly being refuted by the Sunday supplements, which dote on printing pictures of dogs that have adopted cats, and tame foxes that play with chickens. The Philadelphia Zoo has witnessed some remarkable examples of such friendships. There a cat and a Senegal parrot became so attached to each other that they slept together. Another cat struck up an acquaintance with a deer, and chose the deer cage to have her kittens. The deer took special care not to step on the litter. A female goat was cautiously introduced by the zoo keepers to a female black rhinoceros, a creature of very savage temperament. The rhino, instead of attempting to harm the goat, befriended her. The two were inseparable for the rest of their lives.

Perhaps the most remarkable story of the effects of companionship comes from the Ohio Bureau of Fish Propagation. The Bureau chief, T. H. Langlois, has persuaded the bass in the Bureau's rearing ponds to give up cannibalism—a practice long supposed to be instinctive with these fish. Langlois noticed that if bass are put into weedy ponds, they tend to become separated by the vegetation and fail to form large social groups. Some of the fish take up lodgings in secluded spots and apparently develop a gangster psychology. Any small outsider unlucky enough to stray into these restricted territories gets eaten. The cannibalism does not stop when other food is thrown into the water by the fisheries men. The gangsters either fail to see the food because of the intervening vegetation, or are just not interested. Langlois' solution was simply to clear the vegetation out of the ponds before stocking them with bass. Now all the fish had to mingle. When food was thrown to them, they all ate together. With everybody well fed and everybody acquainted with everybody else, nobody tried to eat anybody.

These examples and scores of others recorded by scientists in many parts of the world emphasize how strong and deep-seated is the urge toward social life and mutual aid throughout animal life. What is the basis of this urge? The answer proposed here is that the social nature of all living things has its origin in the relationship between offspring and parent—the fact that the one is for a time dependent on the other. This hypothesis appears to bind together a large mass of facts not previously known to be related.

Consider a unicellular organism, the amoeba. When the amoeba reaches a certain size, it can avoid death only by dividing. Its continued existence is dependent on the proper formation of the daughter cells, and their existence in turn is dependent on the proper functioning of the parent through the various stages of mitosis. Here is a real instance of interdependent, social life; it exhibits in miniature the pattern of co-operative behavior that we see throughout nature. Co-operation is the mechanism by which every new individual is formed, whether sexually or asexually. Co-operation is the means by which it keeps alive through the first precarious stages of existence. Co-operation is as basic to its nature as are irritability and motility.

Let us consider our theory in terms of man. In the first weeks of life the human infant appears solely concerned with satisfying its physical needs, such as food and warmth. But gradually its feelings of satisfaction are transferred to the person or persons who make the satisfactions possible. From then on the baby is not content with merely getting enough to eat; it also needs a close emotional connection with the provider—the mother or mother substitute. It cannot live by bread alone. Thus the mutuality that governed the infant's life in the uterus is raised to the psychic level. The baby now has a social "inclination." This characteristic can never be thrown off; it is too closely interwoven with the individual's first encounters with the surrounding world.

This is the pattern in which every adult human being is molded. There are no exceptions; infants who do not go through these stages, who are not cared for or "mothered," do not survive. Hence we may infer that what the human being desires most of all is security. He wants to feel related to something, whether to family, friends, or deity. Man does not want independence in the sense of functioning separately from the interests of his fellows. That kind of independence leads to lonesomeness and fear. What man wants is the positive freedom that follows the pattern of his life as an infant within the family—dependent security, the feeling that he is part of a group, accepted, wanted, loved, and loving.

In human beings who develop normally, this feeling of love and unity with the group continues to grow all through life. It is a common observation that the happiest persons are those who most strongly feel a sense of connection with the whole community. They are happiest because they are giving fullest play to their innermost tendencies.

Thus we reach the conclusion that the ethical idea of love is no artificial creation of philosophers but is rooted in the biological structure of man. To love thy neighbor as thyself is not only religion's edict but nature's as well. Men who act in disregard of this principle are actually warring against their own bodies. The result is bound to be havoc for themselves and for those around them.

Here is a conclusion fraught with great significance for mankind. It gives support to all forces that are attempting to weld men closer together and so to increase the quantity of security for all individuals. It turns the weight of science against all advocates of separatism, isolationism, aggressive individualism. It brands the theories of the hatemongers not merely as immoral but as unnatural. If this conclusion were widely propagated, it might help strengthen the average man against the appeals of ultranationalist demagogues.

Now it must be acknowledged that the opposite conclusion is deeply rooted in modern thinking, and that a seemingly powerful objection may be offered to our theory. This objection derives from what people suppose to be the Darwinian scheme of evolution. If the dominant impulse in all animals is co-operation, if man's biological structure is rooted in love, what becomes of Darwinism? What about "the struggle for existence," "natural selection," "the survival of the fittest"?

The answer is that these conceptions are only one side of the picture. Certainly aggressiveness exists in nature, but there is a simultaneous drive toward co-operation. And the evidence strongly indicates that the latter is the stronger and biologically the more important. For if struggle and conflict had dominated life back to its very beginnings on this planet, how would unicellular animals ever have joined forces to produce the first multicellular creatures? Without co-operation, evolution as we conceive it could never have started. Furthermore, the coexistence today of so many different species of animals throughout the world is sufficient testimony to the existence of a principle of mutualism, tolerance, live and let live.

It is a narrow interpretation of Darwinism, indeed a perversion of it, that has given rise to the belief that combat and conquest are nature's whole plan, and that as a consequence rivalry, aggression, and imperialism are the inevitable way of personal and social life. Actually Charles Darwin's own attitude was altogether different. He appreciated the powerful role of co-operation, and made this clear in *The Descent of Man*. In a passage to which his disciples have given too little attention he said:

> As man advances in civilization, and small tribes are united into larger communities, the simplest reason would tell each individual that he ought to extend his social instincts and sympathies to all members of the same nation, though personally unknown to him. This point being once reached, there is only an artificial barrier to prevent his sympathies extending to the men of all nations and races.

24. The Myth of the Beast

MAN IS A MYTH-MAKING ANIMAL, or if you prefer, a self-deceiving animal. Through his myths man creates a whole universe of pseudoreality which is as real to him as reality itself—and what can be more real than the unreal? Myth-making is certainly as ancient an occupation as man himself. Myths are devices for the handling of problems which are conformable to the requirements of the individual and of society. This is not the place to consider whether or not myths have on the whole been beneficial to the human race. One thing is certain, and that is that among the many myths current in the present day, perhaps the most unchallenged is what may be called "the Myth of the Beast." This is the myth that animals are "bestial," "bestial" in the sense that they are wild, cruel, nasty, and ever ready to make unprovoked attacks on other living creatures.

A myth is something which is in fact not true, but in which we believe and act upon as if it were true. Almost everyone in the Western world believes that wild beasts live in the jungle and that the jungle is the scene of an unceasing warfare between the animals that live in it. This is the "Nature red in tooth and claw" of which Tennyson sang. It is the "jungle" of countless stories and movies, particularly of the "Bring 'em Back Alive" and Walt Disney variety. The jungle is envisaged as a steaming hot, densely overgrown forest, dark, dank, and dangerous, the lower branches of its trees dripping with poisonous snakes and boa constrictors ready to fall upon whatever unwary wanderer moves below. On the upper branches carnivorous birds

278

await their next victim, and concealed behind the trunks of trees lie any one of an untold number of ferocious beasts ready to leap out upon the next animal and tear it to pieces. It is a war of all against all. This, in brief, is "the Myth of the Jungle," a myth that is closely related to the myth of the beast. It need not be considered further here, except to say that it represents a gross exaggeration of the conditions which actually prevail in the "jungle." The jungle, indeed, of reality is a far safer place for any living thing, including man, to be in than, shall we say, Forty-second Street and Broadway in New York.

Western man's conception of the jungle, it may be suspected, is a projection upon nature of conditions prevailing in eighteenth- and nineteenth-century industrial civilizations—the strife, stress, strain, and competitive struggle for existence which characterized the age of the Industrial Revolution, the "warfare" between individuals, classes, and nations. Certainly the "jungle" of popular imagination and folklore very much more closely resembles industrial civilization of the eighteenth and nineteenth centuries than it does the actual jungle.

Wild animals, like civilized human beings, eat when they are hungry and drink when they are thirsty. They do not wantonly kill, any more than we do when we prefer bacon for breakfast or chicken for dinner. Nor are they exhibiting hostility or aggression when they fall upon their victims any more than we do when we fall upon ours at breakfast or dinner.

The noble-maned lion, far from being the heroic creature that popular tradition has made him out to be, is, in fact, the most arrant coward. When attacked he will run away and abandon the lioness and her cubs to whatever fate may befall them. He neither dares nor cares. It is the lioness who will attempt to repulse the attack and defend her cubs. As for that allegedly most ferocious of all beasts of the jungle, the gorilla, his reputation is based on even less solid foundation than the lion's. The adult gorilla may attain a weight of over 600 pounds, and it is undoubtedly the most powerful of all animals—but it is not in the least ferocious. It doesn't have to be with all that strength. The gorilla has no enemies, except man. The gorilla is a vegetarian, monogamous, a devoted parent, and the male will not run away when attacked but will attempt to defend himself and his family, and he will not unprovokedly attack anything.

When the peaceful gorilla family is suddenly assaulted by the rifle fire of civilized man, it is the gorilla who is described as behaving ferociously when he attempts to defend his family against the unprovoked attack of man. But who, in fact, is behaving like a "wild beast" under such circumstances, the gorilla or man?

The "beast" is a myth we have created, a scapegoat, upon which we project the image of ourselves we are unwilling to acknowledge. When anyone behaves in a peculiarly unpleasant manner we tend to assert that he behaved "like a beast," when the fact, of course, is that no beast ever behaves as iniquitously as man so frequently does. When we wish to show a Nazi behaving in a typically Nazi manner we draw a cartoon of a gorilla with the innocent form of humanity draped over one of his gorilline arms while in his other hand he holds a dagger poised above the inert form. This is a libel upon the gorilla, but it is a factual representation of the manner in which human beings frequently conduct themselves.

The "beast" cannot answer back, so it is perfectly safe to project our sins upon him. He is the perfect scapegoat. The laws of libel afford him no protection, and because it is so psychologically profitable, the myth of the beast is perpetuated from generation to generation. The result is a perversely distorted view of the nature of other animals, and a profoundly impoverishing failure to understand our true kinship with the rest of animated nature. So-called primitive peoples have never lost this kinship with other animals. Without the benefit of a Darwinian theory of evolution our technologically less advanced relatives, the nonliterate peoples of the earth, in their creation myths and in their conduct toward the animal world exhibit a far deeper understanding of the interrelatedness of all living things than does so-called civilized man. The institution of totemism in nonliterate cultures often extends this feeling of relatedness to plants, and even to inanimate nature. This feeling of kinship, of belonging with, being a part of, of relatedness to the whole

of nature, gives the individual a feeling of wholeness, a meaningful rootedness which in purely human terms is as enriching as
it is enlarging.

In the Western world, with the exception of a relatively few
individuals like Saint Francis of Assisi, and Richard Jefferies,
the English writer on nature, the feeling of identity with nature
has been virtually lost. There are "the lower animals" and there
is man; and man, it is considered, not only stands above all other
animals but beyond them—beyond them to such an extent that
he stands apart from them, alone, the solitary monarch of all he
surveys. This self-imposed exclusiveness has cost Western man
dear. It has cut him off from a great part of life, and the growth
in himself that comes with its deeper understanding. The resulting impoverishment has produced a rather parochial view of
himself which isolates him from the rest of nature. There is a
failure of sympathy, a loss of compassion, indeed, a complete
heartlessness develops in relation to the "beast," so that the killing of animals develops into a "sport" in which animals are
rarely, if ever, given a sporting chance, and in which their ex-
termination for commercial purposes is pursued with an unfeel-
ing relentlessness which is perhaps equaled only by the lack of
emotional engagement which characterizes man when he is
occupied with that form of mass murder called war.

I am not here omitting to note that many persons in the
Western world keep domestic animals as pets and are often fond
of them, but this is not what I mean by the feeling of kinship
with animals. Nazi commandants of concentration camps were
very fond of their dogs, but such affections in no way influenced
their behavior toward the human beings whom they ruthlessly
exterminated. A feeling of involvement in the whole of animated
nature is a very different thing from involvement in a pet, and
there need, obviously, be no relation between the two.

From what point of view are "lower" animals lower than man?
Is it, perhaps, from the same point of view that makes a distinction between "higher" and "lower" races of man? The point of
view that begins with a prejudice and terminates with a reinforcement of the prejudice with which one began? The use of
such terms as "higher" and "lower" in connection with man or

other animals is prejudicial to clear thinking. These words represent the crassest kind of value judgments. In the evolutionary continuum of development no population of man is either "higher" or "lower" than the other. Technologically, even culturally, some are differently developed than others, and this for reasons which cannot in any valid way be related to such value judgments as "higher" and "lower." Where opportunities for cultural and technological development have varied, so will cultural and technological development have varied. By terming a less developed technology or culture "lower" and a more developed one "higher," the conditions responsible for the differences are obscured. It is similarly so when one speaks of "lower" animals in relation to man. I am not attempting a silly egalitarianism here on behalf of the animal kingdom. What I am trying to do is to suggest that the terms "higher" and "lower" pejoratively suggest, in addition to many differences that do exist between man and the rest of the animal kingdom, some differences which do not in fact exist—one such difference being the assumption that there is an unbridgeable gap between man and the other animals.

On the evidence, this idea is demonstrably unsound; that it has been damaging both to animals and to men should be clear. There is no gap between the animal kingdom and man, for man is a part of that kingdom. Man has simply evolved differently in his genetic capacities for controlling his environment, and in his actual control of that environment, than other animals. In some respects he is superior to all animals, but he is not "higher" and they are not "lower" because of that. The notions of "higher" and "lower" are of considerable antiquity and grew to popularity during the eighteenth century when "scales" or "ladders" of Nature became a fashionable mode of representing the different divisions of the animal kingdom. This hierarchical manner of graphically presenting the animal kingdom, with man at the summit and the remainder of the animal kingdom in descending order on the lower rungs of the ladder, led to the "natural" conclusion that man stood "higher" in the scale of Nature than any other animal. But in fact there is no just ground whatever for the assumption that animals stand in relation to each other in a hierarchial order. The scale, or ladder, of Nature is a highly inaccurate way of representing the process of evolution. Evolution does not proceed in a straight line, but rather in a reticulate manner, crisscrossing in all directions and in all dimensions. All living things evolve by the natural selection of variations which more efficiently adapt the organism to its environment. Though they may live in the same region, different varieties of animals live in different environments. Within the same hundred square yards a mole lives in a different environment from a mouse, and a mouse from a man, and each one is thoroughly adapted to the environment in which it lives. The adaptations and the ways of life of these creatures are different. Each in its own environment can do what the other cannot. In its own environment each functions more efficiently than the other, but this does not make one "higher" than the other, but simply different, and difference does not imply either superiority or inferiority, "higher" or "lower." This, I think, is the important point to grasp. It is the relatedness, and the sense of relatedness, which is the important thing, and the more one realizes this the richer does one's life become.

It is, of course, true that man can adjust himself to many more environments and to a certain extent control them, more efficiently than any other animal, and in that sense he is, indeed, superior to all other animals. It is by virtue of that very superiority that man may yet learn to understand his true place in nature and his relation to the rest of the animal kingdom.

25. The Fallacy of the Primitive

FROM THE RATHER self-conscious heights of our own state of equivocal civilization and of that of the community to which we belong, we men of the latest period of human development have traditionally taken the view that whatever has preceded us was so much the less advanced. Since we are the latest bearers of human development, we reason, therefore, that we are the most fully developed. This rather ortholinear view of development is widely held, and it is, of course, widely believed to be in harmony with the evolutionary facts.

As pointed out in the previous chapter the truth is that evolutionary processes do not proceed in straight lines, but are more accurately observed to assume a reticulate form. And so it has been in the evolution of man, both physically and culturally. So entrenched, however, have our beliefs become concerning the ortholinear evolution of man that our conceptions of "progress," "development," and "evolution" have rendered the assumption automatic that what developed later in time must therefore be more "advanced" and more "evolved" than that which developed earlier. From this the "logical" inference followed that what was less developed must be earlier than that which was more developed, and therefore the earlier was the more "primitive" and the later the more "advanced." Furthermore, since straight-line evolution is taken for granted by so many, it followed that the more advanced developed from the less advanced, from the "primitive," and that the later was "superior" to the earlier.

From *Journal of the American Medical Association*, vol. 179, 1962, pp. 962-963.

Since evolution from the less advanced to the more advanced, or from the simpler to the more complex (not quite the same thing), is a fact beyond dispute (although the reverse has sometimes occurred in evolution), it has been easy to fall into the habit of assuming that the later developed is not only the more evolved but also the better. "Better" is, of course, a value judgment, and value judgments are a quagmire in which one may get hopelessly stuck. And this seems to be the condition into which civilized man has fallen, with respect to those whom he chooses to call "primitive."

We speak of "primitive" peoples—the nonliterate peoples of the earth. What do we mean when we use this term? We mean that such peoples are, in comparison with ourselves, underdeveloped; in many respects that is true. For example, it would be true of reading and writing, of technological progress, and in various cultures it would be more or less true of certain aspects of moral and institutional development. But it is very necessary to point out that in certain respects such cultures are more highly developed than are most civilized cultures. By the standards of values in these matters prevailing in civilized societies, in these respects "primitive" cultures are often "better" than civilized cultures.

For example, Eskimos and Australian aborigines, to take two of the so-called most "primitive" cultures known to anthropologists, are very much more generous, loving, and co-operative than are most of the members of civilized societies. By the standard of our own values in these matters, Eskimos and Australian aborigines are better than we are. Members of these "primitive" cultures are honest, dependable, cheerful, and courageous in all these respects to a degree which comparatively few civilized men manage to be. Who is more developed in these respects? Those who pay lip service to these qualities or those who live them out in their lives?

An additional assumption widely made is that "primitive" peoples are "nearer" and more closely resemble prehistoric man than the so-called "more advanced" peoples. This, too, is a very questionable assumption. The fact is that nonliterate peoples have as long a history as civilized ones. Despite references to "living fossils," no human population can, even by the most violent distortion of the imagination, be considered to be a fossil. All human societies change. The rate of change undoubtedly varies, some being slower than others, but changes must occur. They occur in languages, religion, custom, and technology, and all the changes will be considerably influenced by the varying experiences which each society undergoes. Those that are isolated from the mainstream of cultural change will change slowly; those that are exposed to the fertilizing effects of cultural interchange with other peoples will change rapidly. But even in the absence of such cultural stimulation, the very nature of cultural life involves more or less continuous adjustment and encouragement of change to meet the requirements of changing conditions. We can, therefore, be certain that no culture as we know it today is as it was in prehistoric times. It may even be that some of the so-called "primitive" cultures are much less like those of prehistoric times than some that appear to be more advanced. It cannot be questioned that, in some respects, some nonliterate cultures are closer to the conditions as they prevailed in prehistoric times than are civilized cultures. This, however, does not mean that they are so in all, or even most, respects.

Each culture in the course of time makes the progress necessary to enable its members to live as comfortably as possible in the environment in which the culture functions. The environment generally sets certain limits beyond which it is almost impossible for the culture to develop unless radical changes are introduced from the outside. Metal tools, for example, will not be developed in an environment in which metal ores are unknown. As I have already said, cultures differ from one another in the history of the experiences they have undergone and, therefore, in the kind of development they have realized. This does not mean that any culture, that is, the human beings through whom the culture is expressed, given the same history of conditions, is incapable of realizing or achieving the same degree of development as any other culture, but merely that most cultures have not had the same or similar opportunities to do so, and largely for that reason differ from one another.

Too often we identify "primitive man" with contemporary

nonliterate peoples when the only legitimate use of the phrase "primitive man" is when it is applied to prehistoric man. But even here there are dangers in the use of terms which are so loaded with erroneous ideas. Primitive man, that is, prehistoric man, is too often thought of as a beetle-browed monster, with little brain, a bull neck, knock-knees and a nasty habit of dragging his womenfolk around by their hair. Sad to say, all these ideas were perpetrated upon the innocent public by leading scientists of their day. Beetle-brows there undoubtedly were, but it should have been explained that behind those beetle-brows beat a brain of considerable power and, as in the case of Neanderthal man, larger in size than our noble own! The monster, the bull neck, the knock-knees and the hair-dragging of women are all figments of the imaginations of those who wished to see these things the way they thought they ought to be. But the true scientist endeavors to see things the way they are, not the way they ought to be or what is considered desirable.

One of the consequences of the belief that primitive man was so much less developed than ourselves is the failure to understand that prehistoric man of fifteen thousand years ago was in some aspects of his life capable of achievements which have scarcely been surpassed by men since. An outstanding example of this is prehistoric art, especially the art of the Upper Old Stone Age. When this was first discovered at the beginning of this century, it was at first attributed to modern artists who, for some reason, had crept into a natural crypt and decorated its ceiling in the manner of Michelangelo in the Sistine Chapel. But, as other discoveries were made in the dark recesses of caverns and caves under conditions which pointed to an extreme antiquity, the weight of evidence could no longer be resisted, and prehistoric man was finally acknowledged as the creator of these wonderful works of art, paintings, sculptures, and engravings. As Sir Herbert Read has said, "The best paintings in the Altamira, Niaux and Lascaux caves exhibit a degree of skill which is not less than that of a Pisanello or a Picasso." Anyone who has seen the originals or even reproductions will agree that this is no overstatement. In addition to the technical skill displayed by the artists, their work exhibits a vitality and expression which has seldom been equaled in any age. Be that as it may, in the works of art of prehistoric men, who lived between 15,000 and 30,000 years ago, we have the clearest evidence that these men, as artists, were as accomplished as any who have lived since. When it is remembered that these works were not really executed as works of art but as magico-religious rituals calculated to yield success in the hunt, that the conditions under which these works were created were usually of the most difficult kind, high up on walls and ceilings, often with the artist lying on his back, and doing his work by the uncertain light of a smoky oil flame, the achievement becomes all the more remarkable. There can be little doubt that individuals capable of such skills were endowed with an intelligence potentially no less great than that possessed by contemporary civilized man. Because the term "primitive" not only tends to obscure that fact, but also militates against the possibility of understanding the true significance of the facts, it will readily be understood why, if the term is used at all, it should be used with the greatest caution.

Primitive man as prehistoric man is most certainly a reality, and the more we learn to understand him, the better we understand ourselves. But to identify existing nonliterate peoples with prehistoric man is an egregious error when it is not an expedient fiction, a fiction which is rather pathetically calculated to provide a lift for the faltering ego. In the rapidly developing world in which we live, in which the underdeveloped regions of the world will witness their most spectacular advances in the areas of human development, it is of the first order of importance that the civilized peoples of the world understand and act upon these facts.

26. Play or Murder?

"GO OUT AND MURDER THEM, BOYS!" How often has the coach or captain of the team uttered those words. How often have they been echoed by the crowd. "I want you boys to win *every* game. If you lose a game, I want you to be bad losers." I have heard the coach of a famous varsity football team enjoin those words upon his players.

From the elementary grades to college "sports" the emphasis in America is on competition. You've got to go out and win. After all, what is the purpose of a game? Is it not to win? Is it not to prove that you are better than the others? Is it not to achieve self-gratification? To reap the rewards of acclaim and prestige? Are not our outstanding college and professional players national heroes? And is it not true that "you've got to be a football hero to get along with the beautiful girls"? Do not college football coaches vie with one another to attain the services of exceptional high school players? And do not colleges often provide scholarships to "scholars" who on the basis of their learning would never have seen the inside of a college? Do not too many of our colleges place a higher valuation on their football coaches than they do on their faculties? Indeed, the president of a great state university some years ago remarked to the incoming members of the football team: "I hope to have a faculty worthy of you boys." The fact is that, on the whole, he has. As one travels about the country one cannot help but be impressed by the fact that by far the largest and most expensive building on university campuses is the football stadium. A season's attendance at football games is likely to exceed the annual attendance at artistic and intellectual events within the university.

Altogether apart from any considerations of the abuses which the game too often represents, college football has become a ceremonial occasion, which one attends as a sort of intertribal gathering during which by feats of derring-do and legerdemain one side vanquishes the other. It is a sort of gladiatorial show in which the rivals are encouraged to win by every means possible. The player who fumbles a ball loses caste. His girl may return his pin to him. His teammates will scarcely conceal their displeasure. There is only one way in which the fallen player can redeem himself, and that is by excelling in helping to win the next game. For the player who makes the spectacular touchdown no reward is great enough. Debutantes will throw themselves at his feet, and corporation alumni will prostrate themselves before him if only he will accept the desk and accompanying emoluments which they offer him.

Thus do our highest educational institutions endorse a style of gamesmanship which sets the pattern for the whole country. It's good business. It helps to keep the alumni interested in contributing to the support of a college which has produced such a good football team. The games serve to bring alumni together, and they serve to give the alumni, their wives and friends, a corking good time—with especial emphasis on the corking. One can really enjoy oneself at a football game. One can shout, shriek, whistle, urge, expostulate, catcall, let off steam, be hostile, roar with laughter and with fury—in short, run the whole gamut of the emotions, and experience a catharsis that is worth half a dozen psychiatrists or trips to the Isles of the Blessed. Then, of course, there are the celebrations after the game. It is then that often the most heroic feats are performed. Undergraduates get pickled, and many of them remain pickled all the rest of their lives— "pickled undergraduates." Whenever they return to the campus and sing soulfully, "Back to dear old . . ." one can only wonder *why*, since they appear never to have left "dear old . . ." whatever the campus may be. It is really rather touching. It is no mystery why so many alumni are devoted to football—some of their most cherished and enjoyable memories are associated with it, though they may never have touched a ball in all their college days.

There is, of course, nothing wrong with joy as such. What *is* wrong is joy in the wrong things and for the wrong reasons.

When one adds to college football the influence of professional sports, particularly baseball—of which college football is the colder season's representative—one may perceive what a powerful combination of forces is at work in molding the ideals and purposes for which, and the standards by which, games are played.

In professional baseball, as everyone knows, whole teams and individual players are bought as one buys a stable or a race horse. The purchase is generally made as an open business deal with the avowed object of making a commercial profit. The fact that individual players receive salaries and bonuses which equal or exceed those paid to the President of the United States is publicly widely advertised. Games, quite obviously, pay off. There's big money in professional games, and there's fame and prestige. You get your picture in the papers and in the movies, and everyone talks about you. Professional baseball players rate on a par with the royalty of Hollywood; even though they may not always be as beautiful, they are not the less glamorous, and as their final achievement often acquire unto themselves a Hollywood wife. What could be more rewarding than to play the game as successfully as that?

During the final league games the whole of America is in the grip of baseball. Radios and portable television sets appear where they were never seen before and will not be seen again until the next series. Public-address systems and television bring the games to millions of listeners and watchers, who with fevered anxiety observe the progress of their side, vicariously participating in the game play by play. Strangers exchange the news and sometimes get into fights. Those who attend the games can scarcely be called "spectators," for their passionate partisanship involves them so deeply in the game—or is it the outcome?—that they are virtually beside themselves when things go wrong. In addition to catcalls, Bronx cheers, raspberries, and other expressions of rage and frustration, they will throw anything that can be thrown, not excluding vegetables and lethally dangerous bottles. Not only this, players in their own rage and frustration have been known to hurl their bats into the bleachers with resulting serious injury to the spectators.

And this is sport in America! And these are the reasons why one plays games in America. For what other good reasons can there be than those in which one is brought up to believe? How can anyone know any better—if any better reasons are to be known—when one has no other examples held before one than those which our society prescribes?

In America, in all games the idea is to win. One plays not for aesthetic pleasure but for prestige, with methodical and calculated ruthlessness, with a plan geared unashamedly to success. If you know that one of the key men on the other side has sustained a knee injury in a previous game, it is your job, you are taught, to go after him and get him out of the game as soon as possible. This is "sportsmanship." Win, win, win. Whatever you do—*win*.

If you never hit a man when he's down, it's perfectly all right to hit him as soon as he gets up. What's wrong with that, isn't that all right?

In answer to that question and all the others, I would begin by saying that everything is wrong about the spirit in which Americans play games. And the first point I would make is that, unless he is a gambler, *no one should ever play any game in order to win.* No one should ever participate in any sport in order to win. I have no doubt that this will be a startling statement to many, but I do not make it in order to startle anyone. I make it as a sober statement calculated from the beginning of the discussion of the meaning and purpose of games to indicate what is wrong with the attitude with which Americans enter into the playing of any game.

The principal reason for playing any game is that it is fun. If it isn't fun, then it ceases to be a game and becomes something else —a business, an investment, a technique, a means of acquiring kudos or whatever it is that one wants to acquire—anything but a game. Without fun one has about the same interest as the gambler who is interested in the game only as a means to the end of winning the stakes involved.

In all games one should take pleasure in playing one's best. One should play one's best not in order to win but to bring out the best in the other (commonly called the opponent) who in turn may bring out the best in him—and may the best man win. Going into a game with such an attitude between the players is reciprocally creative—*not* reciprocally destructive.

How little we understand these things in this country! Even some of the experts have been heard to remark that since the rewards of life cannot go to everyone, and children as well as adults have to work off their frustrations and hostility somehow, it is a good thing that they have competitive games through which they can get rid of some of their frustrations and hostility. Some there are who have gone so far in misunderstanding as to suggest that competitive games are a good way of reducing the amount of general competitiveness. On the contrary, I should have thought it obvious that training is competition, whatever form it may take, is likely, in general, to make the individual more rather than less competitive.

We belong to a society which prides itself on being competitive. It is often asserted that America is the great country it is because of competition. To me this is a gross misreading of the history of America. America's genuine greatness has not been achieved *because* of competition, but in *spite* of competition. The robber-baron spirit is not the spirit representative of America. America, on the other hand, is the outstanding example of what can be *achieved* by the co-operation of people of the most diverse origins and backgrounds that have ever been assembled on one team.

Of course competition exists as a way of life for many people in America, and in many respects America is one of the most competitive societies in the world—but it is also one of the most co-operative. The fact is that there has been a great deal of confusion in America concerning the meaning of what has generally gone by the name of "competition." We need to clarify our thinking on this subject.

Competitive competitors have, in America, often recognized the inefficiency of such competition, and have pooled their resources by combining to compete co-operatively—to compete co-operatively with each other, and to co-operate competitively against the problems which independently of each other they could not meet as efficiently. General Motors is a good example of such a combination, and there are many others.

Because of our confusion between co-operative competition and competitive competition, and because of our failure to recognize and give co-operative competition a name, we have mostly attributed to competitive competition what properly belongs to co-operative competition. In addition to co-operative competition there is such a thing as *competitive co-operation* in which one vies with others to achieve for the benefit of all the advantages one seeks together. This form of competition also often goes unrecognized and is also often confused with competition pure and simple. And so competition is understood by most people to mean principally the struggle against others for existence. And since we live in a "competitive" society, it is argued, what more natural than that our games should be competitive? And should not our children be trained to play competitively as a preparation for the competitive struggle for existence? This is to worship confusedly at the shrine of a false god. Competition doesn't *have* to be of the competitive variety—unless one wants it so. But if one believes that it is the only kind of competition, then Americans are likely to want it so.

In the middle of the twentieth century we have to recognize that the competitively most valuable quality of human beings is co-operation, and that in a world that stands so much in need of co-operation we are teaching our children to become competitive competitors. We have to change our own views and conduct as adults if, recognizing the desirability, we are to change those of our children and of our culture. And toward this end where games are concerned we can begin by attempting to understand the true meaning and significance of playing games for human beings.

Being taught to play games, in addition to the fun they can provide, should constitute one of the most important of all educational devices for the training of character and personality. In the education of our English cousins, games have long been considered an indispensable part of the training of character. The rules by which one learns to play the game are the rules one sticks by all one's life. The expression "It isn't cricket" is familiar wherever the English language is spoken. What the words mean is not so much that "It isn't fair" as that "It isn't decent." And it is the production of decency which should be one of the principal aims of education through play—to be decent, and considerate, and civilized in one's relations with others. This is not what through play we teach our children. Our way of playing games teaches them to be indecent, hostile, selfish, combative, and anything but kind and considerate. In American games, with the all-out emphasis on winning, the tendency is to take every advantage one can, and if the other side has any weaknesses to go after them. The idea is to ride the other man's weakness until he is worried into defeat—for is it not known that if you don't cut your competitor's throat he will cut yours?

Surely, what is needed in the game, as in the game of life, is not the skill to overcome the other because of his weakness, but rather the ability to know how to use one's own strength in relation to the other fellow's strength as well as his weaknesses. One doesn't have to mollycoddle the other's weaknesses, nor should one overlook them, but one should not play one's strengths off against the other's weaknesses exclusively. Let us play to the whole man, to his strengths and his weaknesses, and always in such a manner as to help the other to play his best, and particularly in such a manner as to help make him strong where formerly he was weak. This, surely, is or should be part of the fun of playing the game.

If a skilled tennis player can win games on his service alone, I should think it would hardly be fun or good sportsmanship to do so. The essence of those very words "good sportsmanship" means to give the other a chance, to be fair and more than fair. It is being neither fair nor giving the other a chance to ride his weakness or to take undue advantage of his strength. It is silly. Any slugger can without skill knock a better man out in a boxing match. If it is brute strength or stamina that one values in boxing, then I suggest it is the wrong thing that is valued. In all sports it is the general skill and the pleasure one takes in the development of that general skill that is both valuable and admirable. Brute strength may be valuable in a weightlifter or in a shot-putter, but if it is not accompanied by skill it is, in sport, far less valuable a quality than it is in a longshoreman. Similarly, a "murderous service" in a tennis player may be a valuable asset, but if that is the only skill he possesses, if he doesn't play the whole game well, he is no more admirable a player than his single skill permits him to be. It is the general skill which is admirable, just as the general development of the personality is rather than a particular or special aspect of it. And that is just the point of all sports and games so far as their educational value is concerned: that is the role they should play in the development of character.

As Americans we must make up our minds as to the kind of character we would like our citizens to have and to do what is indicated to bring those characters into being, to recognize that a most important preparation for the game of life is the training one receives in playing the game in childhood and youth. We need to realize that the present training we give our children through competitive games tends to bring out the worst rather than the best in them. We deplore the decline of chivalrous behavior, of good manners, and general thoughtfulness, while at the same time we see to it—without being aware of it—that our children are thoroughly trained in the atrophy of just those qualities. We lament the increase in violence and general ruthlessness, but through our games we encourage these traits. We falsely create the idea that you must win. But an essential part of education is learning how to lose gracefully, and more important than winning or losing, how to play the game gracefully. The old adage will always remain true: It's not who wins that matters but how you play the game.

27. The Go-Getter Spirit

IT IS OFTEN URGED that America owes its greatness to the spirit of competition which characterizes its citizens. "Rugged American individualism," "the go-getter spirit," and other such phases give implicit recognition to this idea. Commerce, it is said, through competition, is the lifeblood of a nation.

These ideas, I am going to suggest, are erroneous, tragically erroneous. I am going to suggest that such greatness as America has achieved it has achieved *not* through competition but in spite of competition; that the lifeblood of a nation is not commerce through competition, but social welfare through co-operation; that, indeed, commerce through competition can be the death of a nation, and that only through the dominance of the co-operative motive can any people or nation survive. Finally, that in a competitive society freedom of inquiry is not genuinely possible; that freedom of inquiry is proportional to the development of co-operation within any society, in which there is an absence of dictatorship of any sort, and the person is free to arrive at and express his own judgments without fear of punishment, and in the expectation of the desire in his fellows to understand.

In view of the fact that there exists, at the present time, a widespread belief in the innate nature of competition, that is to say, that competition is a form of behavior with which every organism is born, and that this is particularly true of man, it will be necessary to discuss such facts, with which scientific studies have recently acquainted us, which throw light upon this notion.

Just when the idea of the innate competitiveness of man came

From *The Christian Register*, vol. 131, 1952, pp. 17-19.

into being I have not the least idea. It is at least several thousand years old, and was probably in circulation long before The Old Testament came to be written.[1] It is quite possible that the idea of the innate competitiveness of man is as old as man himself. There are some existing nonliterate cultures, such as the Zuni of the American Southwest, which abhor competition and in which the idea of innate competitiveness is nonexistent.[2] It is quite possible that many prehistoric peoples held similar notions. But here we are largely in the field of conjecture. One thing, however, is certain, and that is the scientific validation of the idea of the innate competitiveness of man was provided in the nineteenth century by Darwin and his supporters, and particularly by Spencer and the whole school of Social Darwinists who followed his lead.

"Competition" was the cornerstone of the whole edifice of the theory of evolution by means of natural selection. And Darwin took the whole concept over from the social thinkers of late eighteenth-century England. It is important to understand that the prevailing notion that Darwin influenced the social thinkers of the nineteenth century to develop Social Darwinism is only partially true. In a very real sense the ideas which corresponded to Social Darwinism were already in existence before the birth of Darwin in 1809. The essential conception of natural selection—the very phrase "the struggle for existence"—Darwin took, as he readily acknowledges in The Origin of Species (1859), from Thomas Malthus' Essay on the Principle of Population (1798).

The "struggle for survival" of a geometrically increasing population in a world in which the food supply increases only in arithmetic progression, and in which war, pestilence, and famine are the natural checks to human increase, renders competition inevitable and natural. Hence, "commerce, through competition, is the lifeblood of a nation." What Darwin did was to take over lock, stock, and barrel the ideas of Malthus—who applied them exclusively to man—and apply them to the whole kingdom of

[1] See Kurt Singer, The Idea of Conflict (New York, Cambridge University Press, 1950).
[2] Ruth Benedict, Patterns of Culture (Boston, Houghton Mifflin, 1934), p. 127.

THE GO-GETTER SPIRIT 299

living things. Darwin simply translated the sociological language of his time into the language of biology, so that "commerce, through competition, is the lifeblood of a nation" became "evolution, through competition, in the struggle for existence, is the lifeblood of the species."

War—Nature's Pruning Hook

What Darwin and his supporters, in fact, demonstrated to the satisfaction of most of his contemporaries was that competition is inherent in the nature of living things. At the height of the Industrial Revolution this was a demonstration which fitted the book of laissez-faire capitalism to perfection. It was accepted with enthusiasm. In the struggle for existence the fittest came out on top. Hence, workers could be exploited under the most unspeakable conditions, "inferior races" could be expropriated of their lands and even exterminated, wars were justifiable in that they gave a biologically just decision, a natural arbitrament between peoples, and served as nature's pruning hook to keep her orchard healthy.[3]

Theologians and educators were confirmed in their belief in the inherent naughtiness of men, and the notion that the "brat has to have the inborn 'evil' disciplined out of him and the 'good' disciplined into him," took on a deeper meaning than it had hitherto possessed. In the Freudian psychology—and Freud was much influenced by Darwin—the inherent aggressiveness of man becomes an instinct,[4] and for this reason Freud takes a rather gloomy view of man's future.[5]

In recent years a few scientists, who have been considering

---

[3] See George Nasmyth, *Social Progress and the Darwinian Theory* (New York, Putnam, 1916); Richard Hofstadter, *Social Darwinism in American Thought 1860-1915* (Philadelphia, University of Pennsylvania Press, 1944); Ashley Montagu, *Darwin, Competition and Cooperation* (New York, Abelard-Schuman, 1952).

[4] Sigmund Freud, *An Outline of Psychoanalysis* (New York, Norton, 1949), pp. 21-23.

[5] Sigmund Freud, *Civilization and Its Discontents* (London, Hogarth Press, 1929).

the evidence as a whole, have come to the conclusion that competition or aggressiveness are not innately inherited forms of behavior; that the Darwinists, by overemphasizing the importance of competition and neglecting the factor of co-operation in the evolutionary process, badly put the whole picture out of focus.

Product of Frustration

Competition and aggressiveness are, of course, observable facts of animal and human behavior, but in the sense in which these terms are generally understood and used, that is, competition as a contest for the acquisition of something, and aggressiveness as a more or less hostile attack—in any hereditary sense these forms of behavior can at most be said to exist only as potentialities. Competition and aggressive behavior come into being only under certain conditions, and those conditions are largely, if not entirely, of a frustrating nature.[6]

Frustration may be defined as the thwarting of expected satisfactions. A certain amount of frustration is a very necessary part of the process of development of every person. To learn to postpone immediate satisfactions for long-term ones implies a certain amount of frustration, and this is both unavoidable and desirable if a healthy, mature personality is to be developed. But too much frustration is quite another thing. This is undesirable because it serves to cripple the development of a healthy personality, having either the effect of producing an excessively dependent, shy person, or an overaggressive, highly competitive person.

Different human cultures differ very widely in the kind and amount of frustration to which children and adults are exposed. Significant differences in personality have been observed in correlation with differences in kind and amount of frustration to which children have been exposed in those cultures.[7] In general,

[6] See John Dollard and others, *Frustration and Aggression* (New Haven, Yale University Press, 1939).
[7] See Margaret Mead, ed., *Cooperation and Competition Among Primitive Peoples* (New York, McGraw-Hill, 1937); *From the South Seas* (New York, William Morrow, 1939); Douglas G. Haring, ed., *Personal Character and Cultural Milieu* (Syracuse, New York, Syracuse University Press, 1948).

the rule is, the less frustration children have experienced the better balanced and the less aggressive and competitive they will be.[8]

Foundation for Sociology

So far as the nonhuman animal kingdom is concerned, the corrective to the Darwinian viewpoint has been given by Allee and his co-workers,[9] and by other biologists.[10] The work of those scientists confirms the conclusions put forward by Kropotkin in his famous book, *Mutual Aid* (1902). In the penultimate paragraph of their monumental work, *The Principles of Animal Ecology*, Allee and his co-workers state this conclusion in the following words:

> The probability of survival of individual living things, or of populations, increases with the degree with which they harmoniously adjust themselves to each other and their environment. This principle is basic to the concept of the balance of nature, orders the subject matter of ecology and evolution, underlies organismic and developmental biology, and is the foundation for all sociology.

It seems to me important to grasp the fact that while man is a very different kettle of fish from nonhuman animals, there is no validation to be found in the nonhuman animal kingdom for innate competitiveness and aggression. But even were this not the case, man is unique and there is no necessity to demonstrate his noncompetitiveness on the basis of anything other than his own nature. Even if man were by nature competitive—which he is

[8] See Clyde Kluckhohn and Henry Murray, *Personality* (New York, Knopf, 1948); Gardner Murphy, *Personality* (New York, Harper, 1947).
[9] See W. C. Allee, *Cooperation Among Animals* (New York, Abelard-Schuman, 1951); *Animal Aggregations* (Chicago, University of Chicago Press, 1931); W. C. Allee and others, *The Principles of Animal Ecology* (Philadelphia, W. B. Saunders, 1949), p. 729.
[10] Henry Drummond, *The Ascent of Man* (London, Hodder and Stoughton, 1894); William Patten, *The Grand Strategy of Evolution* (Boston, Badger, 1920); S. J. Holmes, *Life and Morals* (New York, Macmillan, 1948).

most positively not—he is so plastic and malleable a creature[11] that he could channel his competitiveness into co-operative and creative directions. The fact is that man is born neither aggressive nor competitive.

Indeed, the creativeness of the organism is directed toward maturation in terms of co-operation. Lauretta Bender calls it "the inherent capacity or drive for normality." And as she says, "The emphasis on the inborn or instinctive features of hostility, aggression, death wishes, and the negative emotional experiences represents a one-sided approach which has led our students of child psychology astray." Charlotte Bühler has come to similar conclusions.[12]

The nature of life is interdependency, and the organism called man is born in a state of dependency which requires interdependency if it is to survive. If we can teach parents how to co-operate with their children throughout their lives we may yet succeed in producing well-balanced, co-operative human beings.

Strengthen Basic Needs

Our present educational and social failure to recognize new bases of human relationships must change if we are to survive. Human beings who are torn and distracted by internal insecurities and anxieties, who are conditioned to compete on weekdays and to love their neighbors on Sundays, cannot long endure. Such a people must eventually founder on the rock of its own false values. External defenses can never make up for the lack of internal controls. What we need to do is to build internal controls in human beings so that they can withstand external pressures and maintain internal equilibrium. And this can never be done by doing violence to their nature. It can only be done by strengthening those basic needs with which all human beings are born—not by frustrating them.

[11] Theodosius Dobzhansky and Ashley Montagu, "Natural Selection and the Mental Capacities of Mankind," *Science*, vol. 105, 1947, pp. 587-590.
[12] Charlotte Bühler, "Spontaneous Reactions of Children in the First Two Years," *Proceedings and Papers of the 9th International Congress of Psychology*, 1929, pp. 99-100.

The evidence seems to be pretty clear that when the child's basic needs are adequately satisfied, when, in other words, the child is loved, and suffers a minimum of frustrations, he tends to develop as a remarkably well-balanced, nonaggressive, co-operative person, regardless of his class or culture.

We live by a pure flame within us; that flame is love. It is the source from which we draw and convey our warmth to others. It is the light which guides us in relation to our fellow men, it is the flame before which we warm the hands of life, and without which we remain cold all our lives. It is the light of the world —the light which it casts enables us clearly and unequivocally to see our relation to our fellow men. It is up to us to keep that flame burning, for if we fail to do that, there is a very real danger that the light will go out of the world.

The critical social and educational problem of today is one of learning how shared relationships may be fostered and freedom of inquiry accelerated. It seems to me, first, that this must be done through the schools, and second, that there must be a complete change in the attitude toward education. In the United States at the present time we have very little, if anything, resembling education, what we do have is instruction. What are we "educating" for? Obviously we are instructing our future citizens in what it takes to live in the world in which they find themselves. We are equipping them with the elementary skills, reading, writing, and arithmetic, which it takes to maintain that world. More by default than by design, we teach them a kind of cracker-barrel human relations, to become echoes, as it were, of other stereotyped lives already lived. This is to say, in the most important of all relations, human relations, as educators we fail most miserably. For what can be more important than human relations? What is all the instruction in the world worth if it is not accompanied and integrated by an understanding of man's responsibility to man? A scientific approach to education must begin with the basic assumption that values must in the long run be tested by their capacity to contribute to the happiness and creativeness of human beings living together. If we can find a scientific basis in fact for what should be, we should at the very least be willing to give it a try.

I suggest, then, that some of our schools be transformed into institutes for the study of the science and art of human relations. I mean that children be taught the theory and practice of human relations from their earliest years, for whatever is learned should be learned primarily with reference to its significance for human relations, and always with the emphasis on co-operation, on shared relationships. Children should be taught not to become submissive echoes of their teachers and their traditions, but how to evaluate humanely and critically the world in which they are living. They should be taught not only the overt but also the covert values of their society, and they should be taught not only what is right with their society, but that there are a great many things wrong with it, what they are, and that it is going to be their responsibility to put things right, and how they may be put right.

I am often asked how this can possibly be done. Don't I realize the enormous social inertia or even active opposition with which one would have to contend if one attempted to develop such a program? What happened in Pasadena? Look at Bertrand Russell and City College, and the Rugg textbooks. Yes, those are all very serious symptoms, but fortunately not all of the United States exhibits them. It would be wonderful if one could start with a community and work directly through the school system, and this should be our aim wherever and whenever possible; but failing that, a single teacher in a single classroom of a school, multiplied over many schools, could do valuable work.

This would not be enough if it stopped at a single classroom in a few schools, but the hope would be that, with constant awareness of the problem growing, the movement to teach human relations in the school would grow and spread. As I have said, there is not too much time left. The tendency in the United States to equate economic liberty with democracy has helped to disguise the fact that many of our ideas and institutions are under constant threat from ourselves; for persons who are in conflict with themselves, anxious and insecure, tend to be rigid in their ideas and in their behavior, as if to lean upon their rigidity as a rod in compensation for the weak, bending reed of themselves. Such persons cannot be free and they cannot tolerate freedom in others. These are the kinds of persons who tend to become totalitarians; and we have been producing them in fairly large numbers in this country.

We must recognize that the competitive values of our culture put men in opposition to each other, and that under such conditions genuinely free inquiry is retarded. Under co-operative conditions in which men learn to share their interests and experiences, in which altruism rather than egoism is the dominant motive of behavior, there is likely to be no limit to freedom of inquiry or the degree to which we can genuinely love one another.

28. The Annihilation of Privacy

IN RECENT YEARS the increasing isolation of the individual and the fragmentation of social relationships in an age of anxiety have become matters of frequent comment. In his well-known book published in 1941, *Escape From Freedom*, Dr. Erich Fromm pointed out that modern society affects man simultaneously in two distinct, yet related, ways. Man becomes more independent, self-reliant, and critical, and he becomes more isolated, alone, and afraid. Man flees from freedom because freedom has thrown him upon his own resources, to sink or swim by his own efforts—and man in the free Western world has shown that he would rather be supported and maintained in his efforts by his fellow men than be left to his own devices. I am going to suggest that man's flight from this kind of anxious freedom serves to foster the conditions which minister to the shrinkage of his personality and the ever-growing invasion of his privacy.

In T. S. Eliot's *The Cocktail Party*, one of the characters remarks:

> . . . Do you know—
> It no longer seems worth while to *speak* to anyone! . . .
> No . . . it isn't that I *want* to be alone,
> But that everyone's alone—or so it seems to me.
> They make noises, and think they are talking to each other;
> They make faces, and think they understand each other.
> And I'm sure they don't. . . .

The fear of being "desocialized," of being alone, is a healthy fear, for the biosocial nature of man is directed toward *related-*

From *Saturday Review*, March 21, 1956.

ness as the process of living. To be or feel alone is both unnatural and unhealthy.

Hence, in a society in which so many of its members feel lonely, cut off from their fellows, any socially sanctioned means which tends to reduce this feeling is likely to be perfervidly embraced—thus the success of the telephone, movies, radio, and television. For all these are means of communication, and communication is the essence of the social process. Furthermore, if you can have the means of communication on your own terms by simply picking up the receiver, paying your admission, or turning a knob, you can enjoy a much wider range of experience than would ever be possible in face-to-face relationships with your neighbors.

Well might the New Caliban remark:

> You taught me language,
> And my profit on it is
> I know how to read the TV news.

But he doesn't make any such remark. He's glad of his TV news, his television, his radio, and his telephone because they all minister to his sense of security, and they provide him with a one-way means of communication which he can turn on and off at will—he'd rather not turn it off, but fatigue accumulates and one must sleep.

Everyone in the communications industry is out to please the viewer, the much sought-after consumer and final arbiter of what he shall consume. So far there is no record of any viewer ever having been lethally affected by that form of consumption known as TV. But there is reason to believe that the communicators have sometimes had the feeling that their sending stations were discharging into a mass of moribund nonconductors—but this has been the case, mostly, when good programs were involved. On the whole the communicators manage to operate on the same wave length as the communicatees, and all is—communicationally speaking—well. The communicatee is really a receiver, but that is the name usually given to the instrument that picks up the physical waves which the recipient then converts into his own coin of the realm—depending upon the state of his treasury. So we had better call the recipient by his proper name, namely, "recipient." To call him a "receiver" might suggest that he were nothing more than a passive mechanical instrument, or that he was a receiver of stolen goods, when the fact is that they were neither stolen nor good, or even that he was a receiver in bankruptcy, which might suggest that somewhere possibly we were dealing with a bankruptcy of the spirit or even of ideas— to all of which, of course, a loud "perish the thought" might be in order. It depends upon the point of view.

Man is socially the most highly developed of all creatures. Interaction with other human beings is an environmental necessity to him. No man can survive as an island entire of himself. No man wants to be an island. But every human being wants and needs to replenish his resources for being social by having a room of his own, as it were, a sanctuary, to which he can retire, and in which he can be alone with himself, undisturbed by the rumors and alarms of the outside world.

The right to be alone is at least as important as the right to be with others. The delights of occasional periods of solitude have often been celebrated, but by none more notably than the Swiss philosopher, Zimmerman, in his famous but now forgotten book, *On Solitude,* written toward the end of the eighteenth century. Indeed, it is since the end of the eighteenth century that solitude, or what we should in our own day call *privacy,* has become increasingly more difficult of achievement. By privacy we mean freedom from social contact and observation when these are not desired.

Toward the end of the eighteenth century man in the Western world, through painful and long-enduring struggle, through hard-earned thought and bloody battles, had won through to the conception of the sacredness of the individual and his right to "life, liberty, and the pursuit of happiness." Man, for the first time, had the vision of a realizable future in which the rights with which men were equally endowed would afford all an opportunity to realize their potentialities according to the kingdom that was within them.

In the Western world this belief was enshrined in the doctrine of progress. Man, henceforth, could only go "onward and upward." Expanding freedoms, the franchise, education for all— these were all to contribute to the further development of the individual—for surely a society which made it possible to pursue the right to "life, liberty, and happiness" could not lead to anything other than ever-enlarging orders of freedom for the individual?

To be free of bondage or restraint, to live under a government based on the consent of the citizens, these are the basic of all freedoms, because they do, indeed, permit the maximization of the individual's capacity for living. And this is the reason why a democracy is from every possible humane point of view the best form of government for human beings. Providing, as it does, the maximum possibilities for freedom and order, it also provides for the possibility of error and the correction of error.

What so many human beings in the modern world have failed to understand is that freedom is the greatest of all trusts, that it is a great responsibility, not the least important part of which is our responsibility to our fellow men, that freedom does not consist, as Lord Acton pointed out, in the liberty to do what we like, but in the right to be able to do what we *ought*. Surely, freedom consists in the right to discover what we *ought* to do and in the liberty to be able to do it. All this is to say that freedom does not consist in the right to do anything we please, but in the right to discover those things that we ought to do which would please us because they are the right and the healthiest things to do; freedom, as Erich Fromm has said, not in the sense of the ability to make arbitrary choices or freedom from necessity, but freedom to realize what one potentially is, to fulfill the true nature of man according to the laws of his existence.

I am going to suggest that the increasing loss of privacy from which Western man is suffering, particularly in the United States, serves, among other things, to reduce rather than to increase the chances of the individual being able to discover what those things are that are right and healthy for him, as a human being, to do. And that from this fact spring certain serious psychological consequences.

A genuinely healthy society holds together by the respect which men give to men, by the recognition of the biosocial needs of man for relatedness, and the making available of the means by which the relatedness can be achieved. Such a society, instead of providing men with instruments that make them less than themselves, affords them the means of becoming instruments of something greater than themselves. In spite of the superficial appearances our society lamentably fails to afford such opportunities to the majority of individuals. We teach the skills, but we teach them as techniques for the achievement of limited objectives. Our educational attitudes are not directed toward "drawing out" but toward "pumping in." The pursuit of life in reality reduces itself to the pursuit of a living, "liberty" assumes the form of economic liberty, and "happiness' resolves itself into getting whatever one can get out of life by whatever means one can. In the United States we have achieved the highest standard of living in the world—but it is seldom, if ever, added, at the highest cost of ulcers, mental breakdowns, homicide, violent crime, juvenile delinquency, alcoholism, and drug addiction rates, in the entire world. Can it be that something is somewhere wrong, that there are causes for all this breakdown, death, and destruction of human beings—that these causes are traceable ones?

This is not the place to embark upon such a voyage of exploration. I raise the matter simply because in order to understand the causes that have led to the increasing invasion of our privacy, it is desirable to understand how it has come about that man has become so fragmented, so isolated, and so insecure—for that invasion has been a welcomed one.

It will not again be possible to say, as Byron did a century and a half ago, that

> Society is now one polished horde
> Formed of two tribes, the *bores* and the *bored*

for the possibilities of boredom have been reduced to the vanishing point. The world is now amused.

Today, anyone who chooses can cause your phone to ring and invade your privacy whether you like it or not. Whether you like it or not anyone who chooses to do so can know everything—both true and false—that it is possible to know about you, in fact, more than you know about yourself. In this, our government sets the example, for the Federal Bureau of Investigation has millions of such records on file in Washington. The files of the Congressional Committee on Un-American Activities are open to anyone who cares to use them. Then there are the manpower lists, the biographical reference works, specialty lists, telephone books, Black Books, Red Books, Who Knows What Books, the scandal-mongering yellow press, private eyes, public eyes, wire tapping, TV and radio brainwashing, and so on. Privacy has gone with the waves. "Big Brother" of George Orwell's powerful and prophetic novel, *Nineteen Eighty-Four*, is already watching you. A life of one's own is already well-nigh impossible, and the paradox is observed that in a world in which the private life of the individual daily shrinks, and his social life with his fellow human beings is reduced to the narrowest dimensions, that his life should become increasingly more public. Man has become the solitary individual in the lonely crowd.

Small-town gossip was at one time the only medium through which such publicity could be achieved—or rather thrust upon one. But that was a very primitive medium compared with the devices at our disposal in the modern age. Today we have gossip sheets with huge circulations which specialize in the exposure of the most intimate details of the individual's life— whether such details are true or false matters not one bit. Duly elected members of the Congress use their positions for political and private purposes to institute public Congressional Inquisitions during which the reputations of those whom they wish to destroy are nakedly exposed to the public gaze. If the government sets the example for such antinomian indecencies, it is not surprising that innumerable individuals have set themselves up in everything ranging from one-man vigilante committees to group organizations dedicated to the investigation of the private life of any and every individual whom they choose to pillory. These individuals and organizations are more than willing, they are anxious, to supply anyone who asks for it with such information. And if it isn't asked for, they will supply it whenever they can. As a consequence of such publicity many persons have been deprived of the right to earn a living.

It has even been suggested that this kind of desecration of men's privacy be put on a "scientific" basis. Dr. W. H. Sheldon, for example, in a book entitled *Varieties of Delinquent Youth*, has suggested that since "we have begun to forget *who are* the biologically best" people . . . this difficulty could be overcome "if standardized photographic records of even a few hundred thousands of a well-sampled population were to be kept for so short a time as half a dozen generations, together with biographical summaries embracing the physiological, psychiatric, and social adventures of this sample population . . ." And he goes on to suggest that at a very small cost "we could keep central files of standardized photographs of the entire population."[1]

And, of course, these photographs will be in the nude. Thus will the last of our privacies be stripped from us. Our warts and our wrinkles, not to mention more private parts of our anatomy, would become the vicarious property of the public custodian. The possibilities are very interesting.

Since we are now in the Cinderella-land of photography, it should be mentioned that telephoto lenses are now able to pick up scenes over great distances, and that it is now possible to do this with television and sound and other recording devices. Such devices have already been used by crime investigators and the military. Their application to civilian life is already creeping in.

In addition to the one-way glass screens through which one can be observed without being aware of it, there are schools in the United States today in which the principal can listen in on the classroom, and hospitals in which the nurse can listen in on the patient. Television for similar purposes is near at hand. Here, too, the possibilities are very interesting.

In the realm of sound, or rather *noise*, it must be said that the offenses committed this way in the United States are unparalleled for sheer barbarism anywhere else in the world. Many years ago Schopenhauer wrote an essay on Noise. It is many years since I have read it, but I vividly recall how scorching Schopenhauer was on the sudden sharp brain-stopping, thought-killing explosive cracking of the whips of coachmen and others. What Schopen-

[1] W. H. Sheldon, *Varieties of Delinquent Youth* (New York, Harper, 1949), p. 879.

hauer would have had to say on the din and discord created by the automobile horns of today, the noises of starting and gear shifting, the backfiring of trucks and buses, and the whistling and groaning of brakes—all to the accompaniment of a perfusion of essence of gasoline exhaust fumes—can only be guessed.

Public noises, sanctioned and created by public agencies, are among the most barbarous and stupid of destroyers of the individual's inalienable right to quietude. At all times of the day and night their licensed discords are encouraged to break in on one. Consider the piercing shrieks that suddenly fracture the smog-laden air when the police in their cars are bent on getting somewhere in a hurry. The principal function of the sirens, when the police are hurrying to the scene of a crime is, I presume, to announce their impending arrival to the criminals so that the latter may make a leisurely getaway. To these iniquities of the police car sirens add those of ambulance, rescue squads, and the clanging of fire engine bells (the least offensive of the noises).

How thick-skinned must one grow in order not to understand that the sudden noise of sirens constitutes a nerve-racking violation of one's privacy, and a damaging assault upon one's nervous system? For nothing is more effective than such noises in producing an unpleasant jumpiness of the nervous system. It is not without significance that in no other civilized land in the world does one encounter such noisesome sirens as those of the police cars in the United States. How far gone can one be not to know that the last thing on earth a sick or injured person wants to hear while he is being driven to a hospital is the clanging signal or siren of the ambulance, which only serves to disturb him and contribute to his anxiety—as well as to that of everyone else. Surely, some other means could be devised which would enable such vehicles to gain a speedy right of way—if only by the adoption of more pleasant sounds or signals? In many towns it is no longer possible to ride in a cab without the exacerbating accompaniment of the radio-transmitted directions of the central dispatcher. The cab driver not only keeps the din going because he has to, but, apparently, because it helps to alleviate his loneliness.

Another iniquitous intrusion is the continuous blasting from automobile horns that wedding caravans feel obliged to produce. Funeral processions indicate their nature by turning on their lights. Could not the ebullient friends of the newly wedded be induced to settle, say, for Roman candles?

Urbanites who think to escape these impertinences of noise by moving to the country may find that factory whistles or sirens or both can be uncomfortably annoying, and what is perhaps even more hard to bear, every so often one will be awakened from sleep by the community fire siren, which whines, and moans, and groans until all the firemen have appeared—and all sleep has vanished. Effective signals under rural conditions are highly necessary, but, again, surely some less barbarous means to summon firemen could be devised. It is done in other parts of the world.

Ah, public-address systems. These are instruments of torture which are at the disposal of anyone who has anything from moth-eaten rat skins to political self-aggrandizement to peddle. Wherever you may be, your eardrums may suddenly be assaulted by the inescapable abomination issuing from a mobile public-address unit. Seated in your own home your privacy may be similarly blasted by the outbreak of obstreperousness issuing from such a mobile unit.

When, some years ago, a well-known railroad attempted to capture its customers as an unconsulted audience for public-address advertising, the revolt among some of the passengers, led by the late Harold Ross of *The New Yorker,* successfully put the quietus on that profane scheme. But elsewhere, in many parts of the country, the public-address system has successfully established itself in the interest of advertising.

Thus, in whatever environment one may be, the opportunity of being quietly with oneself is inexorably diminishing, for there is no longer any time of the day during which one cannot be broken in on by the uninvited gate crashers of the sound barrier without so much as a by-your-leave.

In addition to the varieties of noise another widespread technique, developed within the last hundred years, for the invasion of privacy is advertising. It may perhaps be legitimately argued that advertising in its proper place is a desirable means of making people acquainted with what they might otherwise fail to know.

But when I want to contemplate the beauties of the land I would prefer that contemplation to be uninterrupted by the impertinence of the hucksters' misshapen and misplaced art, which like some pathological sequestrum too often suggests that it would be better for not being at all. Certainly, there are some landscapes which are so dreary that they are lent greater interest by almost any kind of billboard—there can be no criticism here—but where the natural beauty of the land is picturesque enough, we can dispense with the dubious embellishments of the advertisers. Increasingly, however, as one travels about the country one has occasion to observe that if it is not true that "every prospect pleases" it is because "only man is vile." No other creature defaces and deforms its natural habitat with such unnatural excrescences as does man. Perhaps we shall someday live to see the whole of nature taken over by the advertising fraternity. The sea alone, I believe, has thus far resisted their efforts—but it is only a matter of time before they will conquer even that element. Skywriting, public addresses from the sky, advertising blimps and planes, are no longer novelties. Just think of the advertising possibilities inherent in artificial satellites!

But for the time being let us keep to the earth and the advertisers. One of the most insidious forms which the depletion of privacy takes is mail advertising. I am not for a moment suggesting that large numbers of individuals do not appreciate receiving advertising in their mail. On the contrary, it is clear that innumerable persons do enjoy receiving this kind of mail, especially when other kinds are likely to be somewhat thin—better a letter from a company that wants to communicate with you and wants you, earnestly, to communicate with it, than no letter at all. For the advertising people such persons become like so many puppets who can, in certain numbers, be moved in the desired direction. I will not discuss, but only refer to, the untold thousands of acres of beautiful trees that are sacrificed in order to manufacture the paper upon which the advertisers impress their blandishments. Nature and beauty may suffer, but communications must be maintained.

Those who are affronted by the time-wasting litter represented by so much of the advertising mail they receive are probably in the minority, and I shall not dwell upon this kind of invasion of their privacy, which is after all one of the minor invasions. But I do think that one of the little considered consequences of mail advertising is well worth some attention, and that is the reducing effects it has upon the reading habits of the population. There are large numbers of people whose reading is virtually restricted to the advertising they receive through the mail. Such readers are to be found not only among the isolated rural dwellers, but also among many who live in the larger urban centers of this world. What with the telephone, radio, movies, television, and the other distractions that modern life has to offer, the reading of the advertising mail fits comfortably into the compulsion to be entertained, and will do service for a good deal of the reading of other kinds which might otherwise have been done. The contribution thus made to the increasing spiritual illiteracy of the many is, I believe, a factor to be reckoned with by the few.

The ultimate affront is the smoker who not content with poisoning himself poisons the atmosphere for the nonsmoker. This is an invasion of privacy which should not be tolerated because its effects upon the nonsmoker are organically damaging. If a man suddenly took it into his head to punch me I could have him charged before the law for the offense of assault and battery, but if the same man chooses instead by smoking to pollute the air I am breathing and by this means assault my respiratory system I can do nothing. In trains I invariably seek out the No Smoking car, and quite as invariably there are smokers in it who have clearly seen the No Smoking sign, but choose to disregard it, as they so discreditably never give a thought to the reason why most people have chosen to sit in a No Smoking car.

The other day my wife and I were staying in a hotel in Baltimore. At three in the morning my wife awakened and awakened me with the information that there was a distinct odor of something burning. I called the night manager on the telephone, and it took some two and a half hours before the source was located—a guest had been smoking in bed, fallen asleep, and set his mattress on fire. It was smoldering when finally located. Meanwhile sleep was entirely destroyed—but that was the least of it. Had it not been for the acuity of smell of the superior sex we might have had a somewhat rougher time of it. This utterly iniquitous habit of smoking in bed has been responsible for thousands of deaths, not to mention the incalculable damage done to property.

With the toleration which is increasingly exhibited toward these encroachments upon our privacy goes an increasing callousness to them. We grow accustomed to the transgressions upon our being, the violations of our privacy, and the infringement of our right to be alone with ourselves whenever we choose. This is life as we know it, and the harder it grows the more hardened do we become to it. In becoming so hardened we become cut off from the best that is within ourselves and the best that we could make of ourselves and of the world in which we live. We become increasingly insensitive to all those things to which we should be most sensitive—above all, to human need. In the crowded cities in which we live in loneliness we live more and more for ourselves, in environments in which the modes and opportunities for spontaneous and unreserved social participation are reduced to a minimum. The struggle for existence and the gigantism of our cities have largely served to bring this isolation about, and at the same time to produce the state of mind which invites every kind of intrusion that will serve to reduce one's isolation. It is in this way that isolation comes to be confused with privacy, and the privacy of isolation is unwanted. Since in isolation (which is lack of desired social contact) privacy is excessive, the individual is only too glad to sacrifice his privacy for less isolation.

The unsatisfied desire, the longing, for social participation leads to the fear of being alone, and the desire for occasional solitude tends to be overcome by the fear of being alone. In this manner the need for privacy may eventually be completely submerged in the overpowering need to be with—overpowering because it has been so inadequately satisfied by normal means. When such an annihilation of privacy is achieved man is, indeed, in danger— he is in danger of self-annihilation, of becoming a living automaton at the mercy of anyone who knows how to make him tick. In such a society one becomes grateful to "Big Brother" for assuming the task of directing the life one is no longer capable of directing oneself. In this way does the annihilation of privacy lead to the annihilation of the person, and of society, for the healthy society depends upon the ability of man to think and reflect upon what a true society is—and without the privacy to think and reflect man and society are lost.

Many men in contemporary society are very much in the state of Browning's "Paracelsus":

> I give the fight up; let there be an end,
> A privacy, an obscure nook for me.
> I want to be forgotten even by God.

But what man needs is not to be forgotten, but to be remembered —to be remembered as the one who needs to be needed, who needs to be neighborly, who needs to be responsible to others, who needs to love and to be loved. As Denis de Rougement has remarked in his brilliant book, *The Devil's Share*,

> Without real neighborliness, you are no longer responsible for anything nor for anyone. But without the feeling of responsibility of each toward others, there is no possible civic freedom: dictatorship becomes inevitable in every society whose maxim is 'each for himself and God for all,' which is the maxim of those who do not believe in God. . . . *The sense of one's neighbor, responsibility* and *liberty* are things intimately linked, they engender one another mutually and can not long subsist without one another. And order is born of their alliance.[2]

The return of privacy will be brought about only when the return to neighborliness has been achieved, for as Emerson wrote:

> All are needed by each one;
> Nothing is fair or good alone.

The tragic fact is that, in a society such as ours in which the individual can enjoy the vicarious society of anyone from kings to criminals, the individual is today more than ever alone. The more, as it were, the world is with us the more lonely do we become. We live, and work, and spend, and have our being, but become more and more isolated from mankind and from nature. With Wordsworth well might we say

[2] Denis de Rougement, *The Devil's Share* (New York, Pantheon, 1944), pp. 205-206.

The world is too much with us; late and soon,
Getting and spending, we lay waste our powers;
Little we see in nature that is ours.
We have given our hearts away, a sordid boon.

Shall we ever recover our hearts? It is a question—and it is a question that can be successfully and happily answered only if each of us will do what is required—namely, to return to the fellowship of man. This is the answer to the individual's plaint:

And how am I to face the odds
Of man's bedevilment and God's?
I, a stranger and afraid
In a world I never made.

About the Author

ASHLEY MONTAGU was born in London, England, in 1905, and studied anthropology at the Universities of London and Florence, and Columbia University, where he was awarded the degree of Doctor of Philosophy for a thesis on the Australian aborigines. Professor Ashley Montagu has been scientific worker at the British Museum (Natural History), Curator of Physical Anthropology at the Wellcome Historical Medical Museum, London, Assistant Professor of Anatomy at New York University, Anthropologist to the Division of Child Research at the same university, Associate Professor of Anatomy at the Hahnemann Medical College and Hospital, Philadelphia, and Chairman and Professor of Anthropology, Rutgers University. He has also been a visiting lecturer and professor at Harvard University and the University of Delaware, Regents Professor at the University of California at Santa Barbara, Senior Lecturer in Anthropology on the Veterans Administration Postgraduate Training Program in Psychiatry and Neurology, and was Rapporteur of the UNESCO Committee of Experts on Race which drafted the famous UNESCO Statement on Race. He has been Family Affairs and Anthropological Adviser to NBC, and has appeared on many radio and television programs in his capacity as an anthropologist. He is Chairman of the Anisfield-Wolf Award Committee which awards annual prizes for meritorious works in the field of race relations, Advisory Consultant to the Peace Research Institute, Washington, D.C., Advisory Consultant to the International Childbirth Education Association, and he is an associate and advisory editor of *Acta Geneticae Medicae et Gemellologia*. Professor Ashley Montagu is a member of many scientific and learned societies, and is the author of some twenty-three books, mostly in the field of anthropology. He has also contributed several hundred articles to the scientific and general periodicals of this and other countries. His hobbies are gardening and book collecting.